FREE Test Taking Tips Video/DVD Offer

To better serve you, we created videos covering test taking tips that we want to give you for FREE. **These videos cover world-class tips that will help you succeed on your test.**

We just ask that you send us feedback about this product. Please let us know what you thought about it—whether good, bad, or indifferent.

To get your **FREE videos**, you can use the QR code below or email freevideos@studyguideteam.com with "Free Videos" in the subject line and the following information in the body of the email:

a. The title of your product

b. Your product rating on a scale of 1-5, with 5 being the highest

c. Your feedback about the product

If you have any questions or concerns, please don't hesitate to contact us at info@studyguideteam.com.

Thank you!

SCAN HERE

ACS General Chemistry Study Guide

2 Practice Exams and ACS Test Prep Book
[3rd Edition]

Joshua Rueda

Written and edited by Test Prep Books.

ISBN 13: 9781637759226
ISBN 10: 1637759223

Table of Contents

CHEM 1211

Welcome

Dear Reader,

Welcome to your new Test Prep Books study guide! We are pleased that you chose us to help you prepare for your exam. There are many study options to choose from, and we appreciate you choosing us. Studying can be a daunting task, but we have designed a smart, effective study guide to help prepare you for what lies ahead.

Whether you're a parent helping your child learn and grow, a high school student working hard to get into your dream college, or a nursing student studying for a complex exam, we want to help give you the tools you need to succeed. We hope this study guide gives you the skills and the confidence to thrive, and we can't thank you enough for allowing us to be part of your journey.

In an effort to continue to improve our products, we welcome feedback from our customers. We look forward to hearing from you. Suggestions, success stories, and criticisms can all be communicated by emailing us at info@studyguideteam.com.

Sincerely,
Test Prep Books Team

FREE Videos/DVD OFFER

Doing well on your exam requires both knowing the test content and understanding how to use that knowledge to do well on the test. We offer completely FREE test taking tip videos. **These videos cover world-class tips that you can use to succeed on your test.**

To get your **FREE videos**, you can use the QR code below or email freevideos@studyguideteam.com with "Free Videos" in the subject line and the following information in the body of the email:

a. The title of your product
b. Your product rating on a scale of 1-5, with 5 being the highest
c. Your feedback about the product

If you have any questions or concerns, please don't hesitate to contact us at info@studyguideteam.com.

SCAN HERE

Quick Overview

As you draw closer to taking your exam, effective preparation becomes more and more important. Thankfully, you have this study guide to help you get ready. Use this guide to help keep your studying on track and refer to it often.

This study guide contains several key sections that will help you be successful on your exam. The guide contains tips for what you should do the night before and the day of the test. Also included are test-taking tips. Knowing the right information is not always enough. Many well-prepared test takers struggle with exams. These tips will help equip you to accurately read, assess, and answer test questions.

A large part of the guide is devoted to showing you what content to expect on the exam and to helping you better understand that content. In this guide are practice test questions so that you can see how well you have grasped the content. Then, answer explanations are provided so that you can understand why you missed certain questions.

Don't try to cram the night before you take your exam. This is not a wise strategy for a few reasons. First, your retention of the information will be low. Your time would be better used by reviewing information you already know rather than trying to learn a lot of new information. Second, you will likely become stressed as you try to gain a large amount of knowledge in a short amount of time. Third, you will be depriving yourself of sleep. So be sure to go to bed at a reasonable time the night before. Being well-rested helps you focus and remain calm.

Be sure to eat a substantial breakfast the morning of the exam. If you are taking the exam in the afternoon, be sure to have a good lunch as well. Being hungry is distracting and can make it difficult to focus. You have hopefully spent lots of time preparing for the exam. Don't let an empty stomach get in the way of success!

When travelling to the testing center, leave earlier than needed. That way, you have a buffer in case you experience any delays. This will help you remain calm and will keep you from missing your appointment time at the testing center.

Be sure to pace yourself during the exam. Don't try to rush through the exam. There is no need to risk performing poorly on the exam just so you can leave the testing center early. Allow yourself to use all of the allotted time if needed.

Remain positive while taking the exam even if you feel like you are performing poorly. Thinking about the content you should have mastered will not help you perform better on the exam.

Once the exam is complete, take some time to relax. Even if you feel that you need to take the exam again, you will be well served by some down time before you begin studying again. It's often easier to convince yourself to study if you know that it will come with a reward!

Test-Taking Strategies

1. Predicting the Answer

When you feel confident in your preparation for a multiple-choice test, try predicting the answer before reading the answer choices. This is especially useful on questions that test objective factual knowledge. By predicting the answer before reading the available choices, you eliminate the possibility that you will be distracted or led astray by an incorrect answer choice. You will feel more confident in your selection if you read the question, predict the answer, and then find your prediction among the answer choices. After using this strategy, be sure to still read all of the answer choices carefully and completely. If you feel unprepared, you should not attempt to predict the answers. This would be a waste of time and an opportunity for your mind to wander in the wrong direction.

2. Reading the Whole Question

Too often, test takers scan a multiple-choice question, recognize a few familiar words, and immediately jump to the answer choices. Test authors are aware of this common impatience, and they will sometimes prey upon it. For instance, a test author might subtly turn the question into a negative, or he or she might redirect the focus of the question right at the end. The only way to avoid falling into these traps is to read the entirety of the question carefully before reading the answer choices.

3. Looking for Wrong Answers

Long and complicated multiple-choice questions can be intimidating. One way to simplify a difficult multiple-choice question is to eliminate all of the answer choices that are clearly wrong. In most sets of answers, there will be at least one selection that can be dismissed right away. If the test is administered on paper, the test taker could draw a line through it to indicate that it may be ignored; otherwise, the test taker will have to perform this operation mentally or on scratch paper. In either case, once the obviously incorrect answers have been eliminated, the remaining choices may be considered. Sometimes identifying the clearly wrong answers will give the test taker some information about the correct answer. For instance, if one of the remaining answer choices is a direct opposite of one of the eliminated answer choices, it may well be the correct answer. The opposite of obviously wrong is obviously right! Of course, this is not always the case. Some answers are obviously incorrect simply because they are irrelevant to the question being asked. Still, identifying and eliminating some incorrect answer choices is a good way to simplify a multiple-choice question.

5. No Need for Panic

It is wise to learn as many strategies as possible before taking a multiple-choice test, but it is likely that you will come across a few questions for which you simply don't know the answer. In this situation, avoid panicking. Because most multiple-choice tests include dozens of questions, the relative value of a single wrong answer is small. As much as possible, you should compartmentalize each question on a multiple-choice test. In other words, you should not allow your feelings about one question to affect your success on the others. When you find a question that you either don't understand or don't know how to answer, just take a deep breath and do your best. Read the entire question slowly and carefully. Try rephrasing the question a couple of different ways. Then, read all of the answer choices carefully. After eliminating obviously wrong answers, make a selection and move on to the next question.

4. Don't Overanalyze

Anxious test takers often overanalyze questions. When you are nervous, your brain will often run wild, causing you to make associations and discover clues that don't actually exist. If you feel that this may be a problem for you, do whatever you can to slow down during the test. Try taking a deep breath or counting to ten. As you read and consider the question, restrict yourself to the particular words used by the author. Avoid thought tangents about what the author *really* meant, or what he or she was *trying* to say. The only things that matter on a multiple-choice test are the words that are actually in the question. You must avoid reading too much into a multiple-choice question, or supposing that the writer meant something other than what he or she wrote.

6. Confusing Answer Choices

When working on a difficult multiple-choice question, there may be a tendency to focus on the answer choices that are the easiest to understand. Many people, whether consciously or not, gravitate to the answer choices that require the least concentration, knowledge, and memory. This is a mistake. When you come across an answer choice that is confusing, you should give it extra attention. A question might be confusing because you do not know the subject matter to which it refers. If this is the case, don't eliminate the answer before you have affirmatively settled on another. When you come across an answer choice of this type, set it aside as you look at the remaining choices. If you can confidently assert that one of the other choices is correct, you can leave the confusing answer aside. Otherwise, you will need to take a moment to try to better understand the confusing answer choice. Rephrasing is one way to tease out the sense of a confusing answer choice.

7. Your First Instinct

Many people struggle with multiple-choice tests because they overthink the questions. If you have studied sufficiently for the test, you should be prepared to trust your first instinct once you have carefully and completely read the question and all of the answer choices. There is a great deal of research suggesting that the mind can come to the correct conclusion very quickly once it has obtained all of the relevant information. At times, it may seem to you as if your intuition is working faster even than your reasoning mind. This may in fact be true. The knowledge you obtain while studying may be retrieved from your subconscious before you have a chance to work out the associations that support it. Verify your instinct by working out the reasons that it should be trusted.

8. Key Words

Many test takers struggle with multiple-choice questions because they have poor reading comprehension skills. Quickly reading and understanding a multiple-choice question requires a mixture of skill and experience. To help with this, try jotting down a few key words and phrases on a piece of scrap paper. Doing this concentrates the process of reading and forces the mind to weigh the relative importance of the question's parts. In selecting words and phrases to write down, the test taker thinks about the question more deeply and carefully. This is especially true for multiple-choice questions that are preceded by a long prompt.

9. Subtle Negatives

One of the oldest tricks in the multiple-choice test writer's book is to subtly reverse the meaning of a question with a word like *not* or *except*. If you are not paying attention to each word in the question, you can easily be led astray by this trick. For instance, a common question format is, "Which of the following is...?" Obviously, if the question instead is, "Which of the following is not...?," then the answer will be quite different. Even worse, the test makers are aware of the potential for this mistake and will include one answer choice that would be correct if the question were not negated or reversed. A test taker who misses the reversal will find what he or she believes to be a correct answer and will be so confident that he or she will fail to reread the question and discover the original error. The only way to avoid this is to practice a wide variety of multiple-choice questions and to pay close attention to each and every word.

10. Reading Every Answer Choice

It may seem obvious, but you should always read every one of the answer choices! Too many test takers fall into the habit of scanning the question and assuming that they understand the question because they recognize a few key words. From there, they pick the first answer choice that answers the question they believe they have read. Test takers who read all of the answer choices might discover that one of the latter answer choices is actually *more* correct. Moreover, reading all of the answer choices can remind you of facts related to the question that can help you arrive at the correct answer. Sometimes, a misstatement or incorrect detail in one of the latter answer choices will trigger your memory of the subject and will enable you to find the right answer. Failing to read all of the answer choices is like not reading all of the items on a restaurant menu: you might miss out on the perfect choice.

11. Spot the Hedges

One of the keys to success on multiple-choice tests is paying close attention to every word. This is never truer than with words like almost, most, some, and sometimes. These words are called "hedges" because they indicate that a statement is not totally true or not true in every place and time. An absolute statement will contain no hedges, but in many subjects, the answers are not always straightforward or absolute. There are always exceptions to the rules in these subjects. For this reason, you should favor those multiple-choice questions that contain hedging language. The presence of qualifying words indicates that the author is taking special care with their words, which is certainly important when composing the right answer. After all, there are many ways to be wrong, but there is only one way to be right! For this reason, it is wise to avoid answers that are absolute when taking a multiple-choice test. An absolute answer is one that says things are either all one way or all another. They often include words like *every*, *always*, *best*, and *never*. If you are taking a multiple-choice test in a subject that doesn't lend itself to absolute answers, be on your guard if you see any of these words.

12. Long Answers

In many subject areas, the answers are not simple. As already mentioned, the right answer often requires hedges. Another common feature of the answers to a complex or subjective question are qualifying clauses, which are groups of words that subtly modify the meaning of the sentence. If the question or answer choice describes a rule to which there are exceptions or the subject matter is complicated, ambiguous, or confusing, the correct answer will require many words in order to be expressed clearly and accurately. In essence, you should not be deterred by answer choices that seem excessively long. Oftentimes, the author of the text will not be able to write the correct answer without offering some qualifications and modifications. Your job is to read the answer choices thoroughly and completely and to select the one that most accurately and precisely answers the question.

13. Restating to Understand

Sometimes, a question on a multiple-choice test is difficult not because of what it asks but because of how it is written. If this is the case, restate the question or answer choice in different words. This process serves a couple of important purposes. First, it forces you to concentrate on the core of the question. In order to rephrase the question accurately, you have to understand it well. Rephrasing the question will concentrate your mind on the key words and ideas. Second, it will present the information to your mind in a fresh way. This process may trigger your memory and render some useful scrap of information picked up while studying.

14. True Statements

Sometimes an answer choice will be true in itself, but it does not answer the question. This is one of the main reasons why it is essential to read the question carefully and completely before proceeding to the answer choices. Too often, test takers skip ahead to the answer choices and look for true statements. Having found one of these, they are content to select it without reference to the question above. Obviously, this provides an easy way for test makers to play tricks. The savvy test taker will always read the entire question before turning to the answer choices. Then, having settled on a correct answer choice, he or she will refer to the original question and ensure that the selected answer is relevant. The mistake of choosing a correct-but-irrelevant answer choice is especially common on questions related to specific pieces of objective knowledge. A prepared test taker will have a wealth of factual knowledge at their disposal, and should not be careless in its application.

15. No Patterns

One of the more dangerous ideas that circulates about multiple-choice tests is that the correct answers tend to fall into patterns. These erroneous ideas range from a belief that B and C are the most common right answers, to the idea that an unprepared test-taker should answer "A-B-A-C-A-D-A-B-A." It cannot be emphasized enough that pattern-seeking of this type is exactly the WRONG way to approach a multiple-choice test. To begin with, it is highly unlikely that the test maker will plot the correct answers according to some predetermined pattern. The questions are scrambled and delivered in a random order. Furthermore, even if the test maker was following a pattern in the assignation of correct answers, there is no reason why the test taker would know which pattern he or she was using. Any attempt to discern a pattern in the answer choices is a waste of time and a distraction from the real work of taking the test. A test taker would be much better served by extra preparation before the test than by reliance on a pattern in the answers.

Introduction to the ACS General Chemistry Exam

Function of the Test

The American Chemical Society (ACS) General Chemistry exam is designed to be a culminating final exam for General Chemistry science courses at ACS-accredited chemistry courses at colleges and universities around the country. The program does not need to be ACS-accredited for the student to sit for the test, though it is recommended that the student has completed a rigorous college-level general chemistry course. The full-year exam covers all the topics that undergraduates should encounter in their standard two-semester general chemistry course.

Students are given a percentile score, in addition to their raw and scaled scores, which allows students, professors, and chemistry departments to assess how they are doing relative to other test takers and programs around the United States.

Test Administration

The ACS General Chemistry exam is a paper-and-pencil test. Test takers must bring a #2 pencil, and will fill out a scantron sheet with their answers. Scratch paper will be provided to work through problems; test takers are not allowed to mark up their test booklets.

To register for the exam, students typically contact their school to schedule a date. Schools can set their own policies about deadlines for registering. ACS works with schools to meet the needs and accommodation requirements for students with documented disabilities. Accommodations permitted include options such as additional time, providing an electronic version of the test, allowing an authorized reader, large-print tests, among others. Test takers requiring accommodations should speak with administrators at their school to arrange for the necessary accommodations.

Students are allowed to take the exam three times per year, in most cases, though different colleges and universities may have their own policies and expectations.

Test Format

The test contains 70 multiple-choice questions, each with four answer options. Test takers are given 110 minutes to complete the exam. While it is recommended that test takers be mindful that they only have 1 minute and 34 seconds per question, it is important that they read each question thoroughly and not rush through, as this can result in careless mistakes.

Students are allowed to use a non-programmable calculator only. The Periodic Table, a list of abbreviations and symbols, and the values of common constants are provided. Additionally, test takers are given Integrated Rate Law Equations, the Arrhenius Equation, Graham's Law of Effusion, and the Nernst Equation.

Topics include states of matter, atomic structure and periodicity, molecular structure, solutions, chemical equilibrium, intermolecular forces, redox reactions, nomenclature, resonance and formal charge, stoichiometry, acids/bases, kinetics, thermodynamics, descriptive chemistry, electrochemistry, and laboratory techniques, among others.

Scoring

Scores are calculated based solely on the number of correct responses. Therefore, test takers are advised to guess and fill in answers to every question, even if they are unsure of the answer or are running out of time, because there is no penalty for incorrect responses.

Because students are given a percentile score along with their numerical score, not only are they able to get an assessment of how well they know and understand general chemistry, but they are also able to see how they compare to their peers around the country.

The national average raw score is 38.3. To achieve what is considered an A, the test taker needs to land in the 80th percentile or above, and a B is roughly the 60th to 79th percentile. Scores in the 40th to 59th percentile are generally considered to equate to a C, 20th to 39th percentile are considered a D, and below that is an F.

Study Prep Plan for the ACS General Chemistry Exam

1 **Schedule** - Use one of our study schedules below or come up with one of your own.

2 **Relax** - Test anxiety can hurt even the best students. There are many ways to reduce stress. Find the one that works best for you.

3 **Execute** - Once you have a good plan in place, be sure to stick to it.

One Week Study Schedule

Day 1	Atomic Structure
Day 2	Solutions and Aqueous Reactions
Day 3	Kinetics
Day 4	Thermodynamics
Day 5	Practice Test 1
Day 6	Practice Test 2
Day 7	Take Your Exam!

Two Week Study Schedule

Day 1	Atomic Structure	Day 8	Thermodynamics
Day 2	Electronic Structure	Day 9	Electrochemistry
Day 3	Stoichiometry	Day 10	Practice Test 1
Day 4	Heat and Enthalpy	Day 11	Answer Explanations
Day 5	Structure and Bonding	Day 12	Practice Test 2
Day 6	Kinetics	Day 13	Answer Explanations
Day 7	Acids and Bases	Day 14	Take Your Exam!

One Month Study Schedule

Day 1	Atomic Structure	Day 11	Structure and Bonding	Day 21	Thermodynamic and Kinetic Control
Day 2	The Periodic Table of Elements	Day 12	Electron Delocalization	Day 22	Electrochemistry
Day 3	Electronic Structure	Day 13	States of Matter	Day 23	Predicting the Spontaneous Direction...
Day 4	Orbital diagrams, electron...	Day 14	Kinetics	Day 24	Nuclear Chemistry
Day 5	Formula Calculations and the Mole	Day 15	The Integrated Rate Law	Day 25	Determining Radioactivity Type
Day 6	Elemental Analysis	Day 16	Equilibrium	Day 26	Practice Test 1
Day 7	Stoichiometry	Day 17	Acids and Bases	Day 27	Answer Explanations
Day 8	Solutions and Aqueous Reactions	Day 18	Solubility Equilibria	Day 28	Practice Test 2
Day 9	Heat and Enthalpy	Day 19	Effect of pH with a Common Ion	Day 29	Answer Explanations
Day 10	Enthalpy of Reaction	Day 20	Thermodynamics	Day 30	Take Your Exam!

Build your own prep plan by visiting:

testprepbooks.com/prep

Chemistry Reference Sheet

Name	Formula
Average Atomic Mass	$Average\ Atomic\ Mass\ (amu) = atomic\ mass \times fraction\ abundance$
Avogadro's Number	$1\ mole\ of\ any\ substance = N_A = 6.022 \times 10^{23}\ molecules,\ ions,\ atoms,\ or\ any\ substance$
Cell Potential	$E^\circ_{cell} = E^\circ_{final} - E^\circ_{initial} = E^\circ_{cathode} - E^\circ_{anode}$
Change in Internal Energy	$\Delta U = U_{final(products)} - U_{initial(reactants)}$
Density	$\frac{Mass}{Volume}$
Equilibrium Constant	$aA + bB \rightleftharpoons cC + dD \qquad K_c = \frac{[C]^c[D]^d}{[A]^a[B]^b}$
Gibbs Standard Change in Free Energy	$\Delta G^\circ = nFE^\circ_{cell}$
Mass Percentage	$Mass\ percentage\ of\ E = \frac{mass\ of\ E\ in\ compound}{mass\ of\ compound} \times 100\%$
Molarity	$\frac{Moles\ of\ Solute}{Volume\ of\ Solution}$
Molecular Formula	$n = \frac{molecular\ mass}{empirical\ formula\ mass}$
Moles	$\frac{Given\ Mass\ (g)}{Gram\ Formula\ Mass}$
Nernst Equation	$E_{cell} = E^\circ_{cell} - \frac{0.0592\ \text{V}}{n} \log Q$
Percent Error	$\frac{\lvert True\ Value - Approximate\ Value \rvert}{True\ Value} \times 100\%$
Percent Yield	$Percent\ Yield = \frac{Actual\ Yield}{Theoretical\ Yield} \times 100\%$
Radioactive Decay	$t_{\frac{1}{2}} = \frac{0.693}{k}$

Atomic Structure

Atomic Structure

The structure of an atom has 2 major components: the atomic nucleus and the atomic shells (also known as **orbits**). The **nucleus**, which is made up of protons and neutrons, is found in the center of an atom. The 3 major subatomic particles are protons, neutrons, and electrons, which are found in the atomic nucleus and shells.

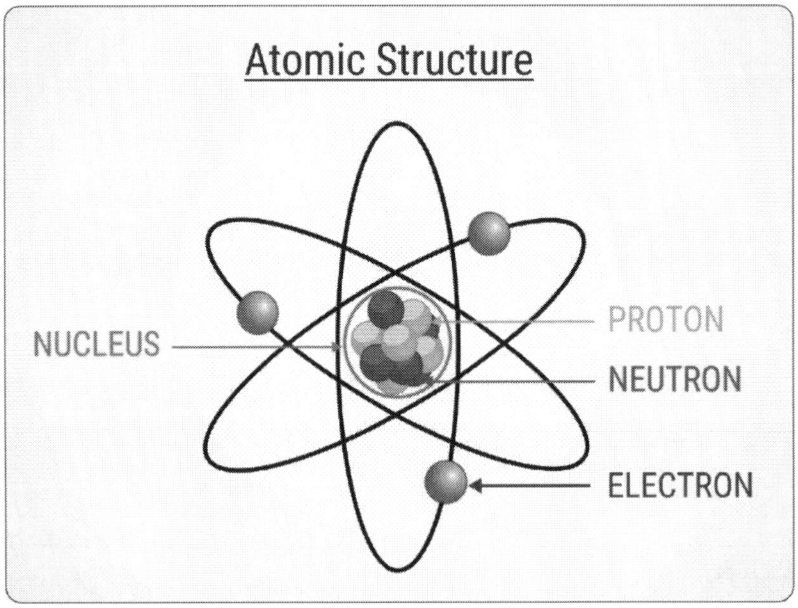

Figure 1. The subatomic particles of the atom

Protons are positively charged particles found in the atomic nucleus. An entirely different element is created when protons are added to or removed from an atom's nucleus. **Neutrons** are also found in the atomic nucleus and are neutral particles, meaning they have no net electrical charge. The addition or removal of neutrons to or from an atom's nucleus does not create a different element; instead it creates a lighter or heavier form of that element, which is called an isotope. **Electrons** are negatively charged particles found orbiting in the atomic shells around the nucleus. A proton or a neutron has nearly 2,000 times the mass of an electron. Table 1 below shows the difference in mass and charge for each subatomic particle.

Table 1. Mass and charge properties of the proton, neutron, and electron

Subatomic particle	Mass (kg)	Mass (amu)	Charge (Coulomb, C)	Charge (e)
Proton	1.67262×10^{-27}	1.00728	$+1.60218 \times 10^{-19}$	+1
Neutron	1.67494×10^{-27}	1.00866	0	0
Electron	9.10939×10^{-31}	0.00055	-1.60218×10^{-19}	−1

The model of the atom in Figure 1 is based off **Ernest Rutherford**'s, **Hans Geiger**'s, and **Ernest Marsden**'s **alpha-particle scattering experiments** (1911), which bombarded helium atoms toward metal foils.

Gold Foil Experiment

These experiments suggested that a majority of the atom's mass (99.95%) was found at the nucleus, which contains the positively charged protons. The electrons move around the nucleus and occupy most of the space in the atom. As an analogy, if a ping-pong ball represented the nucleus, then the electrons would move in a space up to 3 miles in diameter from the nucleus.

It's important to note that Figure 1 is a simplistic atomic representation that shows electrons confined to fixed orbits and moving around the nucleus. A more accurate representation of the nuclear model would show that electrons orbit the nucleus in **atomic shells** or **electron clouds**. These electron clouds can vary in shape and size. For example, the first atomic shell (K shell) has a spherical shape and can accommodate 2 electrons. The second atomic shell (L shell) is farther away from the nucleus and consists of a spherical and dumbbell-shaped electron cloud that can hold a maximum of 8 electrons. The third atomic shell (M shell) is similar to the second shell but is farthest away from the nucleus, and it can house a maximum of 8 electrons.

Figure 2 illustrates the first 2 atomic shells closest to the nucleus, which may be composed of several spherical or dumbbell-shaped orbitals, which are spaces where electrons are. The closest shell to the nucleus is called the "1 shell" (also called "K shell"), followed by the "2 shell" (or "L shell"), then the "3 shell" (or "M shell"). The K shell contains only one spherical or "s" orbital, whereas the L shell contains an "s" orbital and 3 dumbbell-shaped "p" orbitals. The numbers preceding "s" or "p" refer to the first shell (K shell) and second shell (L shell). Only 2 electrons are found per s or p orbital. The last column combines the K and L Shells. The second row shows a simple orbit model of the K, L, and combined shells.

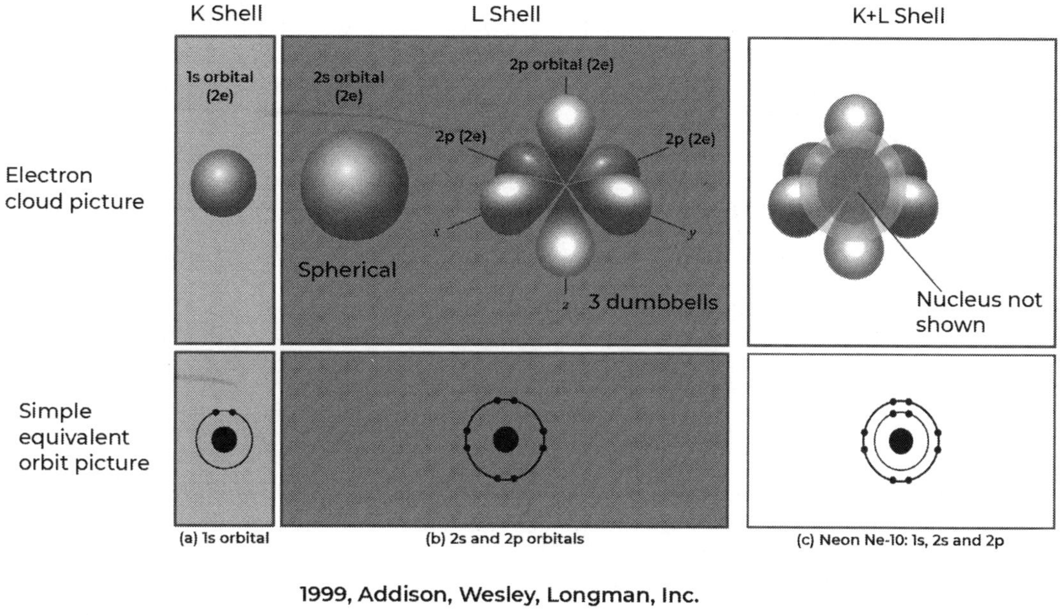

Figure 2. Electron cloud and simple atomic model of the neon atom

The negatively charged electrons orbiting the nucleus are attracted to the positively charged protons in the nucleus via electromagnetic force. The attraction of opposite electrical charges gives rise to chemical bonds, which are how atoms are attached or bonded.

The **atomic number** of an atom is determined by the number of protons in the nucleus. In notation the atomic number is represented by the letter Z. When a substance is composed of atoms that all have the same atomic number, it is called an **element**. In the **periodic table**, elements are arranged by atomic number and grouped by properties. The symbols of the elements in the periodic table are a single letter or a two-letter combination that is usually derived from the element's name.

Figure 3 shows a common chemical symbol represented in some periodic tables. The letter X refers to the specific element. The subscript Z is the element's atomic number. The superscript A is the element's mass number. An atom with a fixed atomic number and mass number is called a **nuclide**. Figure 3 below represents a nuclide.

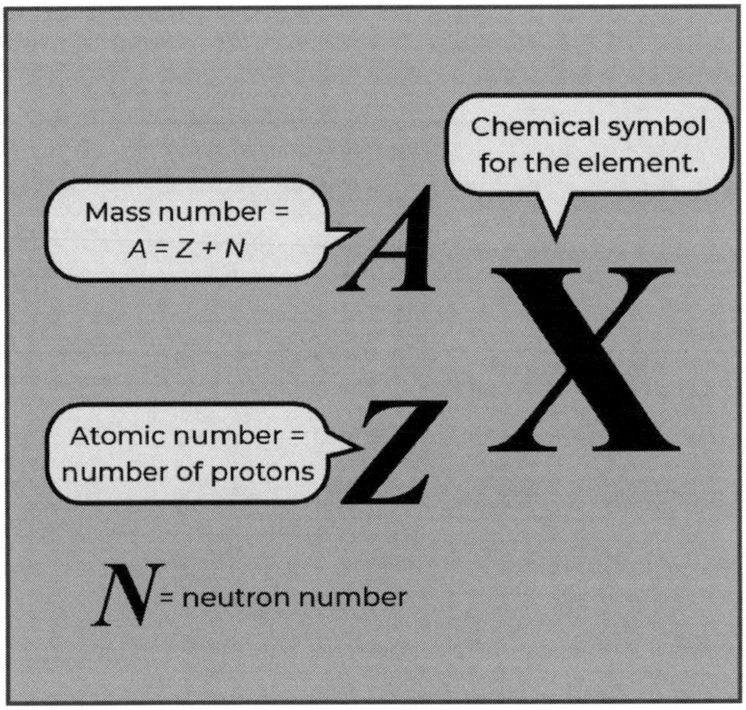

Figure 3. Representation of an element by a symbol X with its associated mass and atomic number

Many of the elements have Latin origins for their names, and their atomic symbols do not match their modern names. For example, iron is derived from the Latin word *ferrum*, so its symbol is Fe, even though it is now called iron. The naming of the elements began with those of natural origin and they have ancient names, often with the ending "-ium." This naming practice has been continued for all elements that have been named since the 1940s. Now the names of new elements must be approved by the International Union of Pure and Applied Chemistry.

An atom's **mass number (A)** is determined by the sum of the total number of protons (Z) and neutrons (N) in the atom. Most nuclei have a net neutral charge, and all atoms of one type have the same atomic number. The neutral charge is due to the equal number of protons and electrons in the atom. Therefore, the atomic number (Z) is often equal to the number of electrons in an atom.

However, there are some atoms of the same type that have a different mass number, due to an imbalance of neutrons. Atoms of this type are called **isotopes**. The atomic number, which is determined by the number of protons, is the same in all isotopes of a given element, but the mass number, which is determined by adding the protons and neutrons, is different due to the irregular number of neutrons. The **atomic mass** of an element is the weighted average of the naturally occurring atoms of a given element, or the relative abundance of isotopes that might be used in chemistry. The mass number of chlorine is 35; however, the atomic mass of chlorine is 35.5 amu (atomic mass unit).

This discrepancy exists because there are many isotopes occurring in nature. For example, the nucleus could have 36 instead of 35 protons. Given the prevalence of the various isotopes, the average of all of the mass numbers turns out to be 35.5 amu, which is slightly higher than chlorine's number in the periodic table. The nitrogen atom contains 2 types of stable isotopes: nitrogen-14 and nitrogen-15. The nitrogen atom has an average mass number of 14.01 amu. Each number following the name of the element indicates the number of neutrons for each nitrogen isotope. Nitrogen-14 is the most naturally occurring isotope, whereas nitrogen-15 is not. Over 10 radioactive isotopes of nitrogen have also been identified, but these isotopes are unstable or short-lived. The chemical symbols for the 2 stable isotopes can also be designated as:

$^{14}_{7}\text{N}$ nitrogen-14

$^{15}_{7}\text{N}$ nitrogen-15

The atomic number of nitrogen is seven ($Z = 7$), $_7\text{N}$. The naturally occurring form of nitrogen has 7 protons, 7 neutrons, and 7 electrons. The mass number A would be attributed to the mass of the protons (7) and neutrons (7), which is equal to 14: $7 \text{ amu} + 7 \text{ amu} = 14 \text{ amu}$. Therefore, the elemental symbol for nitrogen with 7 neutrons is N-14 or $^{14}_{7}\text{N}$, where the left superscript indicates the mass number.

Atomic mass

For each element found in nature, there is a mixture of isotopes, which will each have a characteristic mass, for example, nitrogen-14 is 14 amu and nitrogen-15 is 15 amu. One **atomic mass unit (amu)** is roughly the mass of one proton or neutron, as shown in Table 1, or one-twelfth the mass of the carbon-12 isotope which contains 6 protons and 6 neutrons: $6 \text{ amu} + 6 \text{ amu} = 12 \text{ amu}$. For each element present in the periodic table, the listed mass is an average **atomic mass** because there are other isotopes in addition to the naturally occurring element.

The **mass spectrometer** is an instrument routinely used to measure the atomic mass of different isotopes. The spectrometer works by comparing the mass of a chosen atom to a standard atom such as the carbon-12 isotope, which has a mass of twelve atomic mass units. A mass spectrometer can identify different isotopes in a given element. First, a gaseous form of the specific element is introduced or injected into a tube in the mass spectrometer. The gaseous element is converted to a positive ion (for example, N to N^+), which is accelerated by a negatively charged plate/grid toward an internal magnet. The positive beam of ions is then separated by the magnetic field, from the magnet, based on their mass-to-charge ratio into 2 beams associated with $^{14}_{7}\text{N}$ and $^{15}_{7}\text{N}$. A detector located at the end of the tube will measure the distance between each beam. A computer connected to the instrument then generates a mass spectrum plot that shows the fractional abundance of the isotope with respect to its mass.

Fractional Abundance

Figure 4 shows a mass spectrum of nitrogen, which indicates the presence of 2 isotopes with masses.

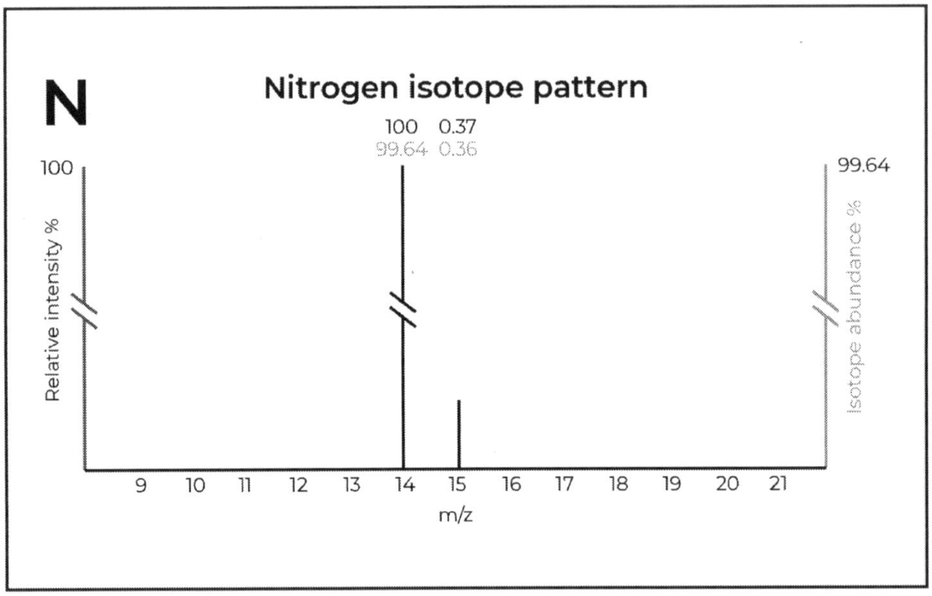

Figure 4. Isotopes of nitrogen: N-14 and N-15. The mass-to-charge ratio is given by m/z

The mass spectrum shows a peak at 14 m/z (14 amu), which corresponds to N-14 with an isotope or fractional abundance equal to 99.64%. The other peak at 15 m/z (15 amu) is N-15, which has one extra neutron compared to N-14 and has a fractional abundance of 0.36%. Table 2 shows the atomic mass and abundance of each isotope.

Table 2. Isotopes of Nitrogen (N)			
Nitrogen isotope	Atomic mass (amu)	Relative intensity %	Fractional abundance
N-14, $^{14}_{7}N$	14.003074005	100	0.9963
N-15, $^{15}_{7}N$	15.000108898	0.37	0.0037

Most of the mass is due to N-14, but the average atomic mass of N will not be exactly 14.0 amu. The atomic mass of N is slightly greater because of N-15. The average atomic mass depends on the intensity or fractional abundance of each isotope. For example, the mass spectrum of N shows 2 isotopes, N-14 (14 amu or m/z) and N-15 (15 amu or m/z), with a fractional abundance of 99.64 and 0.36%. The **fractional abundance** for each isotope is found by dividing the relative intensity of each isotope over the sum of the relative intensities for all isotopes. For example, the fractional abundance of N-14 is:

$$^{14}_{7}\text{N fractional abundance} = \frac{100.0\%}{100.0\%+0.3700\%} = 0.9963$$

Once the fractional abundance is obtained from the relative intensity provided by the mass spectrometer, the **average atomic mass** of can be calculated. Below are calculations for nitrogen.

$$\text{average atomic mass (amu)} = \sum(\text{atomic mass}) \times (\text{fraction abundance})$$

$$(14.003074005) \times (0.9963) + (15.000108898) \times (0.0037)$$

$$14.01 \text{ amu}$$

The average atomic mass of nitrogen (N) is 14.01 amu, which is an approximate value shown in the periodic table.

The Periodic Table of Elements

The **periodic table** catalogs all the known elements known, currently 118 (Figure 5). This table is one of the most important references in the science of chemistry. Information in the periodic table includes elements' atomic number, atomic mass, and chemical symbol. The first periodic table was rendered by **Mendeleev** in the mid-1800s and was arranged in order of increasing atomic mass. The modern periodic table is arranged in order of increasing atomic number and common characteristics.

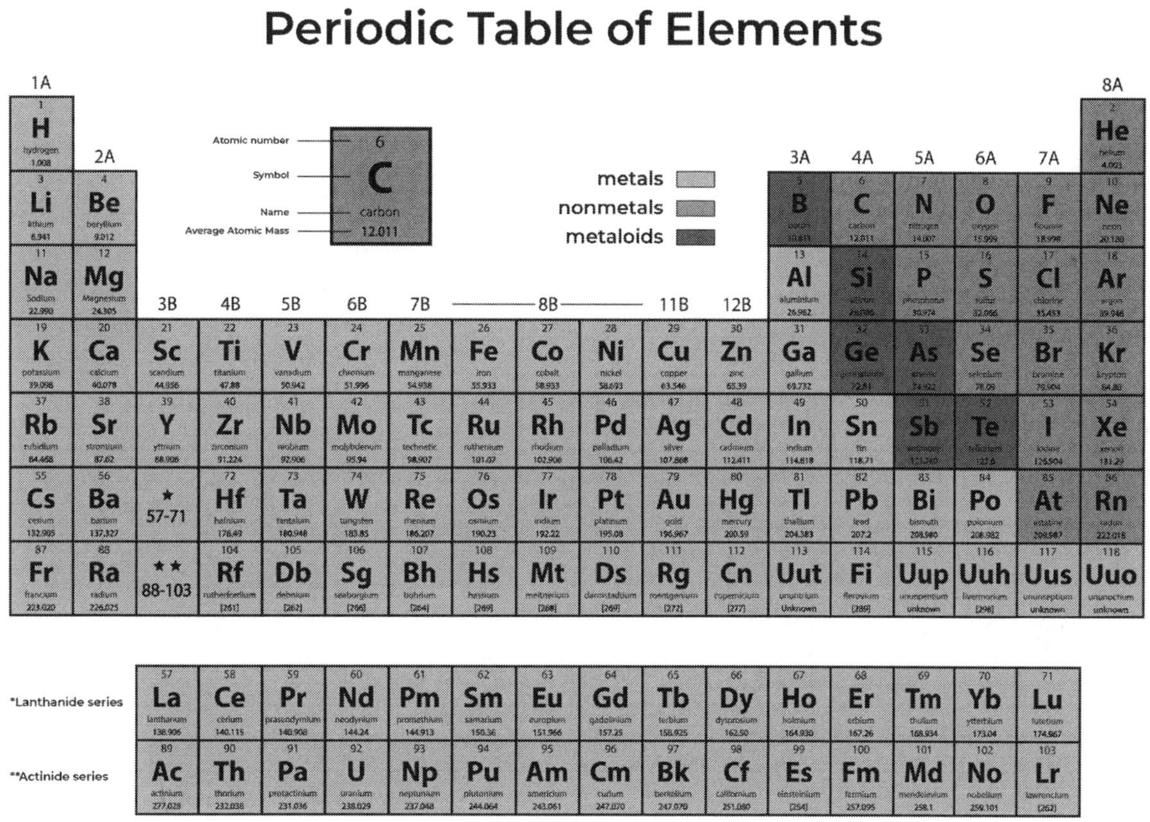

Figure 5. The periodic table of elements

As the atomic number increases, electrons gradually fill the shells of an atom. This is represented in the table from left to right and top to bottom. The horizontal rows, known as **periods**, have different valence electron shell configurations, for example, 1s, 2s, 2p, and 3s. In general, the start of a new period corresponds to the addition of an electron to a new shell. For example, Li: $1s^2\mathbf{2s^1}$ and Na: $1s^22s^22p^6\mathbf{3s^1}$. The sum of superscripts is equal to the atomic number. The periodic table contains 7 periods and 18 families. The vertical columns, called **groups** or **families**, are sorted by similar chemical properties and characteristics such as appearance and reactivity. The elements in the periodic table can also be classified into 3 major groups: metals, metalloids, and nonmetals. The elements in each block (for example, metal, transition metal, and nonmetal) of the periodic table are also group by similar electron configurations. **Metals** are concentrated on the left side of the periodic table, and **nonmetals** are concentrated on the right side (Figure 5). **Metalloids** occupy the area between the metals and nonmetals.

Modern periodic tables have the elements arranged according to their valance electron configurations, which also contribute to trends in chemical properties. These properties help to further categorize the elements into blocks or groups, which include metals, nonmetals, transition metals, alkali metals, alkali earth metals, metalloids, lanthanides, actinides, diatomics, post-transition metals, polyatomic nonmetals, and noble gases. For example, the **alkali earth metals** (Li, Na, K, Rb, Cs, Fr) are found in column one, or group IA, and have one loosely bound electron, low electronegativities, and the largest atomic radii within their period. These metals are soft and highly reactive with water. **Noble gases** (for example, He, Ne, Ar, Kr, Xe, Rn) have a full outer electron valence shell of 8 electrons. The elements in this block possess similar characteristics, such as being colorless, odorless, and having low chemical reactivity. In another block, the metals, elements tend to be shiny, highly conductive, and easily form alloys with each other, nonmetals, and noble gases.

Periodic Trends

The elements in the periodic table are arranged by number and grouped by trends in their physical properties and electron configurations. Certain trends are easily described by the arrangement of the periodic table and include the **atomic radius**, which is defined as one half the distance between the nuclei of atoms of the same element. The **atomic radius** increases as elements go from right to left and from top to bottom in the periodic table (Figure 6). Another trend in the periodic table is the **electron affinity energy**, which is the tendency of an atom to attract electrons. This tendency increases from left to right and from bottom to top of the periodic table, which trend is opposite to the that of atomic radius. **The ionization energy**, the amount of energy needed to remove an electron from a gas or ion, follows a trend similar to that of the electron affinity.

Electronegativity is a measurement of the willingness of an atom to form a chemical bond. Elements on the right side and near the top of the periodic table tend to attract electrons and are more electronegative. Consequently, these elements tend to gain a negative charge since there are more electrons than protons. An atom with a charge is referred to as an **ion**, and if an ion has more electrons than protons, it has a negative charge and is called an **anion**. In contrast, elements on the left and near the bottom of the periodic table lose, or give up, one or more electrons in order to bond and are the least electronegative. If an atom has fewer electrons than protons, it has a positive charge and is a called **cation**. Nonmetals typically form anions and metals form cations. The only exceptions to this rule are the noble gases. Since the noble gases have full valence shells (the outermost orbital shell of an atom), they do not tend to lose or gain electrons.

Chemical reactivity is another trend that can be identified by the groupings of the elements in the periodic table. The chemical reactivity of metals decreases from left to right in the table and while going higher in the table. Conversely, nonmetals increase in chemical reactivity from left to right and while going lower in the table. Again, the noble gases present an exception to these trends because they have very low chemical reactivity.

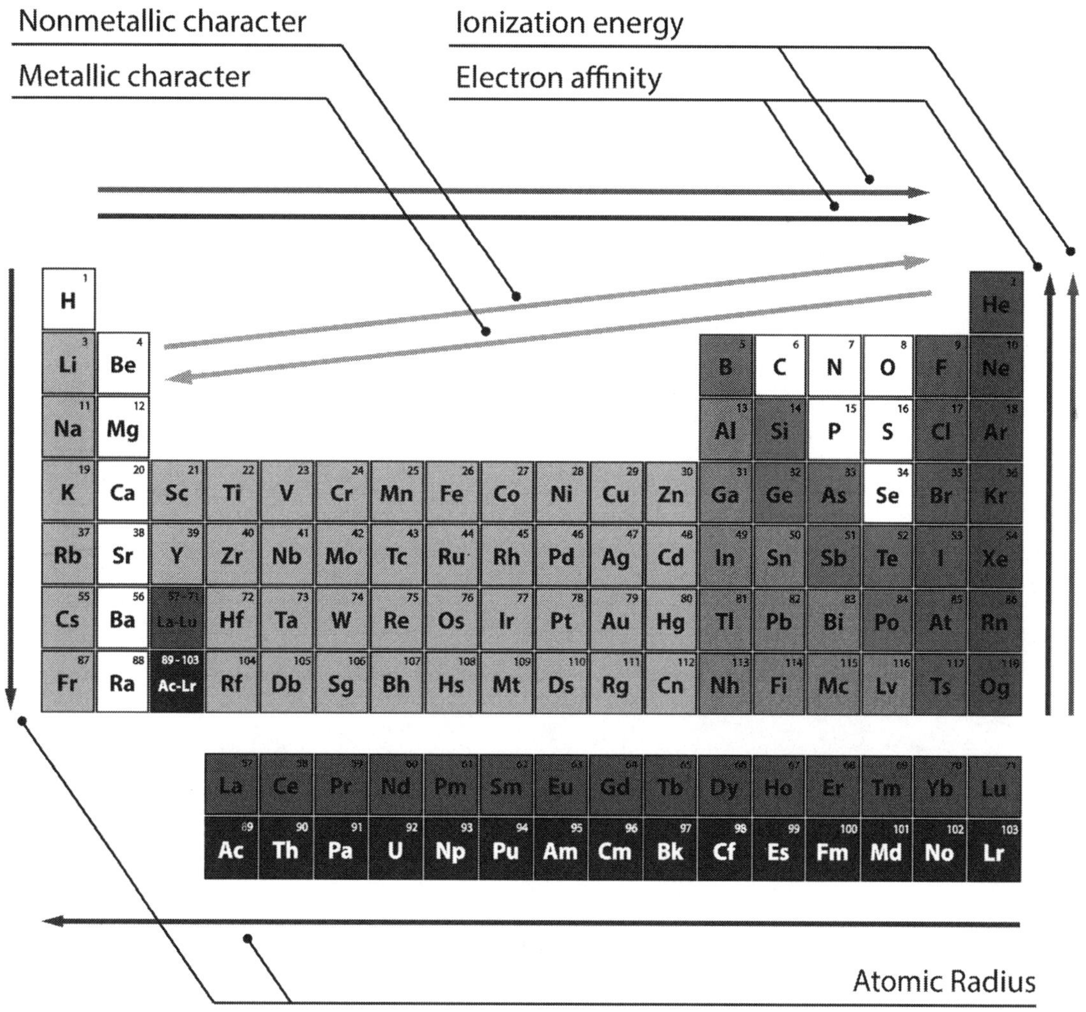

Figure 6. Trends in the periodic table of elements

Chemical Equations

Chemical reactions are represented by **chemical equations**. The equations help to explain how the molecules change during a reaction. For example, when hydrogen gas (H_2) combines with oxygen gas (O_2), two molecules of water are formed. The equation is written as follows, where the plus sign means *reacts with* and the arrow means *produces*:

$$2\,H_2 + O_2 \rightarrow 2\,H_2O$$

Two hydrogen molecules react with an oxygen molecule to produce 2 water molecules. In all chemical equations, the quantity of each element on the reactant side of the equation should equal the quantity of the same element on the product side of the equation. This is due to the law of conservation of matter. If this is true of the equation, the equation is described as balanced. To appropriately label and balance the number of elements on each side of the equation, the coefficient of the element should be multiplied by the subscript next to the element. Coefficients and subscripts are used for quantities larger than one. The **coefficient** is the number located directly to the left of the element.

The **subscript** is the small-sized number directly to the right of the element. In the equation above, on the left side, the coefficient of the hydrogen is 2, and the subscript is also 2, which makes a total of 4 hydrogen atoms. There are 2 oxygen atoms on the left side, so a coefficient of 2 is added in front of water (H_2O) to indicate that there are 2 oxygen atoms. The coefficient multiplied by the subscript in each element of the water molecule also gives 4 hydrogen atoms. This equation is balanced because there are 4 hydrogen atoms and 2 oxygen atoms on each side. The states of the reactants and products can also be written in the equation: gas (g), liquid (l), solid (s), and dissolved in water (aq). If they are included, they are noted in parentheses on the right side of each molecule in the equation.

Electronic Structure

Quantum Numbers

Based on quantum mechanics, an electron can be described by a wavefunction, which gives the probability of locating an electron at several points in space. The **wavefunction** for an electron in an atom is also called an atomic orbital and has a particular shape. Four quantum numbers describe an electron in an atom: the **principal quantum number (n)**, the **angular momentum quantum number (l)**, the **magnetic quantum number (m_l)**, and the **spin quantum number (m_s).** The first 3 quantum numbers describe the wavefunction and are required because there are 3 dimensions in space (Table 3).

An integer or positive whole number designates the principal quantum number (n), which describes a shell and can range from $n = 1$ (K shell), 2 (L shell), 3 (M shell), and so on. The size of the atomic orbital is associated with the principal quantum number and the greater the value, the larger the atomic orbital. The rows or periods in the periodic table are connected to the principal quantum number. Chlorine (Cl) is found in row 3, and the largest permissible value of the quantum number is three ($n = 3$). Chlorine may have several atomic orbitals with the same principal quantum number, which indicates that the orbitals are part of the same shell ($n = 3$).

For orbitals within the same shell (for example, $n = 3$), the angular momentum quantum number distinguishes the orbitals, which can have differing shapes. The value of the angular momentum number is a positive whole number that ranges from 0 to $n - 1$. The chlorine atom ($n = 3$) has 3 different types of orbitals with a specific shape denoted by the angular quantum number (l). The possible values of l for the chlorine atom are 0, 1, and 2 because $n - 1 = 3 - 1 = 2$. For $n = 3$ (M shell), there are 3 possible orbitals, with different shapes, which describe the area where the electron is found. For the M shell found in chlorine (Table 3), there are 3 different subshells denoted by the following letters: s, p, and d.

For an electron within a given shell, the value of the principal quantum number (for example, $n = 3$) is followed by the letter designation for a specific subshell (s, p, or d). For example, the atomic orbitals 3s, 3p, and 3d are 3 different subshells belonging to the M shell ($n = 3$). The quantum numbers associated with the 3p subshell are $n = 3$ and $l = 1$. If the M shell is the outermost shell that has electrons located farthest from the atomic nucleus, then that shell is also called the valence electron shell. Figure 7 shows the different types of atomic orbitals corresponding to a specific value of l.

Table 3 shows the different shells, subshells, and electron orbitals associated with varying quantum numbers.

Table 3. Quantum numbers that describe the wavefunction					
Principal quantum number (n): shell size or energy					
shell	K	L	M	N	
n-value	1	2	3	4	
Angular quantum number (l): orbital shape					
Orbital or subshell	s	p	d	f	g
l value $(n-1)$	0	1	2	3	4
shape	Spherical	Dumbbell	Cloverleaf	Hat	
Magnetic quantum number (m_l): orbital orientation					
Subshell type	s	p	d	f	g
$2l+1$ orbitals	One orbital	Three orbitals	Five orbitals	Seven orbitals	Ten orbitals
Allowed values of m_l from $-l$ to $+l$	0	−1, 0, +1	−2, −1, 0, +1, +2	−3, −2, −1, 0, +1, +2, +3	−4, −3, −2, −1, 0, +1, +2, +3, +4
Maximum number of electrons	2	6	10	14	20

For an atomic orbital with given values for n and l, the magnetic quantum number (m_l) identifies the orientation of that orbital in space. The values of m_l range from $-l$ to $+l$. For example, if the principal quantum number is three ($n = 3$), then the maximum value of l is $n - 1 = 3 - 1 = 2$, which corresponds to the s ($l = 0$), p ($l = 1$) and d ($l = 2$) orbitals. For the d subshell, there are 5 orbitals (equal to $2l + 1$) which have 5 possible orientations. Each d orbital has a specific m_l value: m_l = −2, −1, 0, +1, or +2, corresponding to a different orientation. Table 4 lists the permissible quantum values for $n = 3$, which have a specific subshell notation.

Table 4. Allowed quantum values for $n = 3$ in an atomic orbital				
Subshell notation	n	l $(n-1)$	m_l $-l$ to $+l$	Number of orbitals $= \mathbf{2l+1}$
3s	3	0	0	1
3p	3	1	−1, 0, +1	3
3d	3	2	−2, −1, 0, +1, +2	5

The spin quantum number has a possible value of $-\frac{1}{2}$ or $+\frac{1}{2}$ and refers to the 2 possible orientations that an electron can have about a spin axis. Since the electron spins about its axis, much like the Earth, it generates a magnetic field that corresponds to a spin up value ($+\frac{1}{2}$) or spin down value ($-\frac{1}{2}$).

Atomic Orbitals

For any given value of the principal quantum number ($n = 1, 2, 3$, and so on), the atomic orbital is spherically shaped and increases in size as n increases. Figure 7 shows the 3s orbital; a cutaway portion shows the electron distribution of the orbital. The 3s orbital contains 3 dense or dark regions where the electron is most likely to be found. There are 2 regions in the 3s orbital called nodes where there is zero probability of the electron being found.

The 3s orbital also indicates that there is a relatively small electron distribution around the nucleus and in between the first and second node (small second ring). Therefore, the 3s orbital has a small overlap with the 2s and 1s orbital, which is better illustrated in a total radial probability graph. The l value for the s orbital will always be zero since there is only one possible orientation for a sphere. A p orbital has an l value equal to one, which means there are 3 possible orientations of the p orbitals; they can lie along the x ($m_l = -1$), y ($m_l = 0$), or z ($m_l = +1$) axes. An l value equal to 2 corresponds to the d orbital, which has 5 orbitals and orientations. Figure 7 shows a d_{yz} orbital, indicating that the cloverleaf-shaped orbital lies along the y and z planes.

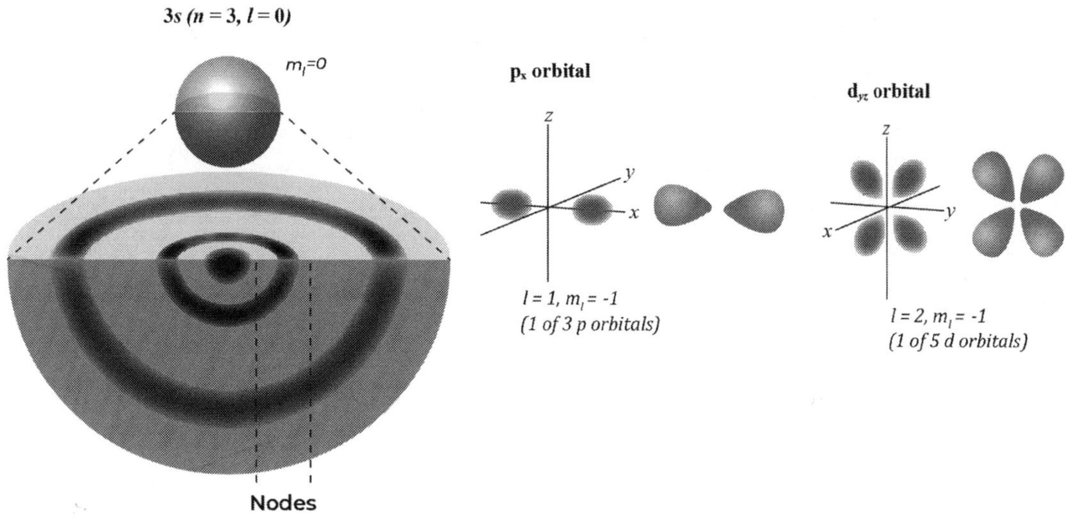

Figure 7. The s, p, and d atomic orbitals

Pauli Exclusion Principle

The circulating electric charge in an electron creates a magnetic field that may point up ($+\frac{1}{2}$) or down ($-\frac{1}{2}$) toward an external magnet. An electron in a hydrogen 1s orbital can have a spin value of $m_s = +\frac{1}{2}$ or $m_s = -\frac{1}{2}$. Multi-electron atoms also contain electrons with only 2 possible spin orientations. The **Pauli exclusion principle** states that for 2 electrons, the quantum numbers n, l, m_l, and m_s must not be identical. For example, no 2 electrons can have the following quantum numbers: $n = 2$, $l = -1$, $m_l = 0$, and $m_s = +\frac{1}{2}$. Each electron must have a different m_s value.

Table 5. Allowed quantum numbers for 2 electrons in the same atomic orbital

	n	l	m_l	m_s
Electron 1	2	1	−1	$+\frac{1}{2}$
Electron 2	2	1	−1	$-\frac{1}{2}$

Table 5 indicates that each electron is located in the L shell ($n = 2$), which can be found in one p atomic orbital ($l = 1$) located along the x-axis (Figure 7). However, the spin values must be opposites.

everything else can be the same, but spins must be opposite

Physically, this means that only 2 electrons can occupy one atomic orbital (for example, 2p) but have opposite spin.

Orbital diagrams, electron configurations, and Hund's Rule

Rather than drawing atomic orbitals (Figure 7) to show how electrons occupy a subshell (2p), orbital diagrams are used for simplification. An orbital is represented by a circle which may be filled by an up or down arrow to indicate that an electron is occupying that orbital. Only 2 electrons or arrows can occupy an orbital but must be opposite in spin or direction. The orbital diagrams for several elements are shown in Figure 8 below. The 1s and 2s orbitals are slightly separated from one another to indicate the difference in energies between each subshell or orbital. The energy of the orbitals increases from 1s to 2p.

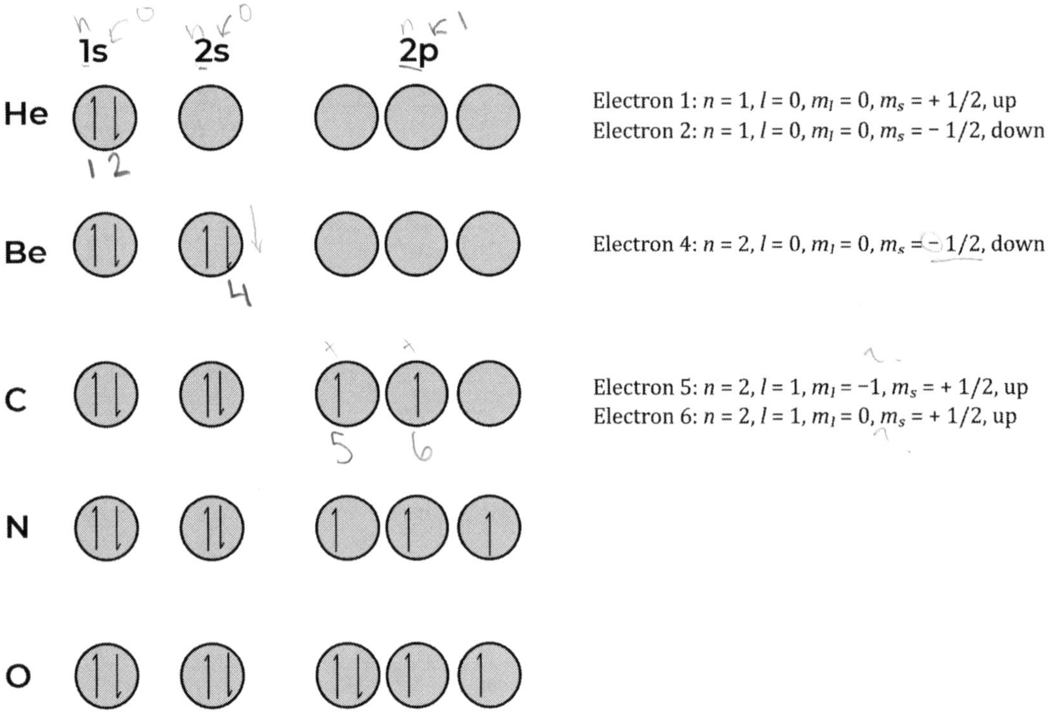

Figure 8. Orbital diagrams for several elements in the s and p subshells

There are three 2p atomic orbitals since there are three ways that orbital can be arranged in space ($m_l = -1, 0, +1$, Figure 7). The three 2p orbitals are close to each other since they are degenerate or similar in energy.

For a neutral helium atom, the atomic number equals 2, so there is a total of 2 electrons, which are represented by 2 arrows in the orbital diagram. These electrons fill the lower-energy 1s orbital first. The quantum numbers for each electron in helium are shown in Figure 8, and each electron has an m_s value opposite in sign. If the arrow points up, then $m_s = +\frac{1}{2}$. If the arrow points down, then $m_s = -\frac{1}{2}$. The electron configuration for helium, which shows the subshell notation followed by a whole number superscript, can be written as He: $1s^2$. The superscript indicates that there are 2 electrons in the 1s shell.

Beryllium has 4 electrons ($Z = 4$), which will fill up the 1s shell and 2s subshell. Electrons fill the 2s orbital first since it is lower in energy compared to the 2p orbital. The third and fourth electron also have opposite spins, as in the 1s orbital. The electron configuration of beryllium is $1s^2 2s^2$. The orbital diagrams of C and N are similar in that the electrons in the 2p orbitals do not pair up into one 2p orbital. Instead, the electrons are dispersed into another 2p orbital. This trend is referred to as **Hund's rule**, which explains that electrons are placed in separate orbitals with a subshell with the same spin. Once all the subshells are occupied with one electron containing the same spin (symbolized by a half arrow, e.g., ↿), then other electrons with the opposite spin (⇂) begin to pair or occupy these same orbitals, for example, oxygen. By following Hund's rule for drawing orbital diagrams, electron repulsion is minimized, and the lowest energy arrangement of electrons is attained. The electron configurations for carbon, nitrogen, and oxygen are similar with the exception to the number of electrons in the 2p subshell:

$\mathrm{C: 1s^2 2s^2 2p^2}$ or $\mathrm{[He] 2s^2 2p^2}$

$\mathrm{N: 1s^2 2s^2 2p^3}$ or $\mathrm{[He] 2s^2 2p^3}$

$\mathrm{O: 1s^2 2s^2 2p^4}$ or $\mathrm{[He] 2s^2 2p^4}$

The electron configuration for C, N, and O can be rewritten with a noble gas configuration (He) since each element contains a filled 1s shell. Writing an electron configuration using a noble gas configuration is especially useful for heavy elements.

The Aufbau Principle and Electron Configurations

Building electron configurations for multi-electron systems will require knowing how many electrons can occupy a subshell. Table 3 shows that the maximum number of electrons per subshell becomes greater as l increases. The d subshell has $l = 2$ with a maximum of 5 orbitals. From the Pauli exclusion principle, the total number of electrons in the d subshell is 10 since $5 \text{ orbitals} \times 2\ \mathrm{e^-} \text{ per orbital} = 10\ \mathrm{e^-}$. The electron configurations shown in Figure 8 are ground state configurations since they represent the lowest energy state. For helium, if one of the electrons moves outside the 1s shell to a 2p subshell, then that electron configuration would correspond to an excited state:

Ground state electron configuration of helium: $1s^2$

Excited state electron configurations of helium: $1s^1\mathbf{2s^1}$ or $1s^1\mathbf{2p^1}$

The total number of electrons in the excited state remains the same. The **Aufbau principle** or **building-up principle** is often used to write and predict the ground state electron configuration by filling subshells with electrons in a successive order based on orbital energies. The ordering of subshells based on the building-up principle is: 1s, 2s, 2p, 3s, 3p, 4s, 3d, 4p, 5s, 4d, 5p, 6s ...

The ordering indicates that the 2s orbital has lower energy than the 3s orbital and that a 3s orbital has lower energy than a 3p subshell orbital. In a multi-electron atom, when the number of electrons is equal to or greater than 21, the 3d subshell is lower in energy compared to the 4s subshell. The decreased energy of the subshell is due to the interaction energy with other subshells.

For a neutral atom, the number of electrons is equal to its atomic number, Z. In the periodic table, when moving successively from one element to the next, O to F, the number of electrons added to the electron configuration increases by one since Z increases by one. Adding one electron to the oxygen configuration would give the fluorine configuration $1s^2 2s^2 2p^5$. Adding 3 electrons to the oxygen electron configuration would give the sodium electron configuration $1s^2 2s^2 2p^6 3s^1$, which can be rewritten using a noble gas core: [Ne] $3s^1$. The electrons outside the noble gas core are called the valence electrons. For oxygen, the valence shell is $2s^2 2p^5$, and for sodium, it is $3s^1$. The main group elements (IA–VIIIA) in the periodic table have a valence shell of $ns^a np^b$ where a and b reflect the number of electrons in the s and p subshells. Chlorine is in the third row and belongs to group VIIA, so $n = 3$ and the sum of a and b must equal 7, the group number. Chlorine's valence shell configuration is $3s^2 3p^5$.

For an electron configuration with $Z = 21$ or greater, the 3d subshell begins to fill. However, when the electron configuration is written, the 3d subshell is placed before the 4s shell, which shouldn't be confused with the building-up principle order. For instance, the ground state electron configuration for calcium is Ca ($Z = 20$):

$$1s^2 2s^2 2p^6 3s^2 3p^6 4s^2$$

The building-up principle says that the 4s subshell is filled before the 3d subshell. The ground state electron configuration for scandium is: Sc ($Z = 21$):

$$1s^2 2s^2 2p^6 3s^2 3p^6 \mathbf{3d^1} 4s^2$$

In electron configuration, 3d is placed before 4s.

The electron configuration for scandium is written in order of increasing principal quantum number. When writing electron configurations for ions, electrons in the highest n-value orbital are removed first: Sc^+ ($Z = 21$):

$$1s^2 2s^2 2p^6 3s^2 3p^6 \mathbf{3d^1} 4s^1$$

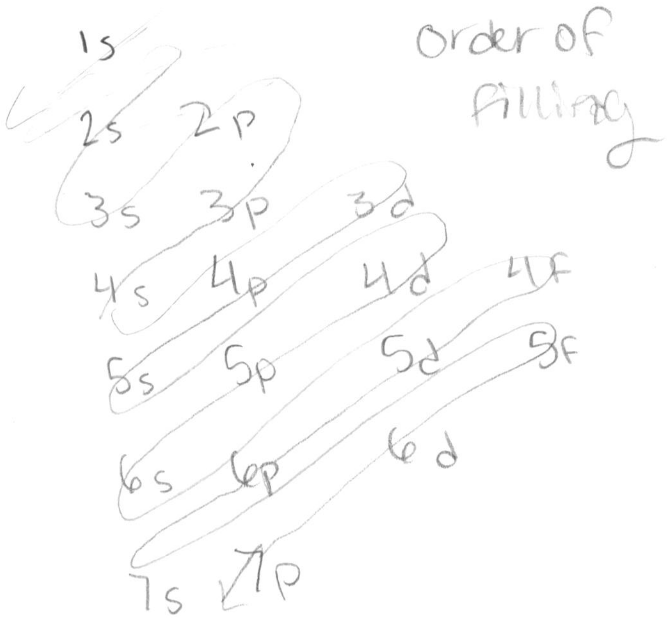

Formula Calculations and the Mole

Molar Mass and Formula Mass

When producing a product or substance in the laboratory, scientists routinely measure the initial mass of that starting material. Soda or pop is composed of 90% water (H_2O) and about 10% sugar. The sugar may be a synthetic substitute called high fructose corn syrup or HFCS-55, which is 55% fructose and 42% glucose ($C_6H_{12}O_6$). A lab scientist at a soda company or a person with a home soda machine would add 39 grams of the sugar to about 330 grams of water to make one can of soda. For mixtures that involve chemical reactions, it becomes important to relate the mass of a substance to the number of atoms or molecules. For example, how many water molecules are in a gram of soda? The concepts of formula mass, molar mass, and mole are often used by chemists to help answer questions related to the quantity of atoms in a substance.

The mass of a single water molecule (H_2O) is the **molecular mass**, which is the sum of the atomic mass of every individual atom in a molecule. There are 2 hydrogen atoms and one oxygen atom in water. The atomic mass of hydrogen and oxygen is 1.008 atomic mass units (amu) and 16.00 amu, so the molar mass is:

$$H_2O \text{ molar mass} = 2 \times 1.008 \text{ amu} + 1 \times 16.00 \text{ amu} = 18.02 \text{ amu}$$

The **formula mass** refers to the sum of the atomic mass of every atom in a given chemical formula unit for any compound. The formula mass can refer to a molecular or ionic compound. For example, the formula mass for glucose ($C_6H_{12}O_6$) and magnesium hydroxide ($Mg(OH)_2$) is:

$$C_6H_{12}O_6 \text{ formula mass} = 6 \times 12.01 \text{ amu} + 12 \times 1.008 \text{ amu} + 6 \times 16.00 \text{ amu} = 180.16 \text{ amu}$$

$$Mg(OH)_2 \text{ formula mass} = 1 \times 24.31 \text{ amu} + 2 \times 16.00 \text{ amu} + 2 \times 1.008 \text{ amu} = 58.33 \text{ amu}$$

The molecular and formula mass of a molecular compound such as glucose are identical. However, the molecular mass of magnesium hydroxide has no meaning since the compound is ionic.

The Mole and Avogadro's Number

It can be useful to simplify large numbers. For example, suppose that you are selling donuts for a school fundraiser. When you place an order with Krispy Kreme, you are likely to say you want an order of 100 dozen donuts rather than 1,200 donuts. Using the unit of a dozen (twelve) is useful when dealing with large quantities. Likewise, the concept of the mole is useful when dealing with a large number of molecules, ions, or atoms in a substance. Like the unit of dozen, the **mole** (or mol) was based on the amount of a given substance that has the same number of atoms as 12 grams of carbon. The specific number is often referred to as **Avogadro's number**, N_A, and is equal to one mole.

$$1 \text{ mole of any substance} = N_A = 6.022 \times 10^{23} \text{ molecules, ions, atoms, or any substance}$$

Like the dozen, the mole can refer to any substance, as shown in the following examples.

$$1 \text{ dozen iPhones} = 12 \text{ iPhones}$$

$1 \text{ mole of iPhones} = 6.022 \times 10^{23} \text{ iPhones}$

$1 \text{ dozen } H_2O \text{ molecules} = 12\ H_2O \text{ molecules}$

$1 \text{ mole of } H_2O \text{ molecules} = 6.022 \times 10^{23}\ H_2O \text{ molecules}$

For one mole of water, the number of water molecules is equal to N_A. The number of oxygen atoms in one mole of water will also be equal to N_A since there is a one-to-one relationship between water and oxygen. However, the number of hydrogen atoms in one mole of water is $2 \times N_A$, which is shown by the following conversion:

$6.022 \times 10^{23}\ H_2O \text{ molecules} \times \frac{2 \text{ H atoms}}{1\ H_2O \text{ molecule}} = 1.204 \times 10^{24} \text{ H atoms}$

The calculation relies on using a conversion that says one molecule of water contains 2 hydrogen atoms. If you were given a question that asked for the number oxygen atoms (O, not molecular oxygen) in one mole of potassium carbonate (K_2CO_3), then it must be understood that for every formula unit of K_2CO_3 there are 3 oxygen atoms.

$1 \text{ mole of } K_2CO_3 \text{ units} = 6.022 \times 10^{23}\ K_2CO_3 \text{ units}$

$$1\ K_2CO_3 \text{ unit} = 3 \text{ O atoms}$$

$$\# \text{ of oxygen atoms} = 6.022 \times 10^{23}\ K_2CO_3 \text{ units} \times \frac{3 \text{ O atoms}}{1\ K_2CO_3 \text{ unit}}$$

$$1.807 \times 10^{24} \text{ O atoms}$$

Unit Conversions with the Mole

Based on the former definition of the mole (equal to N_A), which related the mass of carbon in grams to a mole (12 g/mol), the **molecular mass** of a substance in atomic mass units is equivalent to the **molar mass** in units of grams per mole (g/mol).

$$\text{molar mass} = \frac{\text{mass}}{\text{moles}}$$

In other words, if you were to measure 12 grams of a pencil tip, with a weighing scale, there would be 1 mole of carbon atoms: 12 g/mol of carbon is equal to 12 amu. Note that the "lead" in pencil tips is not lead (Pb) but a pure form of carbon graphite. Since the molar mass relates the mass of a substance to the mole amount, it is possible to calculate the mass of a single molecule. For instance, the molar mass (MM) of a (not ionic) substance such as water (H_2O) is 18.02 amu or g/mol, so the mass of a single water molecule is:

$$\text{mass of one } H_2O \text{ molecule} = \frac{18.02 \text{ g}}{1 \text{ mol } H_2O} \times \frac{1 \text{ mol } H_2O}{6.022 \times 10^{23}\ H_2O \text{ molecules}}$$

$$2.992 \times 10^{-23} \text{ grams per } H_2O \text{ molecule}$$

The previous problem makes use of dimensional analysis, which requires understanding the relationship between mass and moles and the relationship of moles to Avogadro's number. The relationship between the mass and moles of a substance is often used in chemical calculations. If 39.0 g of glucose ($C_6H_{12}O_6$) with a molar mass of 180.16 g/mol is found in a can of soda, then the number of moles is:

$$39.0 \text{ g } C_6H_{12}O_6 \times \frac{1 \text{ mol } C_6H_{12}O_6}{180.16 \text{ g } C_6H_{12}O_6} = 0.216 \text{ mol } C_6H_{12}O_6$$

When you are converting from grams to moles of a substance, the molar mass of the substance is inverted such that the units of mass cancel out. An additional calculation can be carried out to find the number of glucose molecules:

$$0.216 \text{ mol } C_6H_{12}O_6 \times \frac{6.022 \times 10^{23} \ C_6H_{12}O_6 \text{ molecules}}{1 \text{ mol } C_6H_{12}O_6}$$

$$1.30 \times 10^{23} \ C_6H_{12}O_6 \text{ molecules}$$

If the moles of the substance are given, then that value is multiplied by the molar mass, which will cancel out the units of the mole in the denominator. For instance, suppose 0.400 moles of glucose were added to a can of soda, the mass in grams is:

$$0.400 \text{ mol } C_6H_{12}O_6 \times \frac{180.16 \text{ g } C_6H_{12}O_6}{1 \text{ mol } C_6H_{12}O_6}$$

$$72.1 \text{ g } C_6H_{12}O_6$$

Since the amount of glucose in moles is about twice the value of the original amount found in a can of soda, it is expected that the final answer in grams should be roughly 2 times greater in mass.

Determining Mass Percentages from Formulas

Given the formula of a molecular or ionic compound, the mass percentage of a specific element can be determined. The **mass percentage** of an element E can be found using the following equation:

$$\text{mass percentage of E} = \frac{\text{mass of E in compound}}{\text{mass of compound}} \times 100\%$$

The numerator contains only the mass of the element E in grams in the compound, and the denominator contains the mass of the entire compound. The masses of the element and compound are determined from the molar mass given in the periodic table. For example, the molecular formula for caffeine is $C_8H_{10}N_4O_2$, and the mass percentage of nitrogen is:

$$\text{mass percentage of N} = \frac{4 \times 14.01 \text{ g}}{(8 \times 12.01 \text{ g}) + (10 \times 1.008 \text{ g}) + (4 \times 14.01 \text{ g}) + (2 \times 16.01\text{g})} \times 100\%$$

$$28.85\% \text{ N}$$

One mole of $C_8H_{10}N_4O_2$ has a mass of 194.22 grams, which is determined from the individual atomic masses in grams for each element. In the denominator, the molar masses of each element are multiplied by their subscript to obtain the correct molar mass of the compound. There are 8 moles of carbon, 10 moles of hydrogen, 4 moles of nitrogen, and 2 moles of oxygen. In the numerator, since there are 4 nitrogen atoms or 4 moles of nitrogen in the chemical formula of caffeine, the mass of nitrogen must be multiplied by 4 to obtain the correct mass. Other types of problems that relate to mass percentages may give you the mass of the compound and ask you to compute the mass of a specific element. For instance, a cup of coffee has about 95.0 mg of caffeine. How many milligrams of nitrogen are in 95.0 mg of caffeine? The answer to this question requires knowing the percentage of nitrogen in caffeine, which was previously calculated to be 28.85%. To find the mass of the element of interest (N), multiply the mass of caffeine and the percentage of nitrogen in decimal form:

$$\text{mass of nitrogen in 95.0 mg of caffeine} = 95.0 \text{ mg} \times 0.2885 = 27.4 \text{ mg}$$

The mass of nitrogen in 95.0 mg of caffeine is 27.4 mg. If the question asks for the mass of carbon instead, then the mass percentage of C must be determined first.

Elemental Analysis

The mass percentages of elements in a compound containing only C, H, and O can be indirectly found through a combustion process involving oxygen. The combustion of a known mass of a C, H, O-containing compound with molecular oxygen (O_2) will produce a specific amount of carbon dioxide and water. Given the mass of CO_2 and H_2O, the mass of carbon and hydrogen can be found using unit conversions or dimensional analysis. The result will give the original mass of carbon and hydrogen in the original compound, which also allows the mass of oxygen to be found.

For instance, ethylene glycol is a conventional antifreeze or coolant used in automobiles to prevent water from freezing or boiling inside an engine motor. Ethylene glycol is also used as a coolant to lower the temperature in graphical processing units, which are commonly used in PC gaming or scientific computing. If 19.14 g of ethylene glycol ($C_2H_6O_2$) is combusted in a furnace with 27.18 g and 16.74 g of CO_2 and H_2O collected, what is the mass percentage of C, H, O in $C_2H_6O_2$? A useful roadmap to solving this problem for the combustion of any C, H, O compound is outlined below:

$$\text{Step 1: mass of } CO_2 \rightarrow \text{moles of } CO_2 \rightarrow \text{moles of C} \rightarrow \text{mass of carbon}$$

$$\text{Step 2: mass of } H_2O \rightarrow \text{moles of } H_2O \rightarrow \text{moles of H} \rightarrow \text{mass of hydrogen}$$

In step 1, three unit conversions must be used. The first unit conversion requires converting the mass of CO_2 to moles of CO_2 using the molar mass of CO_2 (44.01 g/mol) obtained from the periodic table. The second unit conversion says that one mole of CO_2 contains one mole of carbon. The final unit conversion is simply the molar mass of carbon taken from the periodic table. These unit conversions must be arranged so that units cancel out accordingly:

$$27.18 \text{ g } CO_2 \times \frac{1 \text{ mol } CO_2}{44.01 \text{ g } CO_2} \times \frac{1 \text{ mol C}}{1 \text{ mol } CO_2} \times \frac{12.01 \text{ g C}}{1 \text{ mol C}} = 7.417 \text{ g C}$$

Step 2 is applied similarly using the correct unit conversions.

$$16.74 \text{ g } H_2O \times \frac{1 \text{ mol } H_2O}{18.016 \text{ g } H_2O} \times \frac{2 \text{ mol H}}{1 \text{ mol } H_2O} \times \frac{1.008 \text{ g H}}{1 \text{ mol H}} = 1.873 \text{ g H}$$

Knowing the mass of carbon and hydrogen enables the mass percentage of C and H to be calculated, which was shown above. The mass percentages are:

$$\% \text{ mass of C} = \frac{\text{mass of collected C}}{\text{initial mass of ethylene glycol}} \times 100\%$$

$$\frac{7.417 \text{ g}}{19.14 \text{ g}} \times 100\% = 38.75\% \text{ C}$$

$$\% \text{ mass of H} = \frac{\text{mass of collected H}}{\text{initial mass of ethylene glycol}} \times 100\%$$

$$\frac{1.873 \text{ g}}{19.14 \text{ g}} \times 100\% = 9.786\% \text{ H}$$

The percent mass of oxygen can now be found indirectly:

$$\text{mass \% oxygen} = 100\% - (38.75\% \text{ C} + 9.786\% \text{ H})$$

$$51.47\% \text{ O}$$

Given the molecular formula of ethylene glycol, the percentages of each element could have easily been calculated by finding the total mass of each element:

$$\frac{\text{molar mass of oxygen}}{\text{molar mass of } C_2H_6O_2} \times 100\% = \% \text{ mass of O}$$

However, in elemental analysis, the identity or molecular formula of the compound is not always known.

Finding the Empirical and Molecular Formulas

Suppose a sample weighing 41.8 g contains 16.7 g of sulfur with the remaining amount being oxygen.

$$\text{mass of oxygen} = 41.8 \text{ g unknown compound} - 16.7 \text{ g S} = 25.1 \text{ g O}$$

Note that subscripts are not placed on S or O since only the mass of the elements is considered. Instead, the value of the subscripts in the compound S_xO_y must be determined. The empirical formula can be found from the molar amounts by carrying out the following conversions:

$$16.7 \text{ g S} \times \frac{1 \text{ mol S}}{32.07 \text{ g S}} = 0.521 \text{ mol S}$$

$$25.1 \text{ g O} \times \frac{1 \text{ mol O}}{16.00 \text{ g O}} = 1.57 \text{ mol O}$$

find mols of elements

The **empirical formula** contains the simplest whole number ratio of atoms in a compound, so each calculated molar value must be divided by the smallest molar value, for example, 0.521 mol S.

$$x = \frac{0.521 \text{ mol S}}{0.521 \text{ mol S}} = 1$$

find ratio to smallest amount

multiply until you have all whole # ratios

$$y = \frac{1.57 \text{ mol O}}{0.521 \text{ mol O}} = 3.01 \approx 3$$

The empirical formula for the sulfur-oxygen containing compound is S_1O_3 or SO_3 and the empirical formula mass 80.07 g/mol. If another experiment determined the molecular mass to be 160.14 g/mol, then the actual **molecular formula**, which contains the exact number of each atom, can be obtained from the following:

$$n = \frac{\text{molecular mass}}{\text{empirical formula mass}} = \frac{160.14 \text{ g mol}^{-1}}{80.07 \text{ g mol}^{-1}} = 2.0$$

The molecular formula is:

$$(SO_3)_n = (SO_3)_2 \text{ or } S_2O_6$$

multiply empirical formula by n to get molecular formula

Stoichiometry

Stoichiometry

Stoichiometry investigates the quantities of chemicals that are consumed and produced in chemical reactions. Chemical equations are made up of reactants and products; stoichiometry helps elucidate how the changes from reactants to products occur, as well as how to ensure the equation is balanced.

When a chemical equation is written, it can be interpreted in terms of the number of molecules/formula units or the number of moles. For example, in Table 6, consider the reaction of hydrogen sulfide gas (H_2S) and molecular oxygen (O_2), which forms the products sulfur dioxide (SO_2) and water (H_2O). The reaction says that 2 molecules of H_2S react with 3 molecules of oxygen to produce 2 molecules of SO_2 and 2 molecules of H_2O. Alternatively, this could have been phrased as "two moles of H_2S reacts with 3 moles of O_2 to yield two moles of SO_2 and two moles of H_2O." Recall that one mole is equal to Avogadro's number ($N_A = 6.022 \times 10^{23}$ molecules), so the equation can have several interpretations, as shown in Table 6.

Table 6. Interpretations of a chemical equation

	$2\ H_2S(g)$ $+$	$3\ O_2(g)$ $\rightarrow$	$2\ SO_2(g)$ $+$	$2\ H_2O(g)$
mass	2×34.09 g H_2S	3×32.00 g O_2	2×64.07 g SO_2	2×18.02 g H_2O
molar	2 moles H_2S	3 moles O_2	2 moles SO_2	2 moles H_2O
molecular	2 molecules H_2S	3 molecules O_2	2 molecules SO_2	2 molecules H_2O
Avogadro's	$2 \times N_A$	$3 \times N_A$	$2 \times N_A$	$2 \times N_A$

Based on Table 6, how many grams of H_2S will be needed to react with 96.00 g (3×32.00 g) of O_2? Based on the mass interpretation, 68.18 g of H_2S will react completely with 96.00 g of O_2. Note that the question is specific to 2 moles of H_2S and 3 moles of O_2, which will remain fixed. In other words, the stoichiometric molar or mass ratio of H_2S to $O_2$is 2:3 and 68.18 g to 96.00 g.

Relating the Amounts of Substances

In chemical equations, molar relationships can be represented as a unit type conversion when performing stoichiometric calculations that require the molar conversion of one species to another. From Table 6, the reactant molar relationship is:

$$\frac{2\ \text{mol}\ H_2S}{3\ \text{mol}\ O_2} \quad \text{Converting moles of } O_2 \text{ to } H_2S$$

$$\frac{3\ \text{mol}\ O_2}{2\ \text{mol}\ H_2S} \quad \text{Converting moles of } H_2S \text{ to } O_2$$

These relationships can be read as saying, "For every three moles of O_2 (denominator), two moles of H_2S are required (numerator)." The terms in the denominator are mentioned first because this will be converted to the desired unit in the numerator. The stoichiometric relationship comes from the balanced chemical equation, which remains unchanged. Different stoichiometric relationships can be written, from the coefficients for each species, between the reactants and products, or just between the products.

$$\frac{2 \text{ mol } SO_2}{3 \text{ mol } O_2} \quad \text{Converting moles of } O_2 \text{ reactants to } SO_2 \text{ products}$$

$$\frac{2 \text{ mol } H_2S}{2 \text{ mol } SO_2} \quad \text{Converting moles of } SO_2 \text{ product to } H_2O \text{ products}$$

Consider the scenario where 4.00 moles of H_2S react with O_2. How many moles of H_2O are produced? The following roadmap helps clarify how to solve the problem:

$$\text{moles of } H_2S \text{ reactant} \rightarrow \text{moles of } H_2O \text{ product}$$

To figure out how many moles of H_2O are produced, an initial amount of reactant or product must be given. The only starting amount given is 4.00 moles of H_2O. Since the initial amount of O_2 is not stated, you can exclude O_2 from your calculations and assume that O_2 is present in excess. Based on the balanced equation shown in Table 6, the stoichiometric relationship between the reactant and product is 2 moles of H_2S for every 2 moles of H_2O. Therefore, using dimensional analysis, the moles of H_2O produced are:

$$4.00 \cancel{\text{mol } H_2S} \times \frac{2 \text{ mol } H_2O}{2 \cancel{\text{mol } H_2S}} = 4.00 \text{ mol } H_2O$$

Since the relationship between H_2S and H_2O is 1:1, the final answer will not change. Based on looking at the balanced equation, multiplying the equation by a factor of 2 doubles the amount of H_2O produced (2:2 H_2S to H_2O, and then one multiplies the equation by 2 to get 4:4 H_2S to H_2O). Stoichiometric calculations become more necessary when dealing with fractional molar amounts and when chemists are dealing with the mass of chemical substances.

Chemical reactions are limited by the amount of starting material, or reactants, available to drive the process forward. The reactant that has the smallest amount of substance is called the limiting reactant. The **limiting reactant** is completely consumed by the end of the reaction. The other reactants are called **excess reactants**. For example, gasoline is used in a combustion reaction to make a car move and is the limiting reactant of the reaction. If the gasoline runs out, the combustion reaction can no longer take place, and the car stops.

Suppose 3.5 moles of H_2S react with 2.0 moles of O_2. Which of the reactants is limiting or in excess? In other words, based on the stoichiometric relationship between the reactants, which reactant will be completely consumed first? One way to answer these questions is to figure out how much product (SO_2 or H_2O) will be produced from each reactant, H_2S and O_2. The product that is produced in the least amount would indicate that the starting reactant was limiting. A roadmap of each general calculations is shown below.

$$\text{Step 1: moles of } H_2S \text{ reactant} \rightarrow \text{moles of } H_2O \text{ product}$$

$$\text{Step 2: moles of } O_2 \text{ reactant} \rightarrow \text{moles of } H_2O \text{ product}$$

The general calculation may use SO_2, but the final answer regarding which reactant is limiting is still the same. For each step, each reactant must be converted to the same product. When converting the specified reactant in moles to the product (or another reactant), a stoichiometric ratio must be used. Since the chosen product is water, the relationships are:

$$\text{Step 1: } \frac{2 \text{ mol } H_2O}{2 \text{ mol } H_2S}$$

$$\text{Step 2: } \frac{2 \text{ mol } H_2O}{3 \text{ mol } O_2}$$

Each ratio is taken from the balanced chemical equation. Now multiply the initial molar amounts of each reactant with the stoichiometric relationships:

$$\text{Step 1: } 3.5 \cancel{\text{mol } H_2S} \times \frac{2 \text{ mol } H_2O}{2 \cancel{\text{mol } H_2S}} = 3.5 \text{ moles } H_2O$$

$$\text{Step 2: } 2.0 \cancel{\text{mol } O_2} \times \frac{2 \text{ mol } H_2O}{3 \cancel{\text{mol } O_2}} = 1.3 \text{ moles } H_2O$$

In step 2, no more than 1.3 moles of H_2O can be produced, which is less than the amount of H_2O produced in step 1. The results indicate that O_2will be consumed entirely, and there will be some excess H_2S left over. Therefore, the limiting reactant is $O_2$and the excess reactant is H_2S. The moles of the chosen product will be the initial amount of the limiting reactant. In practice, one may not be given the molar amounts of H_2S and O_2 but rather the mass amounts in grams. In such a scenario, the mass of each substance must be converted to the molar amount by using the molar mass of each reactant. Consider the following example:

$$119.32 \cancel{\text{g } H_2S} \times \frac{1 \cancel{\text{mol } H_2S}}{34.09 \cancel{\text{g } H_2S}} \times \frac{2 \text{ mol } H_2O}{2 \cancel{\text{mol } H_2S}} = 3.5 \text{ mol } H_2O$$

The quantity of product that is produced after consuming the limiting reactant can be calculated and is called the **theoretical yield of the reaction**. In practice, the reactants do not always convert to 100% of the products, and the produced sample may be lost during collection. So, the actual amount of the resulting product, called the **actual yield**, will be less than the theoretical amount. The actual yield is divided by the theoretical yield and then multiplied by 100 to find the **percent yield** for the reaction.

$$\text{percent yield} = \frac{\text{actual yield}}{\text{theoretical yield}} \times 100\%$$

Suppose you devise an experiment that collects SO_2 from the reaction shown in Table 6. If the amount of SO_2 collected from the experiment is 150.0 g, what is the percent yield of SO_2if you start with 120.0 g of H_2S and 125.0 g of O_2? A useful guide for steps involved in a stoichiometric calculation is shown below:

$$\text{grams of A} \xrightarrow{C1} \text{moles of A} \xrightarrow{C2} \text{moles of B} \xrightarrow{C3} \text{grams of B}$$

Each arrow or conversion (for example, C1) represents multiplication of a conversion factor, as shown below:

$$\text{Conversion 1: } \frac{\text{1 mole of A}}{\text{mass of A}} \quad \text{(Molar mass from periodic table)}$$

Conversion 2: $\frac{\#\text{ moles of B}}{\#\text{ moles of A}}$ (Stoichiometric ratio or coefficients taken from equation)

Conversion 3: $\frac{\text{mass of B}}{\text{1 mole of B}}$ (Molar mass from periodic table)

To determine the theoretical yield of O_2 produced, first figure out which reactant is the limiting one by using the first 2 conversions shown above for the following reaction:

$$2\ H_2S(g) + 3\ O_2(g) \rightarrow 2\ SO_2(g) + 2\ H_2O(g)$$

$$\text{Step 1: grams of } H_2S \overset{C1}{\rightarrow} \text{moles of } H_2S \text{ reactant} \overset{C2}{\rightarrow} \text{moles of } SO_2 \text{ product}$$

$$120.0\ g\ H_2S \times \frac{1\ mol\ H_2S}{34.09\ g\ H_2S} \times \frac{2\ mol\ SO_2}{2\ mol\ H_2S} = 3.520\ mol\ SO_2$$

$$\text{Step 2: grams of } O_2 \overset{C1}{\rightarrow} \text{moles of } O_2 \text{ reactant} \overset{C2}{\rightarrow} \text{moles of } SO_2 \text{ product}$$

$$125.0\ g\ O_2 \times \frac{1\ mol\ O_2}{32.00\ g\ O_2} \times \frac{2\ mol\ SO_2}{3\ mol\ O_2} = 2.604\ mol\ SO_2$$

Since the amount of SO_2 produced in step 2 is less, the limiting reactant is O_2, and the excess reactant is H_2S. To obtain the theoretical yield in grams, convert moles of SO_2, taken from Step 2, using the third conversion (C3) to convert to grams:

$$2.604\ mol\ SO_2 \times \frac{64.07\ g\ SO_2}{1\ mol\ SO_2} = 166.8\ g\ SO_2$$

The percent yield is:

$$\text{percent yield} = \frac{150.0\ g}{166.8\ g} \times 100\% = 89.93\%$$

Such a yield is good by collection standards. For the same problem, you could have been asked to find out how much of the excess reactant remains. Most of the 120.0 g of H_2S will react with all 125.0 g of O_2, but what is the mass of the remaining H_2S? Using steps 1 and 2 above, by finding the difference in moles of SO_2, the excess amount of H_2S left over from the reaction can be found. The theoretical excess moles of SO_2 are:

$$\text{excess moles } SO_2 = \text{moles of } SO_2 \text{ calculated from } H_2S - \text{moles of } SO_2 \text{ calculated from } O_2$$

$$= 3.520\ mol\ SO_2 - 2.604\ mol\ SO_2 = 0.916\ mol\ SO_2$$

Note that the excess moles of SO_2 refer to the extra amount of SO_2 obtained if the reactant H_2S was completely consumed. The excess amount of SO_2 can now be converted to grams of H_2S, and the calculation is similar to step 1 but done in reverse.

$$\text{excess moles of } SO_2 \rightarrow \text{excess moles of } H_2S \rightarrow \text{excess mass of } H_2S$$

$$0.916\ mol\ SO_2 \times \frac{2\ mol\ of\ H_2S}{2\ mol\ of\ SO_2} \times \frac{34.09\ g\ H_2S}{1\ mol\ H_2S} = 31.2\ g\ H_2S$$

Of the 120.0 g of H_2S used in the reaction, 31.2 g of H_2S is left over, so the amount consumed is:

$$120.0 \text{ g } H_2S - 31.2 \text{ g } H_2S = 88.8 \text{ g of } H_2S$$

Solutions and Aqueous Reactions

Solutions and Solution Concentrations

A homogeneous mixture, also called a **solution,** has uniform properties throughout a given sample. An example of a homogeneous solution is salt fully dissolved in warm water. In this example, salt is the **solute**, or the material being dissolved, and water is the **solvent**, or the material dissolving the solute. In this case, any number of samples taken from the parent solution would be identical.

One **mole** is the amount of matter contained in 6.022×10^{23} of any object, such as atoms, ions, or molecules. It is a useful unit of measure for items in large quantities. This number is also known as **Avogadro's number**. One mole of ^{12}C atoms is equivalent to 6.022×10^{23} ^{12}C atoms.

Molarity is the concentration of a solution. It is based on the number of moles of solute in one liter of solution and is written as the capital letter M. A 1.0 molar solution, or 1.0 M solution, has one mole of solute per liter of solution. The molarity of a solution can be determined by calculating the number of moles of the solute and dividing it by the volume of a chemical solution in liters. Molarity equals moles divided by liters:

$$\mathrm{M} = \mathrm{mol} \div \mathrm{L}$$

The resulting number is the mol/L or M for molarity of the solution. Alternatively, **percent concentration** can be written as parts of solute per 100 parts of solvent.

Another means of expressing concentration is **molality**, sometimes symbolized as an italic m or b to distinguish it from molarity (M). Units of molality are expressed in moles of solute per kilogram of solvent (mol/kg):

$$m = \frac{\text{moles of solute}}{\text{mass of solvent}} = \frac{\text{mol}}{\text{kg}}$$

Because this measure uses the mass of the solvent rather than the volume of the solution, it does not vary with temperature, such as the molarity of a liquid solution, which can slightly expand or contract. Note that the units for molality use the mass of the solvent, not the whole solution.

Concentrations may also be presented as parts per mass, the mass of a solute per mass unit of the solution. This can be given as **parts per billion (ppb)**, **million (ppm)**, or **hundred (percent mass)** of a solute in solution. When representing concentrations of highly dilute solutions, it can be useful to give it as parts per mass.

Additionally, **molar volume** measures the volume (in liters) occupied per mole of a substance, typically a gas, at a known temperature and pressure.

Chemical Reactions

Chemical reactions are characterized by a chemical change in which the initial reactants are transformed into new products. Chemical reactions may involve a change in color, the production of gas, the formation of a precipitate, or changes in heat content. The following are the 4 basic types of chemical reactions:

- **Decomposition reactions:** A compound is broken down into smaller elements. For example, $2\ H_2O \rightarrow 2\ H_2 + O_2$. This is read as saying, "Two molecules of water decompose into two molecules of hydrogen and one molecule of oxygen."

- **Synthesis reactions:** Two or more elements or compounds are joined together. For example, $2\ H_2 + O_2 \rightarrow 2\ H_2O$. This is as saying, "Two molecules of hydrogen react with one molecule of oxygen to produce two molecules of water."

- **Single displacement reactions:** A single element or ion takes the place of another element in a compound. It is also known as a substitution reaction. For example, $Zn + 2\ HCl \rightarrow ZnCl_2 + H_2$. The equation is read as saying, "Zinc reacts with two molecules of hydrochloric acid to produce one molecule of zinc chloride and one molecule of hydrogen gas (H2)." In other words, zinc will replace the hydrogen in hydrochloric acid.

- **Double displacement reactions:** Two elements or ions exchange a single element to form 2 different compounds, resulting in different combinations of cations and anions in the final compounds. It is also known as a metathesis reaction. For example:

$$H_2SO_4 + 2\ NaOH \rightarrow Na_2SO_4 + 2\ H_2O$$

  - Special types of double displacement reactions include:

    - **Oxidation-reduction (or redox) reactions:** Elements undergo a change in oxidation number. For example:

$$2\ S_2O_3{}^{2-}(aq) + I_2(aq) \rightarrow S_4O_6{}^{2-}(aq) + 2\ I^-(aq)$$

    - **Acid-base reactions:** These involve a reaction between an acid and a base, which produces a salt and water solution. For example:

$$HBr + NaOH \rightarrow NaBr + H_2O$$

    - **Combustion reactions:** A hydrocarbon (a compound composed of only hydrogen and carbon) reacts with oxygen (O_2) to form carbon dioxide (CO_2) and water (H_2O). For example:

$$CH_4 + 2\ O_2 \rightarrow CO_2 + 2\ H_2O$$

Oxidation-Reduction

Oxidation-reduction reactions, also known as **redox reactions**, are those in which electrons are transferred from one element to another. Batteries and fuel cells are 2 energy-related technologies that utilize these reactions. When an atom, ion, or molecule loses its electrons and becomes positively charged, it is described as being oxidized. When a substance gains electrons and becomes more negatively charged, it is reduced. In chemical reactions, if one element or molecule is oxidized, another must be reduced for the equation to be balanced. Although the transfer of electrons is evident in some reactions in which ions are formed, redox reactions also include those in which electrons are transferred but the products remain neutral.

Keep track of oxidation states or oxidation numbers to ensure the chemical equation is balanced. **Oxidation numbers** are assigned to each atom in an ion or neutral or uncharged substance. For a single atomic ion, the oxidation number is equal to the charge of the ion. For atoms in their original elemental form, the oxidation number is always zero. Each hydrogen atom in an H_2 molecule, for example, has an oxidation number of zero. The sum of the oxidation numbers in a molecule should be equal to the overall charge of the molecule. If the molecule is a positively charged ion, the sum of the oxidation numbers should be equal to the overall positive charge of the molecule. In ionic compounds that have a cation and anion joined, the sum of the oxidation numbers should equal zero.

All chemical equations must have the same number of elements on each side of the equation to be balanced. **Redox reactions** have an extra step of counting the electrons on both sides of the equation to be balanced. Separating redox reactions into oxidation reactions and reduction reactions is a simple way to account for all of the electrons involved. The individual equations are known as **half-reactions**. For the redox reaction to be balanced, the number of electrons lost in the oxidation reaction must be equivalent to the number of electrons gained in the reduction reaction.

The oxidation of tin (Sn) by iron (Fe) can be balanced by the following half-reactions:

$$\text{Oxidation: } Sn^{2+} \rightarrow Sn^{4+} + 2\ e^-$$

$$\text{Reduction: } 2\ Fe^{3+} + 2\ e^- \rightarrow 2\ Fe^{2+}$$

$$\text{Complete redox reaction: } Sn^{2+} + 2\ Fe^{3+} \rightarrow Sn^{4+} + 2\ Fe^{2+}$$

Diluting Solutions

When preparing acidic or basic solutions with specific molarity, the mass of that acidic or basic substance must be measured in the laboratory with a weighing scale followed by dilution with water. Such a solution is necessary when preparing standard solutions for use in acid-base titrations. For instance, suppose you prepared a concentrated solution of NaOH (40.00 g/mol) by adding 50.0 g of NaOH to 250.0 mL of distilled water. How would you prepare a 2.00 M NaOH solution? First, find the molarity of the initial concentrated NaOH solution:

$$\text{molarity of NaOH} = \frac{\text{moles of NaOH}}{\text{volume of NaOH in liters}} = \frac{50.0\text{ g NaOH} \times \dfrac{1\text{ mol NaOH}}{40.00\text{ g NaOH}}}{250.0\text{ mL} \times \dfrac{1\text{ L}}{1000\text{ mL}}}$$

$$= \frac{1.25\text{ mol NaOH}}{0.2500\text{ L}} = 5.00\text{ M NaOH}$$

In the numerator, the mass of NaOH is converted to moles of NaOH using the molar mass of NaOH. In the denominator, the volume of the solution is converted to liters. To make a 2.00 M solution of NaOH from a 5.00 M NaOH solution, use the following equation:

$$M_{\text{initial}}V_{\text{initial}} = M_{\text{final}}V_{\text{final}}$$

Dilutions

In practice, you would start with a molarity (M_{initial}) and volume (V_{initial}) of 5.00 M and 0.2500 L in a large beaker and add water up to a specific volume (V_{final}) to obtain a 2.00 M solution (M_{final}). To find the final volume, rearrange the dilution equation:

$$V_{\text{final}} = \frac{M_{\text{initial}}V_{\text{initial}}}{M_{\text{final}}} = \frac{(5.00\text{ M})(0.2500\text{ L})}{2.00\text{ M}} = 0.625\text{ L or }625\text{ mL}$$

Before diluting with distilled water, the beaker is filled with water up to the 250 mL marker. To obtain a 2.00 M solution, you would add water until it reaches the 625 mL marker. Suppose you were asked, "How much water must be added to a 250 mL 5.00 M solution of NaOH to make a 2.00 M solution?" The answer would be $625\text{ mL} - 250\text{ mL} = 375\text{ mL}$. On the other hand, suppose the question were, "What is the total volume needed to make a 2.00 M NaOH from a 250 mL 5.00 M NaOH solution?" Then, the answer would be 625 mL.

Quantitative Analysis: Volumetric Analysis (Stoichiometry in Solutions)

Solution stoichiometry deals with quantities of solutes in chemical reactions that occur in solutions. The concentrations of solutions are often expressed in molarity, which is equal to the number of moles per one liter of solution. The solute is HCl, and the solvent is water. Both components make up the solution. For instance, a 1.5 M solution of hydrochloric acid (HCl) contains 1.5 moles per one liter of solution. The quantity of a solute in a solution can be calculated by multiplying the molarity (M) of the solution by the volume in liters (L). If the molarity of a 2.0-liter solution of HCl is equal to 1.5 M, then the number of HCl moles is:

$$\text{Molarity }(M) = \frac{\text{moles}}{\text{Volume }(V)}$$

$$\text{moles HCl} = M \times V = 1.5\text{ M} \times 2.0\text{ L} = 3.0\text{ moles}$$

Similar to chemical equations involving simple elements, the number of moles of the elements that make up the solute should be equivalent on both sides of the equation. If a salt or solute such as sodium chloride (NaCl) or sodium hydroxide (NaOH) is added to water, it will completely dissociate into cations and anions.

$$\text{NaCl(s)} \xrightarrow{\text{H}_2\text{O}} \text{Na}^+\text{(aq)} + \text{Cl}^-\text{(aq)}$$

$$\text{NaOH(aq)} \xrightarrow{\text{H}_2\text{O}} \text{Na}^+\text{(aq)} + \text{OH}^-\text{(aq)}$$

Based on the conservation of mass, the chemical equation is written such that each element is present in equal molar amounts on both sides of the equation. **Solution stoichiometry** plays an essential role in identifying the concentration or amount of solute in a solution. When the concentration of a particular solute in a solution is unknown, a **titration** is used to determine that concentration. In a titration, the solution with the unknown solute is combined with a standard solution or **titrant**, which is a solution with a known solute concentration. The point at which the unknown solute has completely reacted with the known solute or titrant is called the **equivalence point**, which is the point in the titration where the moles of the unknown and known solute have equal molar amounts. Using the known information about the standard or titrant solution, including the concentration, volume, and the volume of the unknown solution, the concentration of the unknown solute is determined in a balanced equation.

For example, in the case of combining acids and bases, the **equivalence point** is reached when the resulting solution is neutral. HCl, an acid, combines with NaOH, a base, to form water and a neutral salt or a solution of Cl^- ions and Na^+ ions. Suppose that you are given a standard 2.0 M solution of sodium hydroxide, NaOH, and were asked to identify the concentration of a 25.00 mL solution of an unknown monoprotic acid (for example, an acid with one proton like HCl, Figure 9).

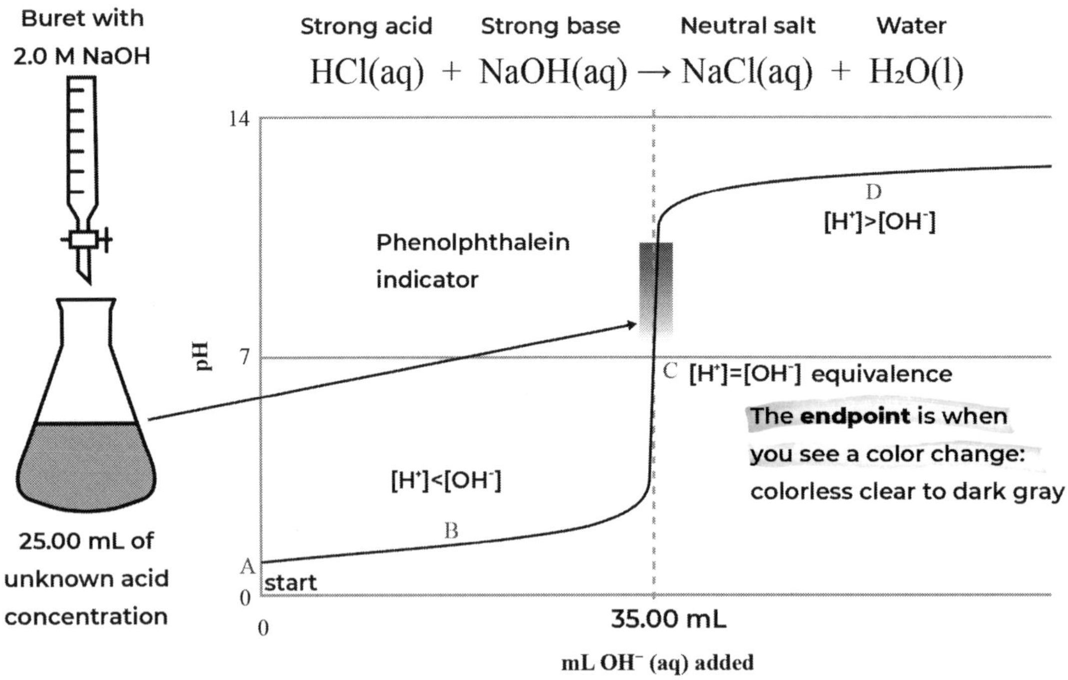

Figure 9. Titration of a strong acid by a strong base

Figure 9 represents a pH curve for the reaction of HCl and NaOH. The left inset figure shows a burette and an Erlenmeyer flask. The burette can hold up to 50.00 mL of the titrant, 2.0 M NaOH. The flask contains 25.00 mL of HCl acid of unknown concentration and a color indicator that changes to a pink color when the pH increases. A valve on the burette is opened to control how much base is added. The graph shows the pH value (0-14) with respect to the amount of NaOH or OH^- added in milliliters (mL). Initially, the number of NaOH moles added to the colorless solution of HCl is zero (point A in Figure 9), but as NaOH is gradually added, the pH of the solution increases slightly and becomes more basic (point B). At point B, about 17.50 mL of NaOH are added to the flask. The number of moles NaOH added is:

$$\text{mol NaOH or OH}^- = M \times V$$

$$2.0\text{ M} \times 17.50\text{ mL} \times \frac{1\text{ L}}{1000\text{ mL}} = 0.035\text{ mol OH}^-$$

The volume must be converted to liters since, by definition, the units for molarity are in moles per liter. If 0.035 moles of the hydroxide ion (OH^-) are added to the flask, what is the new concentration? The concentration of OH^- cannot be 2.0 M since adding NaOH to the acid increases the overall volume. The concentration or molarity of the hydroxide ion $[OH^-]$ is:

$$\text{molarity of } OH^- = \frac{0.035 \text{ mol } OH^-}{(17.50 \text{ mL} + 25.00 \text{ mL}) \times \frac{1 \text{ L}}{1000 \text{ mL}}} = 0.82 \text{ M } OH^-$$

Before the equivalence point, there is an unequal number of cations (H^+) and anions (OH^-), so the solution is not neutral. If equivalence occurs when 35.00 mL of the base are added, what is the concentration of the acid? Since there are an equal number of cations (H^+) and anions (OH^-), the following is true:

$$\text{moles of base } OH^- = \text{moles of acid } H^+$$

$$\text{molarity of acid} = \frac{\text{moles of acid } H^+}{\text{original volume of acid in flask (liters)}}$$

To find the unknown concentration of the acid in the 25.00 mL flask, first find the moles of OH^-, which is equal to the moles of acid, and then calculate the concentration of the acid:

$$\text{mol } OH^- = M \times V = 2.0 \text{ M } \times 35.00 \text{ mL} \times \frac{1 \text{ L}}{1000 \text{ mL}} = 0.070 \text{ mol } OH^-$$

$$\text{molarity of acid} = \frac{0.070 \text{ mol } H^+}{25.00 \text{ mL} \times \frac{1 \text{ L}}{1000 \text{ mL}}} = 2.8 \text{ M } H^+ \text{or HCl}$$

The answer is reasonable because it required 35.00 mL of a 2.0 M NaOH to neutralize a smaller volume of acid or 25.00 mL of a 2.8 M HCl solution. Note that the equivalence point and endpoint are not the same. The equivalence point is the theoretical or actual point at which the moles of acid and base are equal. The endpoint refers to the point at which the titration is stopped due to an observed color change. So, the actual volume you add may be near 35.00 mL but not exactly 35.00 mL.

Heat and Enthalpy

Energy and Heat of Reaction

Thermodynamics is a science that describes the relationship between heat and many forms of energy, such as kinetic and potential energy. **Energy** can be described as a physical property that has the ability to move matter and can be interconverted to electrical/light, mechanical, and chemical/thermal energy. These forms of energy are the most common ways that chemical reactions occur. **Chemical systems** or **molecules** are made up of moving electrons and nuclei and have a specific amount of potential and kinetic energy. The **kinetic energy** is due to the motion of the electrons and nuclei, and the potential energy is due to the bonding of atoms or molecules.

The **internal energy (U)** of a chemical system is defined as the sum of the molecules or particles of kinetic and potential energy. Every chemical bond in a chemical system has an associated amount of internal energy, and its chemical rearrangement, for example, bond forming and breaking, during the formation of the products can change its final internal energy. **Thermochemistry** is a branch of thermodynamics that refers to the study of how much heat is released or absorbed during a chemical reaction or physical change, which may result in a change in internal energy ΔU.

For example, physical changes in a chemical system such as water, $H_2O(g) \rightarrow H_2O(l)$, will release or absorb heat. The condensation of water vapor from the air onto the outer container of a cold beverage is an example of heat absorption. Water vapor has higher kinetic energy or internal energy than liquid water, and, consequently, the individual water molecules will be farther apart. The kinetic energy decreases for water undergoing a phase change from gas to liquid, and the chemical bonds in water vapor vibrate and rotate with less frequency. The final internal energy of liquid water is lower, and ΔU is negative.

To track heat flow for a chemical or physical change in a substance, it's important to define a system and the surroundings, since heat moves between these physical spaces. The **thermodynamic system** is typically defined as the substances under study that undergo a chemical or physical change. For example, the substances can be a chemical system that changes from reactants to products. The **surroundings** are everything else or the space around the chemical system. **Heat (q)** is described as the energy that flows between the system and the surroundings due to a difference in temperature. For example, when a match is struck against a matchbox, a small flame is created at the tip of the match and the surroundings suddenly become warmer. The reaction is described as follows:

$$P_4S_3(s) + 8\ O_2(g) \rightarrow P_4O_{10}(s) + 3\ SO_2(g) + \text{heat}$$

Tetraphosphorus trisulfide, $P_4S_3(s)$, and an oxidizing agent such as potassium chlorate are found on the match tip. When the tip is rubbed against the box, $P_4S_3(s)$ burns with the oxygen, $O_2(g)$, found in the air and produces heat. Chemical reactions or physical changes that release heat are called **exothermic reactions** and have a sign of $-q$, meaning heat is removed. Figure 10 shows a schematic of the chemical system (match), the surroundings, and the direction of heat flow. In this example, heat moves from hot (system) to cold (surroundings).

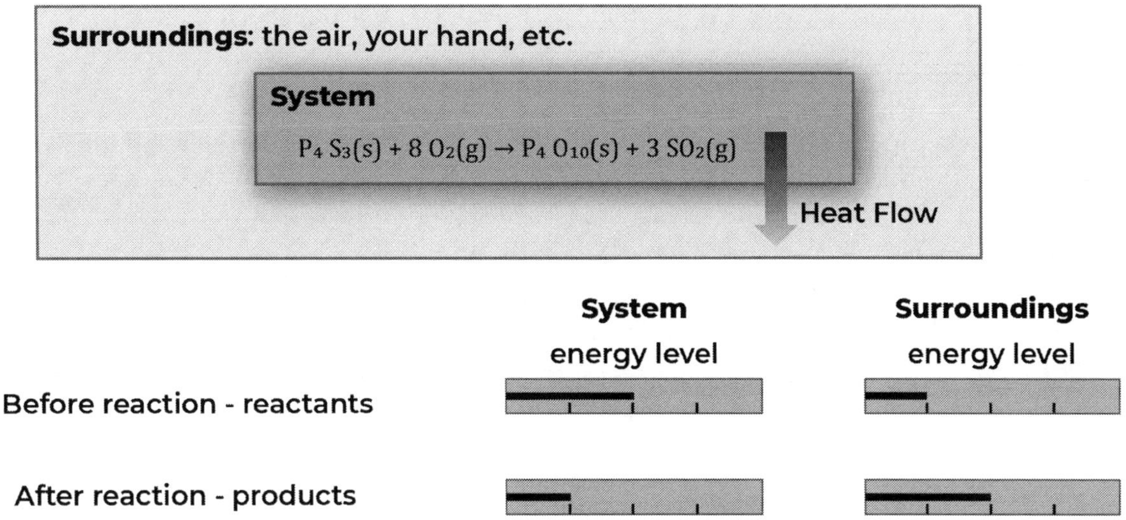

Figure 10. Schematic of the system and surroundings

The chemical system is the reactants, which have a specific amount of internal energy U_i. The surroundings include everything other than the reactants and the products. The burning of a match causes a change in the system's internal energy and releases heat to surroundings. Note that the change in internal energy is:

$$\Delta U = U_{\text{final (products)}} - U_{\text{initial (reactants)}}$$

As the reaction proceeds, heat will move from the system to the surroundings or from hot to cold, and the internal energy of the chemical system will decrease ($-\Delta U$) since it is transferred to the surroundings. Heat (q) for the system has a negative value since it is lost to the surroundings, $-q_{\text{system}}$. The value of q for the surroundings must be positive and is designated as $+q_{\text{surroundings}}$. The **law of conservation of energy** states that energy is neither created nor destroyed but merely transferred from the system to the surroundings or from the surroundings to the system. In other words, energy is conserved and $-q_{\text{system}} = +q_{\text{surroundings}}$. The magnitude of heat transferred is the same and only opposite in sign.

Consider the movement of heat in reverse or from the surroundings to the system. For instance, cold packs work by combining a specific salt, ammonium nitrate, $NH_4NO_3(s)$, with water. The water is initially separated by an inner pouch. When the pouch is broken, a chemical reaction between the salt solution and the water occurs, and the cold pack lowers to a temperature close to freezing due to heat absorption, meaning, heat is added to the reactants:

$$\text{Heat} + NH_4NO_3(s) \xrightarrow{H_2O(l)} NH_4^+(aq) + NO_3^-(aq)$$

The chemical system is the salt and water, and the surroundings are everything else, such as the pouch and your hand. Heat moves from the surroundings, such as your hand or the air, to the chemical substituents, which explains why a cold pack suddenly becomes cold. A chemical process that involves the absorption of heat ($+q$) is called an **endothermic reaction**. Since the chemical system gains heat, it must have been lost by the surroundings according to the conservation of energy:

$$\text{cold pack: } +q_{\text{system}} = -q_{\text{surroundings}}$$

Figure 11 provides a general summary regarding the sign for the **heat of reaction**, which is the value of q needed to return the chemical system to a specific temperature after the reaction takes place.

Reaction type	Sign of q	System result	Experimental observations
Exothermic	-q	Energy removed	Flask gets hot because heat is evolved
Endothermic	+q	Energy added	Flask gets cold because heat is absorbed

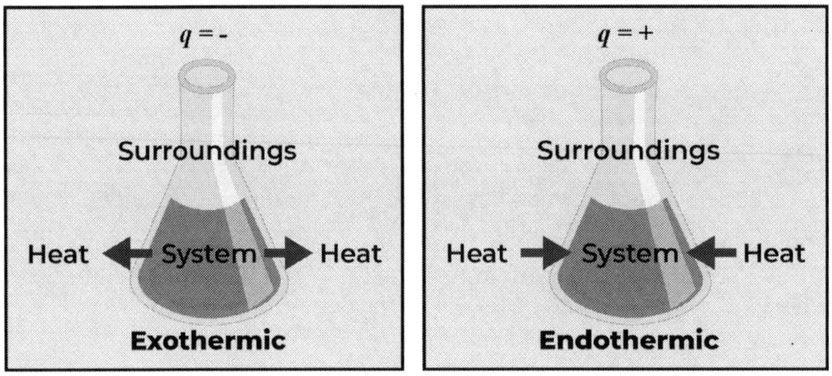

Figure 11. The direction of heat flow between the chemical system and the surroundings

Enthalpy of Reaction

Many chemical reactions that take place in a small laboratory setting or even in nature occur in the open atmosphere at constant pressure (~1.0 atm). Therefore, the "heat of the reaction" at constant pressure, q_p, is constantly moving between a specific system and its surroundings. The subscript p refers to the transfer of heat at constant pressure. Chemists often associate the heat of reaction, q_p, with a thermodynamic state function called **enthalpy (H)** which is related to the bond strength of a molecule. The enthalpy depends on the amount of the substance and is an extensive property that can be used to determine the amount of heat evolved or absorbed in a chemical reaction. For a given pressure and temperature, the difference in enthalpy between the reactants and products is called the **enthalpy of reaction ΔH (or $\Delta H^{\circ}_{\text{rxn}}$)**, which includes mass or mole units. The difference in enthalpy is related to the heat of reaction q_p by the following equation:

$$\Delta H = q_p$$

When the pressure is kept constant, the enthalpy of reaction is equal to the heat of reaction. The change in internal energy ΔU is equal to the enthalpy of reaction ΔH when there is no volume change (no work) in the chemical system. The change in internal energy ΔU is roughly the same when there is a small volume change. The chemical potential energy is associated with the positions of the nuclei and electrons. Since the internal energy, ΔU, is made up of the chemical potential energy, it is approximately equal to the enthalpy of reaction, ΔH, in the absence of work. For this reason, the **enthalpy** in a chemical sense refers to the strength of a molecular bond. Figure 12 below shows a synthesis reaction and the relationship between ΔU, ΔH, and q_p.

$$C(s) + O_2(g) \rightarrow CO_2(g)$$

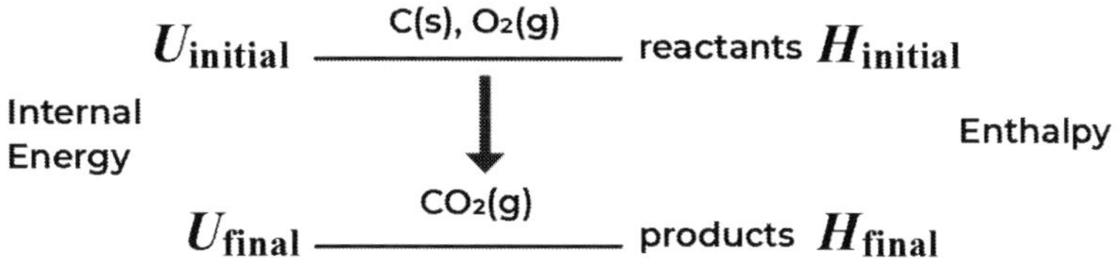

$$\Delta H = H_{final} - H_{initial} = q_p$$

$$\Delta U = U_{final} - U_{initial}$$

Figure 12. Relationship of ΔU and ΔH between the reactants and products

The reaction of pure carbon (C, diamond) with molecular oxygen, O_2, produces carbon dioxide, CO_2. The reactants have a specific amount of internal energy ($U_{initial}$) and enthalpy ($H_{initial}$). When the reaction proceeds to the products, the values of $U_{initial}$ and $H_{initial}$ decrease. If we were to look at the reactants and products (enthalpy) in terms of bond strength, more bonds are present in the reactants than in the products. Carbon (diamond allotrope) contains 4 single bonds, and molecular oxygen has one double bond, which gives a total of 6 bonds. In contrast, carbon dioxide contains 2 double bonds and a total of 4 bonds. It is expected that the initial bond enthalpy will be greater due to the number of bonds. As the reaction proceeds, the products have less bond enthalpy, and heat is released to the surroundings. The final values of internal energy and enthalpy will decrease. In practice, **thermochemical equations** are often written by showing the balanced chemical equation, which includes all phases and the calculated value for the enthalpy of reaction, which is based on the molar amounts. For example, the synthesis of carbon dioxide is written as:

$$C(s, diamond) + O_2(g) \rightarrow CO_2(g)$$

$$\Delta H = -395.4 \text{ kJ/mol}$$

For every one mole of C and one mole of O_2 that reacts, one mole of CO_2 is produced, which releases 395.4 kJ/mol to the surroundings. The reaction is exothermic since heat is released from the system to the surroundings. Recall that ΔH is an extensive property and will, therefore, depend on the molar amount. So, if the equation is multiplied by 2, then ΔH will double in magnitude:

$$2\ \mathrm{C(s, diamond)} + 2\ \mathrm{O_2(g)} \rightarrow 2\ \mathrm{CO_2(g)}$$

$$\Delta H = -790.8\ \mathrm{kJ/mol}$$

Enthalpies of Formation

Enthalpy of reactions ΔH or $\Delta H^{\circ}_{\mathrm{rxn}}$ is typically calculated at a **standard state (°)**, which refers to a standard temperature and pressure of 298.15 K and 1.0 atm. If the products (for example, CO_2) are produced from pure reactant elements (for example C and O_2) in their reference form, then the enthalpy ΔH, at a standard state, is referred to as the **standard enthalpy of formation, $\Delta H^{\circ}_{\mathrm{f}}$**. The **degree sign**, °, refers to standard conditions, and the subscript letter f refers to "**formation**." The **reference form** refers to a stable form of an element under standard conditions. For example, the reference form of carbon is the graphite allotrope C(s, graphite). If carbon dioxide is produced from elements which exist in a stable reference form, the standard enthalpy of formation of CO_2(g) is: $\Delta H^{\circ}_{\mathrm{f}} = -393.5\ \mathrm{kJ/mol}$.

$$\mathrm{C(s, graphite)} + \mathrm{O_2(g)} \rightarrow \mathrm{CO_2(g)}$$

$$\Delta H^{\circ}_{\mathrm{f}} = -393.5\ \mathrm{kJ/mol}$$

Notice that this value is different from the enthalpy of reaction, ΔH, shown above for the production of CO_2 (g) from carbon (s, diamond). Enthalpy of reactions, ΔH or $\Delta H^{\circ}_{\mathrm{rxn}}$, is typically calculated at their standard states and does not necessarily involve elements in their reference forms. Standard enthalpies of formation, $\Delta H^{\circ}_{\mathrm{f}}$, are important because they are used to calculate $\Delta H^{\circ}_{\mathrm{rxn}}$, which typically involve more complex reactions that do not include reactants or products in their reference form.

Enthalpies of Reaction

The **standard enthalpy of reaction, $\Delta H^{\circ}_{\mathrm{rxn}}$**, can be calculated from the enthalpies of formation, $\Delta H^{\circ}_{\mathrm{f}}$, for each reactant and product. The general formula for calculating $\Delta H^{\circ}_{\mathrm{rxn}}$ is:

$$\Delta H^{\circ}_{\mathrm{rxn}} = \sum n_{\mathrm{p}} \Delta H^{\circ}_{\mathrm{f}}(\mathrm{products}) - \sum n_{\mathrm{r}} \Delta H^{\circ}_{\mathrm{f}}(\mathrm{reactants})$$

The first term explains that ΔH_f° for one product must be multiplied by its stoichiometric coefficient, which is indicated by n_p (or n_r for reactants), to obtain a numerical value with units of kJ/mol. If there is more than one product, then each numerical value from each product is added, which is indicated by the summation term Σ. The second summation term applies to the reactants. For instance, we can find ΔH_{rxn}° for the production of carbon dioxide from 2 allotropes of carbon, C(s, graphite) and C(s, diamond). The enthalpies of formation are listed in Table 7 below.

Table 7. Enthalpies of formation for some compounds at 25 °C.	
Substance or Ion	$\Delta H_f^\circ \left(\frac{kJ}{mol}\right)$
$C(s, graphite)$	0
$C(s, diamond)$	1.897
$O_2(g)$	0
CO_2	−393.5

As a useful note, the enthalpy of formation, ΔH_f°, for some pure molecular elements is zero since these are reference elements. The ΔH_{rxn}° for the following reaction is shown below.

$$C(s, graphite) + O_2(g) \rightarrow CO_2(g)$$

$$\Delta H_{rxn}^\circ = \left[\overbrace{1 \times -393.5 \frac{kJ}{mol}}^{CO_2}\right] - \left[\overbrace{\left(1 \times 0 \frac{kJ}{mol}\right)}^{C(s,\,graphite)} + \overbrace{\left(1 \times 0 \frac{kJ}{mol}\right)}^{O_2}\right] = -393.5\ kJ/mol$$

Two terms are expected in the second parenthesis since there are 2 different reactants. The ΔH_{rxn}° for carbon dioxide produced from the carbon allotrope, graphite, is equal to ΔH_f°. However, for the production of carbon dioxide from the carbon allotrope, diamond, we have:

$$C(s, diamond) + O_2(g) \rightarrow CO_2(g)$$

$$\Delta H_{rxn}^\circ = \left(\overbrace{1 \times -393.5 \frac{kJ}{mol}}^{CO_2}\right) - \left(\overbrace{1 \times 1.897 \frac{kJ}{mol}}^{C(s,\,diamond)} + \overbrace{1 \times 0 \frac{kJ}{mol}}^{O_2}\right) = -395.4\ kJ/mol$$

The reaction above (involving graphite) is slightly less exothermic. Recall that the heat of reaction is related to enthalpy of reaction by $q_p = \Delta H$. The ΔH_{rxn}° is typically calculated from ΔH_f°, which can be found from an experimental q_p. In constant pressure calorimetry experiments, the heat of reaction, q_p, is given by:

$$q_p = m \times C_s \times \Delta T$$

The terms m, C_s, and ΔT ($\Delta T = T_f - T_i$) are the mass (grams), specific heat capacity (units of $\frac{J}{g\,°C}$), and the change in temperature (°C). The **specific heat capacity** is the amount of heat needed to raise the temperature (T) by 1 °C for every one gram of a specific material, for example, a silver coin. By calculating q_p, which has units of J or kJ, the enthalpy of reaction with respect to the amount of material can be found.

If ΔH_{rxn} is near standard conditions, then the value is equivalent to $\Delta H^{\circ}_{\text{rxn}}$. Suppose you were hiding a few silver coins in your freezer. If you removed one coin which has a mass of 28.35 g (1 ounce) from your refrigerator, which had an initial temperature of −18.0 °C (T_{i}), what is ΔH_{rxn} if the final temperature (T_{f}) is 37.0 °C? The specific heat capacity, C_{s}, of pure silver is 0.235 $\frac{\text{J}}{\text{g °C}}$. ΔH_{rxn} is calculated as follows:

$$q_p = \Delta H = (28.35\ \text{g}) \times 0.235 \frac{\text{J}}{\text{g °C}} \times \big(37.0\ \text{°C} - (-18.0\ \text{°C})\big) = -366\ \text{J}$$

$$\Delta H_{\text{rxn}} = \frac{-366\ \text{J}}{28.35\ \text{g}} = -12.9\ \text{J/g}$$

Note that if you're grabbing the coin and placing it on your hand, then the coin loses heat while your hand gains it:

$$-q_{p,\,\text{coin}} = +q_{p,\,\text{hand}}$$

Although the subscript rxn in ΔH_{rxn} is used, it doesn't always indicate an actual reaction but can be better understood as the gaining or loss of heat per amount of substance.

Structure and Bonding

Chemical Bonding

Chemical bonding typically results in the formation of a new substance, called a **compound**. Only the electrons in the outermost atomic shell can form chemical bonds. These electrons are known as **valence electrons**, and they determine the chemical properties of an atom.

Chemical bonding occurs between 2 or more atoms that are joined together. There are 3 types of chemical bonds: ionic, covalent, and metallic. The characteristics of the different bonds are determined by how electrons behave in a compound. **Lewis structures** were developed to help visualize the electrons in molecules; they are a method of visually representing a compound's structure and its electron composition. A Lewis symbol for an element consists of the element symbol and a dot for each valence electron. The dots are located on all 4 sides of the symbol, with a maximum of 2 dots per side, and a maximum of 8 dots, or electrons, total. The octet rule explains that atoms tend to gain, lose, or share electrons until they have a total of 8 valence electrons.

Ionic bonds are formed from the electrostatic attractions between oppositely charged atoms. They result from the transfer of electrons from a metal on the left side of the periodic table to a nonmetal on the right side. The metallic substance often has low ionization energy and will transfer an electron easily to the nonmetal, which has a high electron affinity. An example of this is the compound NaCl, which is sodium chloride or table salt, in which an electron from the Na atom moves to the Cl atom. Due to strong bonding, ionic compounds have several distinct characteristics, such as high melting and boiling points. Ionic compounds are brittle and crystalline, and they are arranged in rigid, well-defined structures, which allow them to break apart along smooth, flat surfaces. The formation of an ionic bond is an exothermic reaction since it releases heat. In the opposite scenario, the energy it takes to break up a one-mole quantity of an ionic compound is referred to as lattice energy, which is generally endothermic. The Lewis structure for NaCl is written as follows:

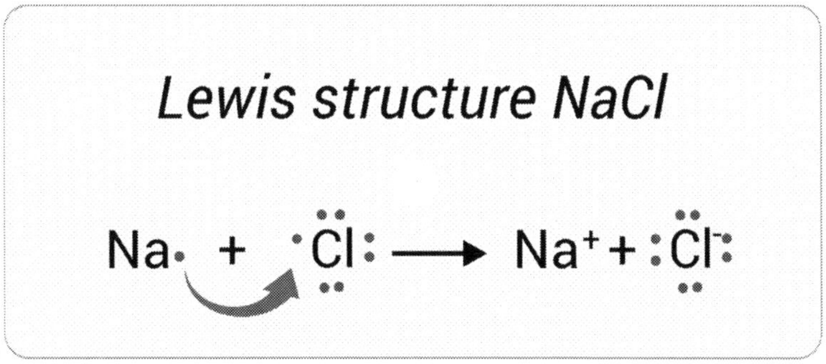

Figure 13. The Lewis structure for NaCl

Metallic bonds are formed by electrons that move freely through metal. They are the product of the force of attraction between electrons and metal ions. Many metal cations share the electrons and act like glue holding the metallic substance together, similar to the attraction between oppositely charged atoms in ionic substances, except the electrons are more fluid and float around the bonded metals and form a sea of electrons. Metallic compounds have characteristic properties that include strength, conduction of heat and electricity, and malleability. They can conduct electricity by passing energy through the freely moving electrons, creating a **current**. These compounds also have high melting and boiling points. Lewis structures are not common for metallic structures because of the free-roaming ability of the electrons.

Covalent Bonds

Covalent bonds are created when 2 atoms share electrons, instead of transferring them as in ionic bonds. The atoms in covalent compounds have a balance of attraction and repulsion between their protons and electrons, which keeps them bonded together. Two atoms can be joined by single, double, or even triple covalent bonds. As the number of electrons that are shared increases, the length of the bond decreases. Covalent substances have low melting and boiling points and are poor conductors of heat and electricity.

A **Lewis electron dot formula** can be used to represent the sharing of valence electrons between 2 atoms. These valence electrons may be a **bonding pair**, where 2 atoms share an electron pair, or a **lone or nonbonding pair**, which are electrons that are found on an atom and not shared. Consider the Lewis formulas for the compounds borane, BH_3, and ammonia, NH_3, which are shown in Figure 14.

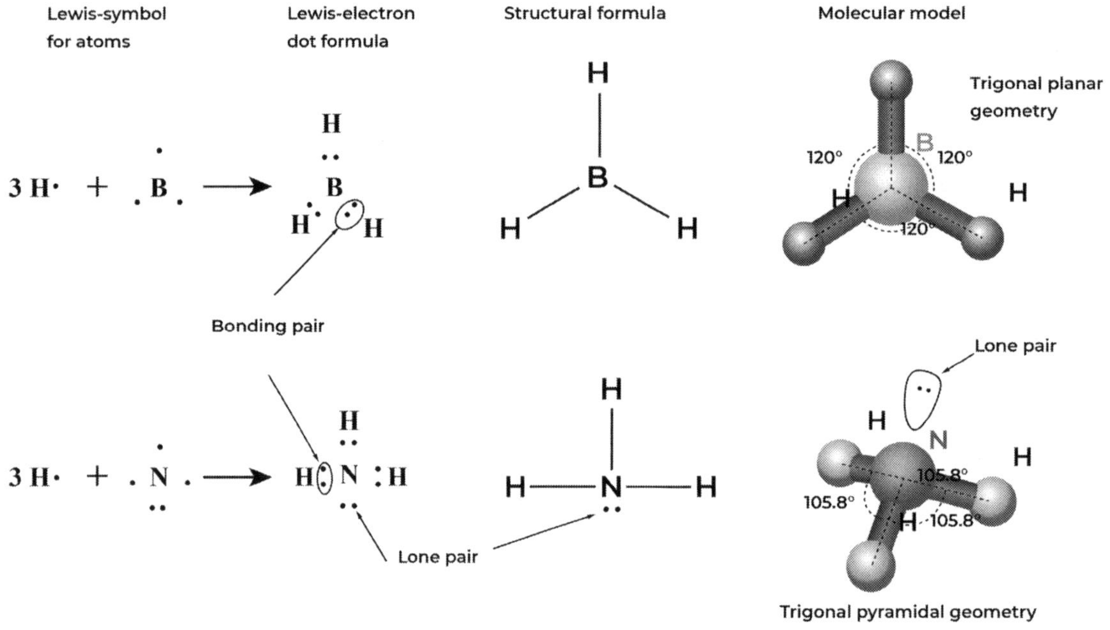

Figure 14. Covalent Lewis structures

The Lewis symbol for hydrogen contains only one electron. Boron is found in group IIIA of the periodic table and contains 3 valence electrons, which are represented by 3 dots. The Lewis electron dot formula for borane or boron hydride shows 3 covalent bonding pairs, and each atom donates an electron to form one covalent bonding pair. Hydrogen and boron are exceptions to the octet rule. Hydrogen shares 2 electrons (duet) and boron shares 6 valence electrons (sextet). The Lewis symbol for nitrogen will contain 5 dots or electrons since nitrogen is found in group VA of the periodic table. The 5 electrons are spread out around nitrogen, with a maximum of 2 dots on one side.

Only 3 bonding pairs or covalent bonds can form when the Lewis symbols for hydrogen and nitrogen are combined where each atom contributes one electron to form one bonding pair. Nitrogen has one lone pair of electrons that does not participate in chemical bonding with the other hydrogen atoms. Unlike hydrogen and boron, nitrogen follows the octet rule since it is surrounded by 8 valence electrons. Lewis dots are often replaced by a dash or line in a drawing of a chemical structure, as shown in Figure 14. Although the lone pair of electrons does not participate in bonding with other hydrogen-bonded atoms, the lone pair of electrons can be donated to a free hydrogen proton H^+, which can occur in an aqueous solution. Such a bond, which forms when one atom donates its lone pair of electrons, is called a **coordinate covalent bond** (Figure 15.)

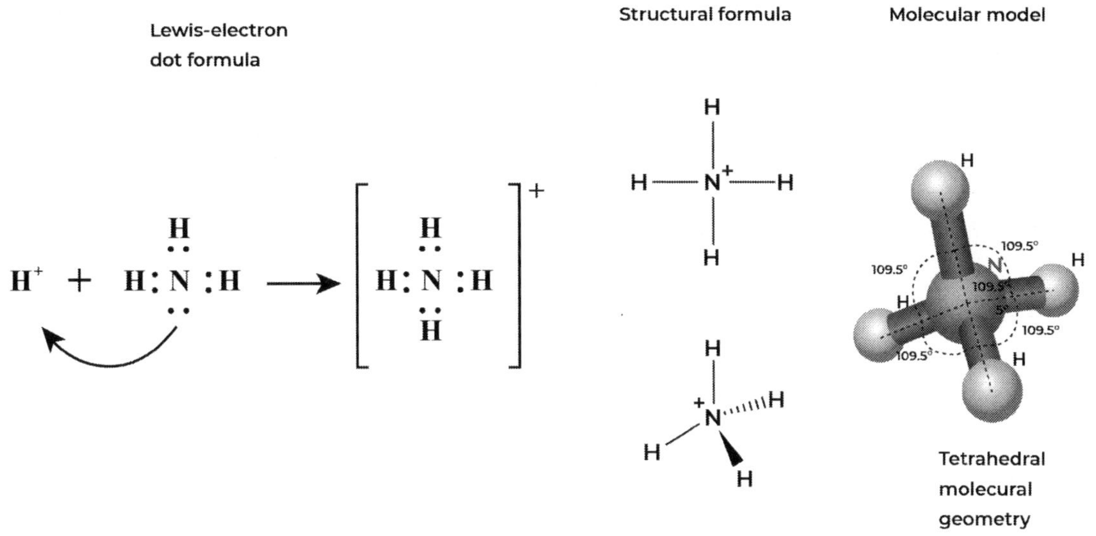

Figure 15. Structural representations of ammonium

The curved arrow in Figure 15 indicates that the nitrogen lone pair electrons are donated or shared with the hydrogen proton to form the ammonium ion. Brackets with a positive superscript are placed around the Lewis formula to indicate that the overall molecule is a cation with a charge of +1. The structural formula bears the positive charge near the nitrogen atom since nitrogen becomes electron deficient when its lone pair electrons are used to form an N-H bond. Two structural formulas for ammonium are shown in Figure 15, but the lower structure uses a bold and hashed wedge to better illustrate the hydrogen atoms in three-dimensional space. The bold wedge refers to an N-H bond that is pointed toward the viewer, while the hash wedge specifies an N-H bond pointed away from the viewer. The remaining dashed N-H bonds lie along the same plane and would be in line or in-plane with this sheet of paper.

Bond Types and Electronegativity

Atoms bonded to one another in a molecule can form multiple bonds. In a Lewis structure, a single bond is represented by the sharing of 2 dots between 2 atoms, with one dot or electron donated from each atom. Other types of covalent bonds include a double and triple bond. A **double bond** contains 2 pairs of shared electrons, which includes a total of 4 electrons or dots shared between 2 atoms. A **triple bond** contains 3 pairs of shared electrons, or a total of 6 electrons or dots shared between 2 different atoms in a molecule. Figure 16 shows an example of a molecule that contains single, double, and triple bonds.

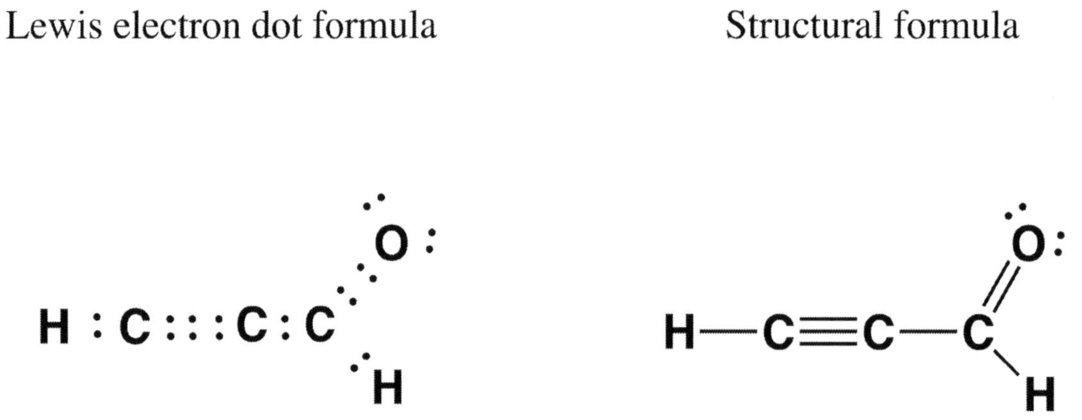

Figure 16. Lewis electron dot formula for a molecule with multiple bonds

Carbon follows the octet rule for single, double, and triple bonding. Triple bonds tend to form with N and C atoms, whereas double bonds are usually formed with C, N, O, and S. **The Lewis dot formulas** tend to show electron pairs that are somewhat equidistant between 2 atoms, for example, C and H. However, certain elements have a greater tendency than others to attract electrons. The extent at which an element in a molecule can attract bonding electrons to itself is called **electronegativity (EN)**. The EN of an element increases from left to right across a row or period in the periodic table. The N atom has greater EN than the C atom, and more than metals such as Be or Li. EN also increases moving bottom to top in a column or group in the periodic table. Boron, B, has a greater EN than gallium, Ga. Each element is assigned an EN value ranging from 0 to 4, as shown in Figure 17.

The F atom, which is found in the upper right corner, has the greatest EN value.

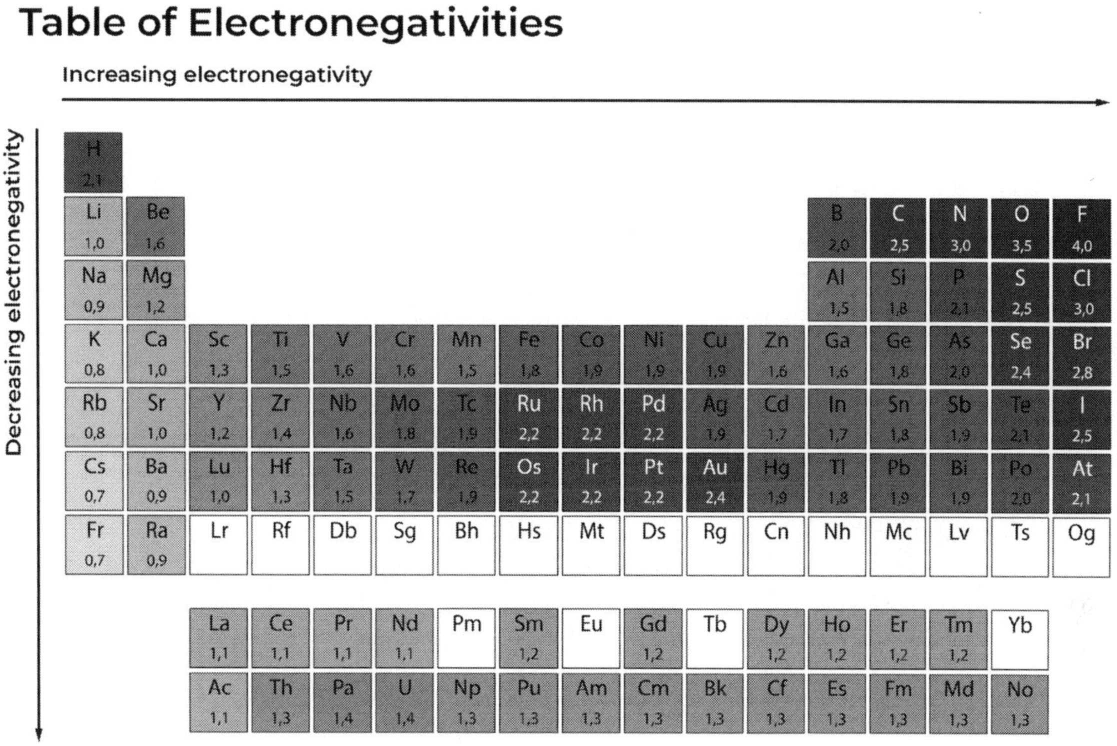

Figure 17. Table of electronegativities

Since each atom has a different EN value, the bonding electrons that are shared between 2 different atoms move closer to the more electronegative atom. A **polar covalent bond** is a bond that contains bonding electrons that move closer to an atom that is more electronegative. Some molecules that have polar covalent bonds are HF and H_2O. The bonding electrons between H and F spend more time near the F atom since it is more electronegative. In water, the bonding electrons are nearer to the oxygen atom compared to the hydrogen atom. Therefore, the electron distribution or electron cloud between 2 different atoms can be unsymmetrical, resulting in a polarity difference, where one side of the molecule is more polar or electron rich.

The hydrogen molecule, H_2, has a symmetrical electron distribution since both atoms have the same EN value, and is called a **nonpolar covalent bond**. Ionic compounds such as potassium chloride, KCl, are ionic because the difference in electronegativity, $\Delta EN = 3.0 - 0.8 = 2.2$, is greater than 2.0. Chlorine has an EN value of 3.0 and potassium has an EN value of 0.8. The difference between each EN value and its absolute value is taken to obtain ΔEN. Table 8 lists different values of EN that are associated with different bond types.

Table 8. Bond types based on electronegativity differences		
Molecule or ionic compound	Bond Type (ΔEN range)	Electronegativity differences
H2	Nonpolar covalent (0–0.4)	$\Delta EN = \lvert 2.1 - 2.1 \rvert = 0.0$
HF	Polar Covalent (0.4–2.0)	$\Delta EN = \lvert 4.0 - 2.1 \rvert = 1.9$
KCl	Ionic (2.0+)	$\Delta EN = \lvert 3.0 - 0.8 \rvert = 2.2$

To determine the bond type, compute ΔEN for the values associated with each atom and compare to the ΔEN range shown in Table 8.

Electron Delocalization

For a given molecule, the bonding electron pairs shown in Lewis structures are not always stationary but may move around or delocalize to other atoms. Such a bonding process is called **delocalized bonding**. Sulfur dioxide, SO_2, is one example where the bonding electrons between each S and O atom can move around (Figure 18).

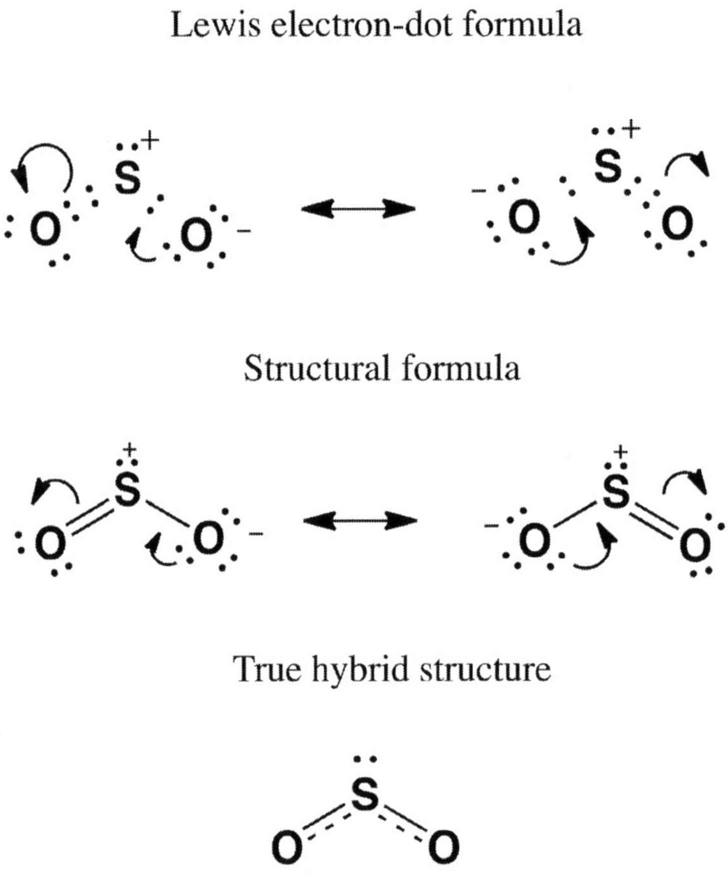

Figure 18. Delocalization of electrons between the S and O atoms

Two possible structures are shown for sulfur dioxide, SO_2: the Lewis electron dot formula and the formula representations. The curved double-barbed arrows indicate the movement of 2 electrons or one bonding pair (a single-barbed or half arrow would indicate one electron moving). The straight double-headed arrow connects 2 possible **resonance structures**, which are all the possible Lewis dot structures that participate in delocalized bonding. For example, in the Lewis structure, the lone pair electrons from the negatively charged O^- atom, to the right of the S atom, are transferred next to the sulfur-oxygen single bond.

Simultaneously, one bonding pair in the sulfur-oxygen double bond is moved to the O atom, which now acts as a lone electron pair on oxygen. The resulting second structure is shown on the right side of the straight double-headed arrow. Delocalization will occur again, as the curved arrows indicate. The structural formula shows the same process. Resonance structures are theoretical descriptions that show the possible electronic structure of a molecule and do not represent the true molecular structures. Sulfur dioxide, SO_2, does not flip between 2 different structures but rather exists as one **hybrid structure**, which is a fusion of all possible resonance structures, as shown in Figure 18.

Formal Charges

When drawing the skeletal structures for a molecule, it is useful to consider the idea of formal charge to choose the best Lewis formula and structural formula. The **formal charge (FC)** is a hypothetical charge assigned to an atom. It is based on the assumption that bonding electrons are shared with atoms bonded to one another but with lone pairs belonging to a specific atom. The formal charge can be computed using the following formula:

$$\text{Formal charge (FC)} = \text{\# of valence e}^- - \left(\frac{1}{2}\text{\# bonding e}^- + \text{\# nonbonding e}^-\right)$$

The preferred structure is one that contains atoms that are devoid of charge or that have the smallest charge. The formal charge for an atom depends on whether it has single or multiple bonds and where the atom is placed in the structure. Figure 19 below shows the formal charges for every atom for 3 different structures of SO_2.

Structure A

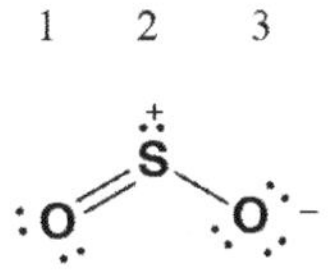

FC (atom 1,O) = 6 - (1/2 (4) + 4)= 0

FC (atom 2,S) = 6 - (1/2 (6) + 2) = +1

FC (atom 3,O) = 6 - (1/2 (2) + 6)= -1

Structure B

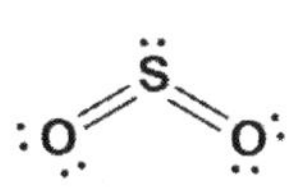

FC (atom 1,O) = 6 - (1/2 (4) + 4) = 0

FC (atom 2,S) = 6 - (1/2 (8) + 2) = 0 exception to octet rule

FC (atom 3,O) = 6 - (1/2 (4) + 4) = 0

Structure C

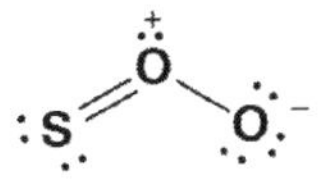

FC (atom 1,S) = 6 - (1/2 (4) + 4) = 0

FC (atom 2,O) = 6 - (1/2 (6) + 2)= +1

FC (atom 3,O) = 6 - (1/2 (2) + 6) = -1

Figure 19. Calculating formal charges in SO_2

In structures A through C in Figure 19, the formal charges are calculated for atoms labeled either 1, 2, or 3, as shown in Figure 19. For instance, structure A contains 3 atoms: O (atom 1), S (atom 2), and another O (atom 3), and each atom has a formal charge. In the formal charge equation, there are 3 different terms to pay attention to, which are the number (#) of valence electrons, # bonding electrons, and # nonbonding electrons. The valence electrons will always stay fixed and is equal to the group number for main group elements. For example, O and S belong to group VIA and have 6 valence electrons. For each formal charge calculation shown in Figure 19, the first term is 6 because O and S belong to the same group. The number of bonding and lone pair electrons typically varies because of the atoms' arrangement and connectivity. It's important to count the number of electrons in the bonding and lone pairs.

In structure A in Figure 19, S (atom 2) has a total of 6 bonding electrons since there are 2 double bonds between S and O and one single bond between S and O^-. Lastly, the S atom in structure A has 2 nonbonding electrons which make up a lone pair, so the number 2 is included in the FC calculation. Even though S and O have a +1 and −1 in structure A, the overall charge of the molecule will be neutral. Structure B is another possible structure. However, S is surrounded by a total of 10 electrons. S is typically an exception to the octet rule since it contains a vacant d orbital, which allows it to accommodate a bonding or nonbonding electron pair. In structure C, even though the formal charges for each atom are computed correctly, there is one oxygen atom that has a +1 charge. Since S is less electronegative than O, it makes more sense to have a structure in which S bears the positive charge (structure A). When building Lewis electron dot formulas and structural formulas, the steps to follow are:

1. Place the least electronegative element in the middle of a skeletal structure.

2. Draw the Lewis symbol for each atom; the number of dots shown should be equal to the number of valence electrons. The total number of electrons in that Lewis structure should be equal to the sum of each atom's valence electrons.

3. Draw the Lewis electron dot formula, or structural formula for simplicity, for various possible structures (for example, Figure 19) and follow the octet rule. It may be easier to draw the bonding electrons first followed by the nonbonding electrons.

4. Compute FC for each atom. A formal chare of zero or a small formal charge on atoms is preferable, and a negative formal charge should be placed on the more electronegative atom.

Valence Shell Electron Pair Repulsion (VSEPR) Theory

Figures 14 and 15 show molecular models for boron hydride, BH_3, ammonia, NH_3, and ammonium, NH_{4^+} , which are three-dimensional models that better depict the space that the atoms occupy, and they also depict the overall geometry of the molecule. The models are based on **valence shell electron pair repulsion (VSEPR) theory**, which explains that groups of electrons found in single/multiple bonds, lone pairs, or even single electrons (radicals) occupy and create a negative region of space. To minimize repulsion, electron groups maximize separation from one another due to the Coulomb force of repulsion, which in turn leads to a specific electron group and molecular geometry. The Lewis electron dot formulas and structural formulas in Figure 18 are drawn a certain way to reflect the repulsion between different electron groups. Figure 20 shows several electron group geometries, which are not the same as molecular geometries. The geometry, whether electron group or molecular, will be determined by the number of bonding groups connected to the central atom in addition to the bonding angles.

Formula	Bonding groups	Lone pairs	Electron-Group Geometry	Bond Angles
CO_2	2	0	linear 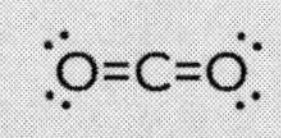 	180°
BH_3	3	0	trigonal planar 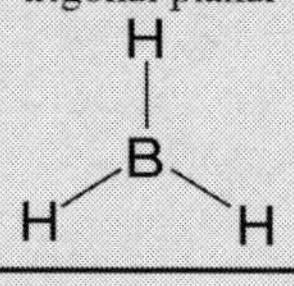 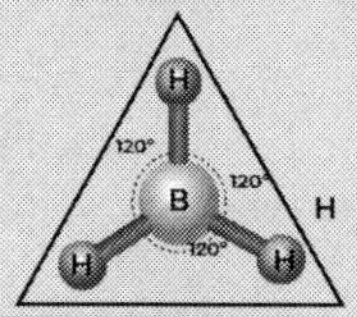	120°
CH_4	4	0	tetrahedral 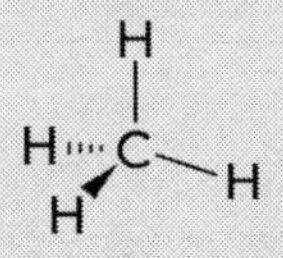 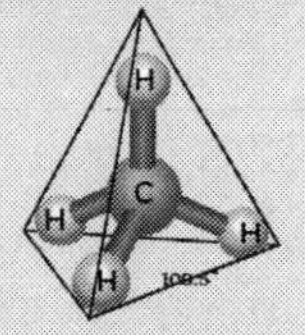	109.5°
PCl_5	5	0	trigonal bipyramidal 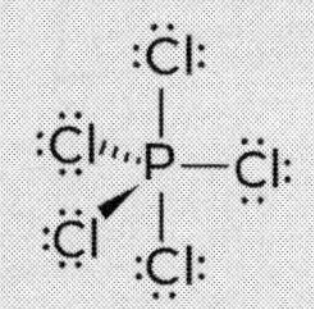 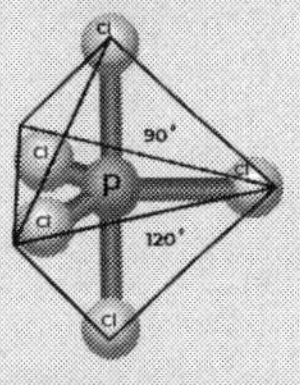	120°/90°
SF_6	6	0	octahedral 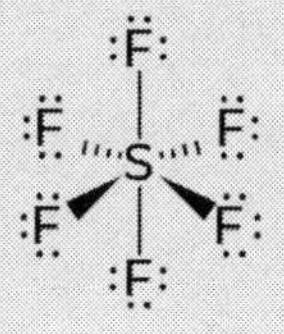 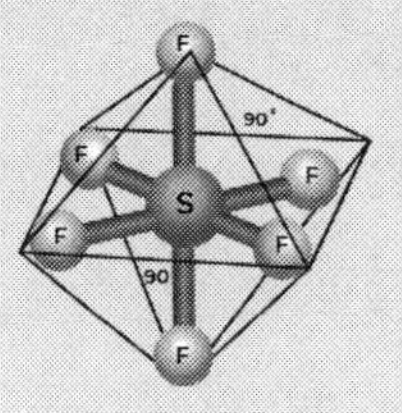	90°/90°

Figure 20. Five electron-group geometries

Boron hydride contains 3 bonding electron groups or pairs and has a trigonal planar electron group geometry. Ammonia has an electron group geometry that is tetrahedral since the lone pair electron occupies a space above the nitrogen atom. However, the molecular geometry of ammonia (N and H atoms only) is trigonal pyramidal, which is not the same as its electron group geometry. For ammonium, the molecular geometry and electron group geometry of the nitrogen atom are both tetrahedral.

States of Matter

States of Matter and Factors that Affect Phase Changes

Matter is most commonly found in 3 distinct states: solid, liquid, and gas. A **solid** has a distinct shape and a defined volume. A **liquid** has a more loosely defined shape and a definite volume, while a **gas** has no definite shape or volume. The **kinetic theory of matter** states that matter is composed of an enormous quantity of small atoms and molecules that are in constant motion. The distance between 2 molecules or atoms, in a substance, will determine the state of the matter: solid, liquid, or gas. In gases, the particles have a large separation and no attractive forces. In liquids, there is a moderate separation between particles and some attractive forces to form a loose shape. Solids have almost no separation between their particles, causing a defined and set shape. The constant movement of particles causes them to bump into each other, thus allowing the particles to transfer energy between each other. This bumping and transferring of energy can help explain the transfer of heat and the relationship between pressure, volume, and temperature.

Phase Transitions

When pressure, temperature, or volume change in matter, a change in state can occur. Changes in state include solid-to-liquid or **melting**, liquid-to-gas or **evaporation**, solid-to-gas or **sublimation**, gas-to-solid or **deposition**, gas-to-liquid or **condensation**, and liquid-to-solid or **freezing**. There is one other state of matter called **plasma**, which is seen in lightning, television screens, and neon lights. Plasma is most commonly formed from the gas state at extremely high temperatures. Examples of each phase change are listed below.

$H_2O(s) \rightarrow H_2O(l)$ melting

$H_2O(l) \rightarrow H_2O(g)$ evaporation

$H_2O(s) \rightarrow H_2O(g)$ sublimation

$H_2O(g) \rightarrow H_2O(s)$ deposition

$H_2O(g) \rightarrow H_2O(l)$ condensation

$H_2O(l) \rightarrow H_2O(s)$ freezing

Intermolecular Forces

The states of matter can be further understood by understanding the forces between them. Three types of intermolecular forces include London dispersion forces, dipole-dipole interactions, and hydrogen bonding. The **London dispersion force** is a weak intermolecular force present in all molecules, but most prevalent in large nonpolar molecules. It is caused by a temporary partial charge due to the asymmetrical movement of electrons. If at some moment the electrons orbiting an atom's nucleus are located on one side rather than spread out, then the atom gains a **temporary dipole**. The positive end of a dipole, which has fewer electrons, is attracted to the negative end, which has more electrons, or to the electrons of other nearby molecules. This attraction to nearby atoms and molecules causes a reduction in movement, slightly raising the boiling points of larger nonpolar molecules—which have a higher number of dispersion interactions. Dispersion forces become stronger in atoms and molecules with higher molecular masses, due to a larger distribution of electrons around the nucleus.

A **dipole** is partial charge caused by a difference in electronegativity of atoms in polar molecules. In a **dipole-dipole interaction**, the positive charge on one end of a dipole will be attracted to the negative end of another dipole. Dipole-dipole interactions are a stronger intermolecular force than the London dispersion force. The larger the net difference in electronegativity across the molecule, the stronger the attraction. This increases the molecule's melting and boiling points and requires more heat or energy to shift to a more energetic state.

Hydrogen Bonding

Out of all the most common intermolecular forces, hydrogen bonding is the strongest. It's important to note that hydrogen bonds are not a type of chemical bond, since valence electrons are not shared. **Hydrogen bonding** is a type of dipole-dipole force, between the dipoles of different molecules, caused by the large electronegativity difference between hydrogen and the highly electronegative non-metals on the right side of the periodic table (e.g., oxygen, fluorine, and chlorine). When these elements share a bond with hydrogen, hydrogen gains a partial positive charge which is attracted to the partial negative charge of atoms in other molecules. The strong but temporary attraction from hydrogen bonds explains the physical properties of water: a high boiling point (relative to its mass), its high adhesiveness (hydrogen bonding to different molecules), and high cohesiveness (hydrogen bonding with other water molecules). Polar molecules are often referred to as **hydrophilic** (meaning "water-loving") or **hydrophobic** ("water-fearing") depending on whether they have hydrogen bonding.

Ideal Gas Law

The **ideal gas law** states that pressure, volume, and temperature are all related through the equation $PV = nRT$, where P is pressure, V is volume, n is the amount of gaseous substance in moles (mol), R is the gas constant, and T is temperature.

Pressure and volume are proportional to temperature ($PV \propto T$), but pressure is inversely proportional to volume. Therefore, if the equation is balanced, and the volume decreases in the system, pressure needs to increase to keep both sides of the equation balanced proportionately. If the equation is not balanced, and the pressure increases, then the temperature also increases since pressure and temperature are directly proportional.

Vapor Pressure

Liquid phase transitions such as evaporation and condensation are constantly occurring, such that the vapor and liquid phase are interconverting with one another:

$$H_2O(l) \rightleftharpoons H_2O(g)$$

As the liquid water molecules evaporate to form water vapor, some vapor water molecules form liquid water. The process is reversible, and when the rates of vaporization and condensation are the same, the chemical system is at **dynamic equilibrium**. If liquid water is enclosed in a container at some temperature, some of the gaseous water molecules exert a force against the container wall and water surface. The force of the water molecules over a specific area at some temperature is called **vapor pressure**, which is the partial pressure of the water vapor over the liquid measured at dynamic equilibrium. The units of vapor pressure are typically in millimeters of mercury (mmHg). The vapor pressure will increase with temperature because the average kinetic energy (K.E.) per mole of an ideal gas is proportional to its temperature (T).

$$\text{K. E.} = \frac{3}{2}RT \quad R = 8.314\frac{\text{J}}{\text{mol K}}$$

At a given temperature, water molecules have a minimum potential energy of attraction to other liquid water molecules. If some of the water molecules have K.E. greater than the minimum energy due to molecular collisions, the water molecules escape into the gas phase. The vapor water molecules then exert a partial pressure over the liquid. Some solid substances (for example, naphthalene mothballs), that can sublimate readily at normal temperatures (for example, 25 °C), are said to be **volatile** due to their high vapor pressure compared to other substances, for example, water.

Melting and Boiling Points

In the laboratory, one of the simplest ways to identify an unknown solid or liquid is by measuring some of its physical properties, for example, melting and boiling points. The **melting point** of a substance refers to the temperature range at which a solid crystalline substance melts or transitions to a liquid. The **freezing point** refers to a physical process in which the liquid changes to a crystalline solid at some specific temperature range. The melting point (measured in Celsius) of many substances is typically listed on safety data sheets as one specific temperature. In practice, as the substance melts, the measurement of the melting point with a thermometer may span a few degrees higher or lower than the specified temperature, perhaps because of the presence of impurities. For a chemical system at dynamic equilibrium between the liquid and the vapor phase, as the temperature increases, the vapor pressure continues to increase.

At a certain temperature the chemical system reaches its **boiling point**, the temperature at which the vapor pressure is equal to the surrounding average atmospheric pressure (1 atm or 760 mmHg). The atmospheric pressure changes depending on whether you are at sea level or in a high-altitude region. For example, in Los Alamos, New Mexico, the average atmospheric pressure is about 0.77 atm, so the boiling point of water is about 93 °C. At sea level, the average atmospheric pressure is 1 atm, so the boiling point of water is 100 °C. The greater the boiling point of a substance, the stronger its intermolecular forces and the lower its vapor pressure with respect to a standard temperature, for example, 25 °C. The lower the boiling point, the weaker its intermolecular forces and the higher its vapor pressure. Ethanol has a higher vapor pressure than water since the hydrogen bonding intermolecular forces in water are greater. Nonpolar substances tend to have lower boiling points than more polar substances in which the intermolecular forces are greater.

Heat of Phase (Fusion and Vaporization) Transition

The amount of energy in the form of heat needed to change matter from one state to another is labeled by **phase change terms**. Suppose you fill a small beaker with water, place a thermometer in it, and freeze it to a temperature of 10 °C. Then you heat the beaker at 20 °C and record the temperature every 3 minutes until the temperature of the beaker is slightly over 100 °C. If you were to plot your data with time on the x-axis and temperature on the y-axis, you would obtain the graph in Figure 21. When heat is added to matter to cause a change in state, there is an increase in temperature until the matter is about to change its state.

During its transition, all the added heat is used by the matter to change its state, so there is no increase in temperature. Once the transition is complete, then the added heat again yields an increase in temperature. Each state of matter is considered to be a phase, and changes between phases are represented by phase diagrams. These diagrams show the effects of changes in pressure and temperature on matter. The states of matter fall into areas on these charts called **heating curves**. The heating curve of water shows 2 flat regions corresponding to the heat of fusion and heat of vaporization.

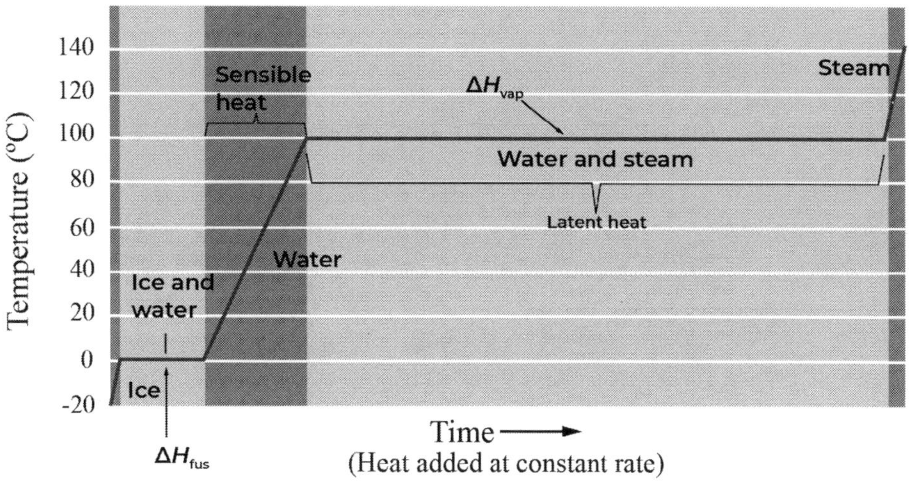

Figure 21. The heating curve of water

As heat is transferred to ice at a constant rate, the temperature increases but will remain constant when it reaches 0 °C. The flat portion of the curve is a phase transition or a region where ice (solid water) and liquid water coexist, and where the temperature remains constant as heat is added to the chemical system. The heat added to the chemical system is the energy needed to melt ice to liquid water or the energy needed to break the hydrogen bonding forces between water molecules in the solid phase. The length of each flat portion of the curve is proportional to the heat of phase transition. The shorter flat portion of the curve, ice and water, represents the **heat of fusion (or enthalpy of fusion),** ΔH_{fus}, and refers to the heat required to melt a solid.

$$H_2O(s) \rightarrow H_2O(l) \quad \Delta H_{\text{fus}} = 6.01 \text{ kJ/mol}$$

For every one mole of water, 6.01 kJ of heat are needed to melt ice. The temperature needed to supply enough energy for matter to change from a liquid to a gas is called the **heat of vaporization (enthalpy of vaporization),** ΔH_{vap}.

$$H_2O(l) \rightarrow H_2O(g) \quad \Delta H_{\text{vap}} = 40.7 \text{ kJ/mol}$$

The flatter region corresponding to water and steam is longer since more heat is needed to separate the water molecules or break most of the hydrogen bonding attractions between most water molecules. The flat portions of a heating curve are often called the **latent heat**. The parts of the curve where the temperature is changing (where the slope is nonzero) or measurable is called the **sensible heat**. Other types of graphs that show stable states of a substance are called **phase diagrams**, which may show the pressure as a function of temperature to summarize the different conditions of that substance.

Figure 22 below shows a water phase diagram. The black curves or lines separate the different phases, and points on these curves represent the coexistence of 2 or even 3 states. For example, 1 atm and 0 °C on the diagram represent a point on the black line (line AB) where the solid and liquid phases are in equilibrium. Any point transitioning from the solid region to the liquid region is called melting. Any point within the liquid region to the gas region is called evaporation. Point A represents a **triple point** where the solid, liquid, and gas phase are in equilibrium. Point C is the critical point and represents a **critical temperature**, which is the minimum temperature where the liquid state is absent no matter the pressure. At point C, the **critical pressure** is the vapor pressure at the critical temperature for that substance.

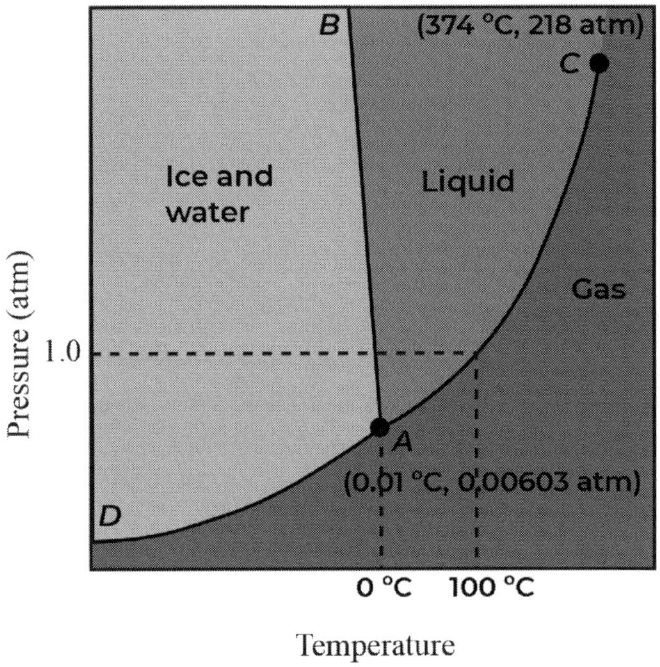

Figure 22. The phase diagram for water

Kinetics

The Rate of a Chemical Reaction

The measure of how fast a chemical reaction can occur, from reactants to products, is called the **rate of a chemical reaction**. The study of how a chemical reaction changes with time within certain set conditions, such as the reactant concentration or temperature, is called **chemical kinetics**. By studying how the rate of a chemical reaction is altered by these conditions, details regarding the reaction mechanism at the molecular level can be obtained. The ability to control the rates of reaction are important for many biological and or chemical processes. In 2018, the spacecraft called the VSS Unity, a spaceplane built by The Spaceship Company for Virgin Galactic, was the first suborbital rocket-powered craft to reach outer space at an altitude of 82.7 km. The rate at which the rocket engines burn fuel is important. A slow rate may mean that the craft will not reach space, and a fast rate may result in an explosion. Suppose we are given the following reaction:

$$2\,\mathrm{A} + \mathrm{B} \rightarrow \mathrm{C}$$

The rate of reaction between a time interval for reactant B is:

- $\text{rate for decomposition of B} = -\frac{[\mathrm{B}]_{t_2} - [\mathrm{B}]_{t_1}}{t_2 - t_1} = -\frac{\Delta[\mathrm{B}]}{\Delta t}$

The brackets [ ] indicate the concentration in moles per liter (mol/L) for reactant B, and the terms, t_2 and t_1, refer to a final and initial point within the time interval. The change in concentration over time is designated by the symbol Δ. The rate equation contains a negative sign because the concentration of the reactant decreases when it combines with A to form C. However, the overall reaction rate is a positive quantity. The reaction rate expression will depend on the coefficients of the balanced chemical reaction. To produce C, two moles of A must react with one mole of B, which means the rate at which A decreases will be one-half compared to reactant B.

- $\text{rate of decomposition of A} = -\frac{\frac{1}{2}[\mathrm{A}]_{t_2} - \frac{1}{2}[\mathrm{A}]_{t_1}}{t_2 - t_1} = -\frac{1}{2}\frac{\Delta[\mathrm{A}]}{\Delta t}$

The fraction, $1/2$, is placed in front of the rate equation of A to indicate that concentration of B decreases twice as fast with respect to A, or the rate at which A decreases is $1/2$ compared to B. The negative sign remains because A is a reactant. Alternatively, the reaction rate can also be written in terms of the product.

- $\text{rate of formation of C} = +\frac{[\mathrm{C}]_{t_2} - [\mathrm{C}]_{t_1}}{t_2 - t_1} = +\frac{\Delta[\mathrm{C}]}{\Delta t}$

The rate equation for the formation of a product will be positive because the concentration of C is increasing. If the concentration of the reactants is plotted as a function of time, the plot will show two curves that have a negative slope because the reactant concentrations are decreasing. For the product, the curve would have a positive slope, because the concentration of C is increasing.

The Instantaneous and Average Rate of Reactions

When performing a reaction rate experiment in the laboratory, the concentration of a specific reactant can be monitored over time with a spectrometer if one of the reactants is colored or through other methods such as a gas chromatograph-mass spectrometer. These instruments will make the measurements of the concentrations and output concentration data on a computer screen. Table 9 represents an example of how the concentration of B changes for every 20 seconds.

Table 9. The concentration of reactant B over time

Time (s)	[B] (Molarity)	Δ[B] (M)	Δt (s)	Rate $= -\frac{\Delta[B]}{\Delta t}$ M/s
0.000	1.000			
20.000	0.675	−0.325	20.000	0.0163
40.000	0.510	−0.165	20.000	0.00825
60.000	0.320	−0.190	20.000	0.00950
80.000	0.210	−0.110	20.000	0.00550
100.000	0.130	−0.080	20.000	0.00400

The units for the rate are molarity per second. The **average rate of reaction** is the change in reactant concentration over the change in time as given by the previous equations and can be determined for any interval of time, as shown in Table 9. For instance, the average rate of reaction between $t_2 = 20$ s and $t_1 = 0$ s is -0.0163 M/s. However, the rate is different between $t_2 = 40$ s and $t_1 = 20$ s. Initially, the rate is relatively fast but begins to decrease or slows down and reaches a steady-state after about 100 seconds. The **instantaneous rate of reaction** refers to the reaction rate at any one point in time and is indicated by an instantaneous slope or slope of the tangent for the rate curve at that point. The reaction rate will be the same regardless of whether the rate is expressed in terms of the reactant or product concentration.

The Rate Law

For the reaction $2\text{ A} + \text{B} \rightarrow \text{C}$, the reaction rate may depend on the reactants A and B. Let's suppose that the reaction rate only depended on B and not A, then the **rate law,** or an equation that expresses the relationship between the concentration of the reactant and rate of reaction, is given by:

$$\text{rate} = k[\text{B}]^n$$

The term k is called a **rate constant** or proportionality constant, and the superscript n is referred to as the **reaction order** for the reactant B. The reaction order can have values of $n = 0, 1,$ or 2. When $n = 0$, the reaction rate is:

$$\text{rate} = k[\text{B}]^0 = k$$

The reaction rate is that of a **zero-order reaction** equal to the rate constant, and it is independent of the concentration of B. If the concentration of B is plotted as a function of time (Figure 23), then the concentration of B will decrease linearly with time with a constant slope equal to the rate constant. The rate constant remains unchanged, which means that the rate does not decrease as B decreases. The sublimation of a substance such as dry ice is an example of a zero-order reaction.

If $n = 1$, then the reaction rate becomes:

$$\text{rate} = k[\text{B}]^1 = k[\text{B}]$$

The reaction is a **first-order reaction** because the rate is directly proportional to the concentration of B. For first-order reactions, the rate begins to decrease or slow down because the reactant concentration decreases, and the slope of the curve (Figure 23) becomes less steep. If the value of $n = 2$, then $\text{rate} = k[\text{B}]^2$ and the reaction is **second-order**, meaning that the rate is proportional to the square of the concentration of B. The reaction rate is more sensitive to the concentration of B, and the slope of the curve will flatten more so. Figure 23 also shows the reaction rate as a function of the reactant concentration B. The rate for a zero-order reaction remains constant, while a first- and second-order reaction will have rates that increase linearly or quadratically.

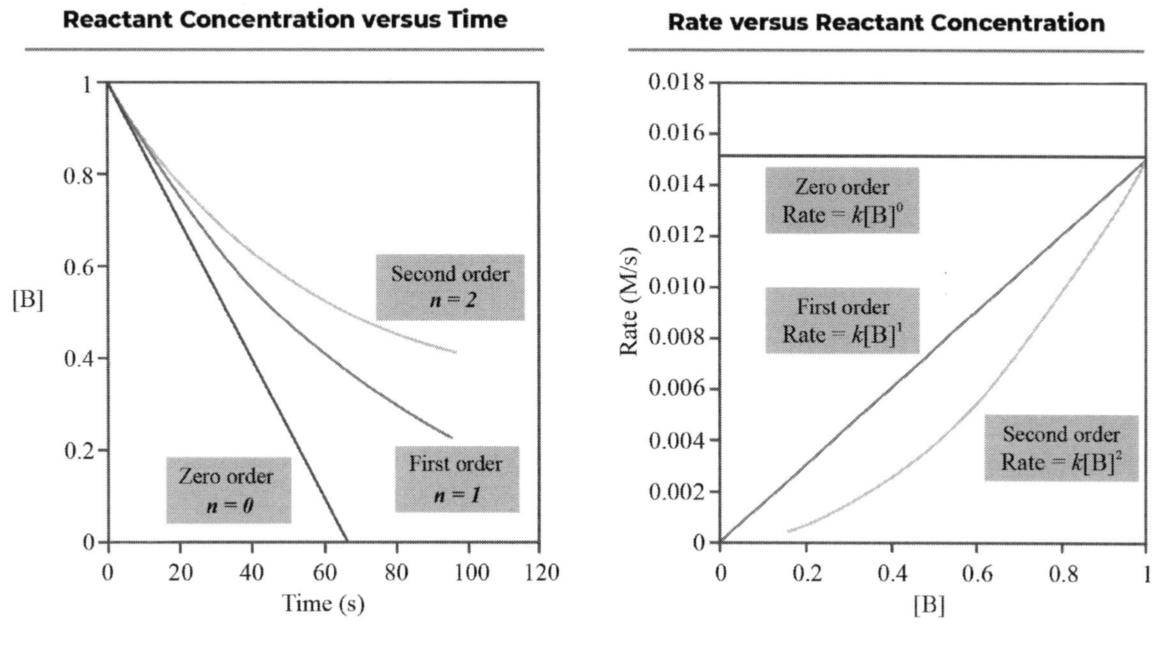

Figure 23. Reactant concentration versus time and rate versus reactant concentration.

Finding the Order of Reaction

Suppose a set of data, e.g., Table 10, is given for the reaction $\text{B} \rightarrow \text{products}$, and you are asked to find the value of the rate constant and the order of the reactant B. The **overall order of the reaction** is simply the sum of the exponents or the value of the exponent if there is only one reactant. Before finding the value of the rate constant, the order of the reaction must be determined from the change in concentration over time. The **method of initial rates** can be used to find the order from an experiment, which requires that an experiment be repeated multiple times with different initial reactant concentrations (Table 10).

Table 10. Initial starting concentration and measured rates		
Experiment	[B] M	Initial Rate (M/s)
1	1.000 M	0.0163
2	2.000 M	0.0326
3	4.000 M	0.0652

The first row represents one experiment with an initial [B] equal to one and an initial rate taken from Table 9. In Experiment 2, when the concentration is doubled, the rate doubles, and when the initial concentration is quadrupled in Experiment 3, so does the initial rate. To find the order of reactant B, two different rate values provided by Table 10 must be chosen and formulated into a new equation where the rates are divided.

$$\frac{\text{rate}_2}{\text{rate}_1} = \frac{k[\text{B}]_2^n}{k[\text{B}]_1^n}$$

The subscript 1 and 2 indicate the first and second initial rates shown in Table 10. The concentrations of B must also be included. The first rate, 0.0163 M/s, will be associated with the [B] equal to 1.000 M.

$$\frac{0.0326\ \cancel{\text{M s}^{-1}}}{0.0163\ \cancel{\text{M s}^{-1}}} = \frac{\cancel{k}(2.000\ \text{M})_2^n}{\cancel{k}(1.000\ \text{M})_1^n} = \left(\frac{2.000\ \cancel{\text{M}}}{1.000\ \cancel{\text{M}}}\right)^n$$

Note that the concentrations are given as positive values here and that the rate constant, k, is canceled out.

$$2.00 = (2.000)^n$$

$$\log_{10}(2.00) = \log_{10}(2.000^n)$$

$$\log_{10}(2.00) = n \times \log_{10}(2.000)$$

$$n = \frac{\log_{10}(2.00)}{\log_{10}(2.000)} = 1$$

The rate law is first order because $n = 1$.

$$\text{rate} = k[\text{B}]^1 = k[\text{B}]$$

The order of the reactant B is one, and the overall order of the reaction is also one ($n = 1$). When determining the order, the two chosen rate values from Table 10 could have been any other rate so long as they differ and the rate corresponding to the later time is placed in the numerator for clarity, e.g., $\text{rate}_3/\text{rate}_2$. Because the rate law equation is now known, the value of the rate constant k can be found.

$$k = \frac{\text{rate}}{[\text{B}]} = \frac{\text{rate}_1}{[\text{B}]_1} = \frac{0.0163\ \cancel{\text{M}}\ \text{s}^{-1}}{1.000\ \cancel{\text{M}}} = 0.0163\ \text{s}^{-1}$$

The value of the rate constant has units of inverse second and will be the same for any other chosen initial rate and corresponding initial concentration. However, the units of the rate constant will vary depending on the order of the reaction.

When the rate law includes more than one possible reactant, the method of initial rates can still be applied to find the overall order of the rate law. For example, consider the following reaction and its associated concentration and rate values shown in Table 11:

$$\mathrm{A + B \rightarrow C + D}$$

Table 11. Initial rates and concentrations for a reaction with two reactants			
Experiment	[A] M	[B] M	Initial Rate M/s
1	0.100	0.100	0.0350
2	0.200	0.100	0.0700
3	0.200	0.200	0.280

The proposed rate law is rate $= k[\mathrm{A}]^m[\mathrm{B}]^n$ and only includes the reactants, but the exponents m and n must be found. To determine the order of one reactant (or the exponent, e.g., m or n), two experiments are chosen such that one of the reactants has a fixed concentration. For example, experiment 1 and 2 have a fixed [B], which will allow the order of reactant A to be found. Applying the method of initial rates, we have:

$$\frac{\mathrm{rate}_2}{\mathrm{rate}_1} = \frac{k[\mathrm{A}]_2^m[\mathrm{B}]_2^n}{k[\mathrm{A}]_1^m[\mathrm{B}]_1^n}$$

$$\frac{0.0700\ \mathrm{M\ s^{-1}}}{0.0350\ \mathrm{M\ s^{-1}}} = \frac{k[0.200\ \mathrm{M}]_2^m\cancel{[0.100\ \mathrm{M}]_2^n}}{k[0.100\ \mathrm{M}]_1^m\cancel{[0.100\ \mathrm{M}]_1^n}}$$

Without performing additional algebraic procedures and based on a previous procedure, the value of m must be one.

$$\frac{0.0700\ \cancel{\mathrm{M\ s^{-1}}}}{0.0350\ \cancel{\mathrm{M\ s^{-1}}}} = \frac{\cancel{k}[0.200\ \cancel{\mathrm{M}}]_2^m}{\cancel{k}[0.100\ \cancel{\mathrm{M}}]_1^m}$$

$$2.00 = (2.00)^m$$

$$2 = 2^1$$

The method of initial rates is repeated again but for a fixed [A] and a varying [B] concentration, e.g., Experiments 2 and 3.

$$\frac{\text{rate}_3}{\text{rate}_2} = \frac{k[\text{A}]_3^m[\text{B}]_3^n}{k[\text{A}]_2^m[\text{B}]_2^n}$$

$$\frac{0.280\ \cancel{\text{M s}^{-1}}}{0.0700\ \cancel{\text{M s}^{-1}}} = \frac{\cancel{k}[\cancel{0.200\ \text{M}}]_3^m[0.200\ \cancel{\text{M}}]_3^n}{\cancel{k}[\cancel{0.200\ \text{M}}]_2^m[0.100\ \cancel{\text{M}}]_2^n}$$

$$4.00 = (2.00)^n$$

$$n = 2$$

The final rate law is rate $= k[\text{A}]^1[\text{B}]^2$, which has an overall order of three.

The Integrated Rate Law

A rate law for a chemical reaction that shows the relationship between reactant concentration and time is called the **integrated rate law**. These types of rate laws are important for some reactions, e.g., decomposition reactions, that may take seconds, days, or even years. It's often important to relate the concentration with the lifetime, which can be done with an integrated rate law. For example, chlorofluorocarbons (CFCs) have been released into the atmosphere as early as the 1930s and have previously been used in refrigeration and aerosol cans. The presence of CFCs in the ozone layers has prompted the banning of these products. However, some CFCs have been calculated to have an average atmospheric lifetime ranging from 45 (CFC-11) to 1700 years (CFC-115). For the reaction

$$\text{B} \rightarrow \text{products}$$

the reaction is zero order and uses the corresponding rate law, rate $= k[\text{B}]^0$ (units of k are M/s). The integrated rate law and its half-life expression are:

$$[\text{B}]_t = -kt + [\text{B}]_0 \text{ and } t_{1/2} = \frac{[\text{B}]_0}{2k}$$

The terms $[\text{B}]_0$ and $[\text{B}]_t$ refer to the initial and final concentration at time t. The half-life, $t_{1/2}$, refers to the point in time where the concentration of B has reached half its amount with respect to its initial value $[\text{B}]_0$. If the rate law happens to be first-order, rate $= k[\text{B}]^1$ (units of k are s^{-1}), then the integrated rate law and $t_{1/2}$ are:

$$\ln[\text{B}]_t = -kt + \ln[\text{B}]_0 \text{ and } t_{1/2} = \frac{0.693}{k}$$

If the reaction is second order, rate $= k[\text{B}]^2$ (units of k are $M^{-1}\ s^{-1}$), then:

$$\frac{1}{[\text{B}]_t} = kt + \frac{1}{[\text{B}]_0} \text{ and } t_{1/2} = \frac{1}{k[\text{B}]_0}$$

Figure 24 shows a straight-line plot for each reaction order.

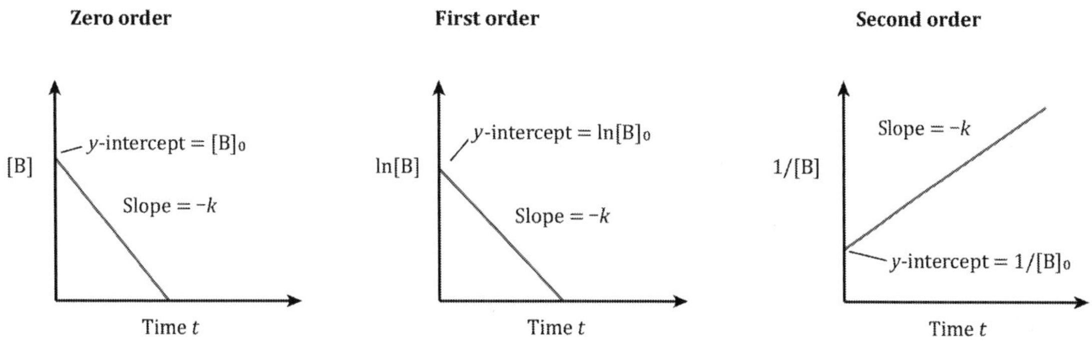

Figure 24. Graphical interpretations of the integrated rate law

The Arrhenius Equation

The **Arrhenius equation** describes the relationship between the rate constant k and the **activation energy**, E_a, which is the energy required for a chemical reaction to proceed from reactants to products.

$$k = Ae^{(-E_a/RT)}$$

The term A is a **frequency factor** that is related to the frequency of collisions or approaches to E_a, and R is the gas constant with a value of 8.314 J/(mol K). The rate constant, k (units of s^{-1}), will change exponentially as the temperature, T, is increased or decreased. For example, suppose that the frequency factor is $1.00 \times 10^9\ s^{-1}$, $E_a = 1.00 \times 10^5$ J mol^{-1}, and $T = 273.15$ K, then $k = 7.52 \times 10^{-11}\ s^{-1}$. If $T = 1000$ K, then $k = 5.98 \times 10^3\ s^{-1}$, which is an exponential increase in the rate with a difference of fourteen orders of magnitude. The greater the temperature, the greater the rate constant, which ultimately leads to a faster rate. Figure 25 shows a **potential energy surface (PES)** that shows the difference between the activation barrier and the enthalpy of reaction. The greater the activation barrier, the smaller the reaction rate.

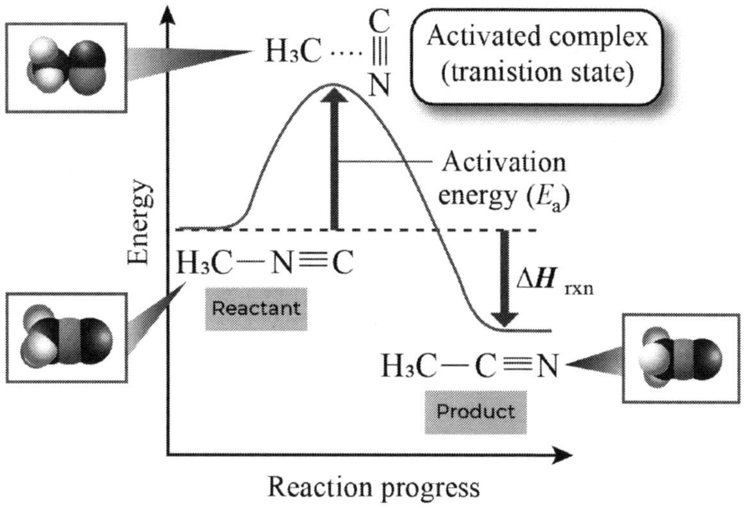

Figure 25. PES showing the activation energy barrier

The reaction is exothermic if it proceeds forward, and the reactant must become a high energy intermediate called an **activated complex**. There are many high energy intermediates, and the molecule corresponding to the highest energy intermediate is called the **transition state**. The Arrhenius equation is often expressed as the following form:

$$\ln\frac{k_2}{k_1} = \frac{E_a}{R}\left(\frac{1}{T_1} - \frac{1}{T_2}\right)$$

The above expression is extremely useful for calculating an experimental activation barrier given the values of the rate constants at two different temperatures.

Influence of Concentration, Pressure, and Temperature on Reaction Rates

The **rate of a reaction** is the measure of the change in concentration of the reactants or products over a certain period of time. Many factors affect how fast or slow a reaction occurs, such as concentration, pressure, or temperature. As the concentration of a reactant increases, the rate of the reaction also increases, because the frequency of collisions between elements increases. High-pressure situations for reactants that are gases cause the gas to compress and increase the frequency of gas molecule collisions, similar to solutions with higher concentrations. Reaction rates are then increased with the higher frequency of gas molecule collisions. Higher temperatures usually increase the rate of the reaction, adding more energy to the system with heat and increasing the frequency of molecular collisions.

Catalysts are substances that accelerate the speed of a chemical reaction. A catalyst remains unchanged throughout the course of a chemical reaction. In most cases, only small amounts of a catalyst are needed. Catalysts increase the rate of a chemical reaction by providing an alternate path requiring less activation energy. **Activation energy** refers to the amount of energy required for the initiation of a chemical reaction.

Catalysts can be homogeneous or heterogeneous. Catalysts in the same phase of matter as its reactants are **homogeneous**, while catalysts in a different phase than reactants are **heterogeneous**. It is important to remember catalysts are selective. They don't accelerate the speed of all chemical reactions, but catalysts do accelerate specific chemical reactions.

Equilibrium

Equilibrium and the Equilibrium Constant

Equilibrium is described as the state of a system when no net changes occur. **Chemical equilibrium** occurs when opposing reactions occur at equal rates. In other words, the rate of reactants forming products is equal to the rate of the products breaking down into the reactants—the concentration of reactants and products in the system doesn't change. Forward and reverse half arrows are used to indicate that the reaction goes in the forward and reverse directions.

$$\mathrm{A + B \rightleftharpoons C}$$

The reaction of some species A and B to produce C or the decomposition of C to produce A and B is called a **reversible chemical reaction**. In **irreversible chemical reactions**, the products cannot be changed back to reactants. Initially A and B react to form C, but the concentrations of A and B begin to decrease, which also decreases the rate of the forward reaction. As the concentration of C increases, the reverse rate begins to increase. At some point in time, as the rate of product formation increases, and the rate of reactant formation decreases, the forward and reverse rate become equal. This type of equilibrium is called a **dynamic equilibrium** where the concentrations of A, B, and C don't change. However, the concentrations of the reactants and products are not necessarily equal. In situations where all reactions have ceased, a **static equilibrium** is reached.

When a reaction reaches dynamic equilibrium, the conditions of the equilibrium are described by the following equation:

$$a\mathrm{A} + b\mathrm{B} \rightleftharpoons c\mathrm{C} + d\mathrm{D}$$

The lowercase terms represent the coefficients of the reaction. At equilibrium, the **equilibrium constant, K**, is used to determine the quantity or concentration of the reactants and products, and is described by the following ratio:

$$K = \frac{[\mathrm{C}]^c[\mathrm{D}]^d}{[\mathrm{A}]^a[\mathrm{B}]^b}$$

The ratio describes the concentration of the products divided by the concentration of the reactants, and each reactant or product is raised to the corresponding coefficient. The equilibrium constant expression is also known as the **law of mass action**, which describes the relationship with K and the balanced chemical equation. The combustion of propane, shown by the balanced chemical equation below, has the following equilibrium constant expression:

$$\mathrm{C_3H_8(g) + 5\ O_2(g) \rightleftharpoons 3\ CO_2(g) + 4\ H_2O(g)}$$

$$K = \frac{[\mathrm{CO_2}]^3[\mathrm{H_2O}]^4}{[\mathrm{C_3H_8}]^1[\mathrm{O_2}]^5}$$

The value of K is calculated by substituting the measured equilibrium concentrations, not the initial concentrations.

Interpretation of K

If the numerical value of K is much less than one ($K \ll 1$), there will be more reactants at equilibrium, and the forward reaction will not move very far to the right. The concentration of the reactants will be greater than the concentration of the products because the denominator is larger than the numerator. If $K \gg 1$ then the products are favored, and the forward reaction proceeds nearly to completion. If $K \approx 1$ then neither the forward nor reverse reaction is preferred, and the reaction will proceed nearly halfway. The equilibrium constant K does not indicate how fast it will take a reaction to reach equilibrium, but only explains the direction or how far a reaction will proceed at equilibrium. Some important relationships between K and the chemical equation are given for the following reaction.

$$a\text{A} + b\text{B} \rightleftharpoons c\text{C} + d\text{D}$$

- Reversing the equation inverts the equilibrium constant.

$$K_{\text{forward}} = \frac{[\text{C}]^c[\text{D}]^d}{[\text{A}]^a[\text{B}]^b} = \frac{1}{K_{\text{reverse}}} \qquad K_{\text{reverse}} = \frac{[\text{A}]^a[\text{B}]^b}{[\text{C}]^c[\text{D}]^d}$$

- Multiplying the equation by $n = 1, 2, 3, \ldots$, raises K to the same factor.
  - $n(a\text{A} + b\text{B} \rightleftharpoons c\text{C} + d\text{D}) \quad K'_{\text{forward}} = \left(\frac{[\text{C}]^c[\text{D}]^d}{[\text{A}]^a[\text{B}]^b}\right)^n = \frac{[\text{C}]^{nc}[\text{D}]^{nd}}{[\text{A}]^{na}[\text{B}]^{nb}}$
- For an overall equation that consists of two steps, multiply each equilibrium constant to obtain the overall K value.
  - $\text{A} \rightleftharpoons 4\,\text{B} \quad K_1 = \frac{[\text{B}]^4}{[\text{A}]}$
  - $4\,\text{B} \rightleftharpoons 2\,\text{C} \quad K_2 = \frac{[\text{C}]^2}{[\text{B}]^4}$
  - $\text{A} \rightleftharpoons 2\,\text{C} \quad K_1 \times K_2 = K_{\text{overall}} = \frac{[\text{B}]^4}{[\text{A}]} \times \frac{[\text{C}]^2}{[\text{B}]^4} = \frac{[\text{C}]^2}{[\text{A}]}$

K Expressed as Pressure

K is typically expressed in concentration with a subscript c to denote concentration in molarity. When the equilibrium constant, K_c is expressed in terms of partial pressures (P, in units of atmospheres, atm), it is designated as K_p. For example, for the combustion of propane, we have:

$$K_\text{p} = \frac{\left(P_{\text{CO}_2}\right)^3\left(P_{\text{H}_2\text{O}}\right)^4}{\left(P_{\text{C}_3\text{H}_8}\right)^1\left(P_{\text{O}_2}\right)^5}$$

The relationship between K_c and K_p for the reaction

$$a\text{A} + b\text{B} \rightleftharpoons c\text{C} + d\text{D}$$

is given by:

$$K_\text{p} = K_\text{c}(RT)^{\Delta n} \qquad R = 0.08206\frac{\text{L} \cdot \text{atm}}{\text{mol} \cdot \text{K}} \qquad \Delta n = c + d - (a + b)$$

The superscript Δn refers to the molar difference between the number of gas products and reactants. For example, the Δn value for the combustion of propane is:

$$\Delta n = 3 + 4 - (1 + 5) = 1$$

K for Solids and Liquids

Chemical equilibriums are also described as homogeneous or heterogeneous. **Homogeneous equilibrium** involves substances that are all in the same phase, e.g., combustion of propane involves species that are in the gas phase. **Heterogeneous equilibrium** means the substances are in different phases when equilibrium is reached. For instance:

$$a\mathrm{A(s)} + b\mathrm{B(l)} \rightleftharpoons c\mathrm{C(aq)} + d\mathrm{D(g)}$$

$$K = [\mathrm{C}]^c[\mathrm{D}]^d$$

When writing equilibrium constant expressions, solid and pure liquid phases are not included in the expression because the concentration remains constant.

Calculating K and Equilibrium Concentrations

Regardless of the initial concentrations for a specific chemical reaction at a fixed temperature, the reactants and products will reach an equilibrium concentration (different from the initial concentration) such that the calculated K will always be the same. The initial concentrations, the changes, and equilibrium concentrations are often written in a table to calculate K. The table is called an ICE table, where $\mathrm{I} = \text{initial}$, $\mathrm{C} = \text{change}$, and $\mathrm{E} = \text{equilibrium}$. Table 12 shows an ICE table along with an example reaction.

Table 12. An ICE table showing the initial and final concentrations of A and B

	$\mathrm{A(g)}$	$\rightleftharpoons$ $3\,\mathrm{B(g)}$
	[A]	[B]
Initial	1.00	0
Change	−0.15	+0.45
Equilibrium	0.85	0.45

Note that if A decreases by -0.15 M, then B must increase by a factor of 3 ($3 \times 0.15\ \mathrm{M} = +0.45\ \mathrm{M}$). The equilibrium expression is:

$$K = \frac{[\mathrm{B}]^3}{[\mathrm{A}]} = \frac{(0.45)^3}{(0.85)} = 0.11$$

The value of K is near zero, which indicates that the reverse reaction is favored. Now suppose that the value of K and the initial concentrations are known, but not the equilibrium concentrations. For instance, Table 13 shows an ICE table where the change in concentrations, indicated by the variable x, is unknown.

Table 13. An ICE table showing the initial concentrations of A, B, and C but with an unknown equilibrium concentration and change indicated by x.

	$2\,A(g)$ $\rightleftharpoons$	$2\,B(g)$ +	$C(g)$
	[A]	[B]	[C]
Initial	3.00×10^{-4}	0	0
Change	$-2x$	$+2x$	$+x$
Equilibrium	$3.00 \times 10^{-4} - 2x$	$2x$	x

The change for reactant and product is indicated by x multiplied with its stoichiometric coefficient. Suppose K is equal to 2.00×10^{-7}, then

$$K = \frac{[B]^2[C]}{[A]^2} = \frac{(2x)^2(x)}{(3.00 \times 10^{-4} - 2x)^2} = 2.00 \times 10^{-7}$$

Solving for x may often require extensive algebraic rearrangement, the use of the quadratic formula, or the method of perfect squares. When the value of K is relatively small (e.g., $\leq 1.0 \times 10^{-3}$) or if $x \leq 5\%$ with respect to the initial concentration of the reactant, x can be neglected for algebraic simplification. In some cases, where x is neglected, the solved value of x is still greater than 5 percent, with respect to the initial concentration of the reactant. In such a scenario, the **method of successive approximations** is applied, which requires solving for x as if it was small, substituting the newly obtained value of x, and then putting it back into the equation where x was initially neglected. For instance, from the previous equation:

$$K = 2.00 \times 10^{-7} = \frac{(2x)^2(x)}{(3.00 \times 10^{-4} - 2x)^2} \approx \frac{4x^3}{(3.00 \times 10^{-4})^2} \quad x \approx 0 \text{ in denominator is neglected}$$

$$(2.00 \times 10^{-7})(3.00 \times 10^{-4})^2 = 4x^3$$

$$x = \left(\frac{1.80 \times 10^{-14}}{4}\right)^{1/3} = 1.65 \times 10^{-5}$$

To determine whether to proceed, resubstitute x to check or apply the 5 percent rule.

$$\frac{(2 \times 1.65 \times 10^{-5})^2(1.65 \times 10^{-5})}{(3.00 \times 10^{-4} - 2 \times 1.65 \times 10^{-5})^2} = 2.53 \times 10^{-7} \qquad \frac{1.65 \times 10^{-5}}{3.00 \times 10^{-4}} \times 100\% = 5.50\% > 5\%$$

Each check indicates that the method of successive approximations must be applied, so for the first iteration, $x = 1.65 \times 10^{-5}$ is placed in the denominator as follows:

$$2.00 \times 10^{-7} = \frac{(2x)^2(x)}{(3.00 \times 10^{-4} - 2 \times 1.65 \times 10^{-5})^2}$$

$$x = 1.53 \times 10^{-5}$$

Based on the 5 percent rule, the first solved value for x gave 5.5 percent, which is still greater than 5 percent. When substituting x into the original equation and applying the 5 percent rule, we have:

$$\frac{(2 \times 1.54 \times 10^{-5})^2(1.54 \times 10^{-5})}{(3.00 \times 10^{-4} - 2 \times 1.54 \times 10^{-5})^2} = 1.96 \times 10^{-7} \quad \frac{1.53 \times 10^{-5}}{3.00 \times 10^{-4}} \times 100\% = 5.09\% \approx 5\%$$

The value for x is closer to the true value of K. A second iteration will give an x value that remains constant with a K value equal to 2.00×10^{-7}. However, it's not necessary to continue further because the value of x is already the best approximation.

Effect of Concentration, Volume, and Temperature on Equilibrium

Le Chatelier's principle explains that for a chemical system that is disrupted at chemical equilibrium, the system will change in a direction that reduces that disturbance. Consider the following reaction:

$$\mathrm{A(g)} \rightleftharpoons 2\ \mathrm{B(g)} + \mathrm{heat}$$

Increasing the concentration of the reactant, i.e., A, will cause the system to shift toward the right to create more products. Increasing the concentration of the product, B, will move the reaction to the left toward the reactant. If the concentration of the reactant, A, is decreased, then the system shifts to the left toward the reactant. If the concentration of B is decreased, then the reaction shifts to the right to produce more products.

Suppose the reaction with A and B shown above occurs inside a small piston chamber. If the volume of the chamber is decreased (the piston moves down), then the reaction will shift in a direction where there are fewer moles of gas, i.e., toward A. However, if the volume of the chamber is increased (piston moves up), then the reaction will shift in the direction where there are more moles of gas particles, i.e., toward B.

If the reaction is **exothermic**, i.e., produces heat, and if the temperature of the chemical system has increased, the reaction will shift to the left, toward the reactants, which will result in the equilibrium constant decreasing. However, if the temperature is decreased in an exothermic reaction, the system will shift toward the right, toward the products, which will cause the equilibrium constant to increase. Consider the following endothermic reaction:

$$2\ \mathrm{A(g)} + \mathrm{heat} \rightleftharpoons \mathrm{B(g)}$$

If the temperature is increased for an endothermic reaction, the system will shift to the right, toward the product, which will cause the equilibrium constant to increase. In contrast, if the temperature of the system is reduced, the system will shift to the left to compensate for the heat loss, toward the reactants, which will cause the equilibrium constant to decrease.

Acids and Bases

Definitions of Acids and Bases

Acids and bases are defined in many different ways. The **Arrhenius definition** of an acid or base provides a molecular description using protons (H^+) and hydroxide (OH^-) ions. An **Arrhenius acid** can be described as a substance that increases the concentration of H^+ ions in an aqueous solution. For instance, consider the dissolution of nitric acid (Table 13), which produces an H^+ ion in aqueous solution. When the strong acid is added to water, it dissolves and acts as a proton donor in the following detailed chemical equation:

$$HNO_3(aq) \rightarrow H^+(aq) + NO_3^-(aq)$$

The reaction may also be written as:

$$HNO_3(aq) + H_2O(l) \rightarrow H_3O^+(aq) + NO_3^-(aq)$$

The first equation is commonly written as a shorthand notation compared to the more detailed second equation. Note that H^+ means H^3O^+. The forward arrow indicates that the reaction proceeds completely to the right, meaning complete ionization or toward the product's side. The nitrate anion, NO_3-(aq), acts as an electron pair acceptor and contains a negative charge. An **Arrhenius base** is a substance that increases the concentration of OH^- ions when it is dissolved in water to form an aqueous solution. The addition of sodium hydroxide to water (Table 13) is an example of an Arrhenius base.

$$NaOH(aq) \rightarrow OH^-(aq) + Na^+(aq)$$

The forward arrow indicates that the base is a strong base where the reaction proceeds completely to the right.

Some examples of acids are shown in Table 13, and each acid is typically written with an H in front.

Table 13. Common Acids and Bases	
Name	Application or occurrences
Acids	
HCl (Hydrochloric acid); strong acid	Stomach acid for digestion
HNO_3 (Nitric acid); strong acid	Common fertilizer
H_3PO_4 (Phosphoric acid); strong acid	Food preservative
H_2SO_4 (Sulfuric acid); strong acid	Used in automobile batteries
H_2CO_3 (carbonic acid); weak acid	Found in carbonated beverages
$HC_2H_3O_2$ (acetic acid); weak acid	Found in vinegar
Bases	
NH_3 (Ammonia)	Detergent
$NaOH$ (Sodium hydroxide), strong base	Used for making plastic and soaps
$NaHCO_3$ (Sodium bicarbonate)	Antacid and found in baking soda

The **Brønsted-Lowry definition** defines an acid or base depending on whether a particular species donates or accepts a proton. A **Brønsted-Lowry acid** is a species that is a proton (H^+) donor, and a

Brønsted-Lowry base is a species that is a proton acceptor. The Brønsted-Lowry definition of an acid fits well for the reaction of nitric acid and water whereby a proton is donated to water as shown above. Generally, for any acid that donates a proton, the general reaction can be written:

$$\overbrace{\mathrm{HA}}^{\substack{\text{Brønsted–}\\\text{Lowry}\\\text{acid}}} + \overbrace{\mathrm{H_2O(l)}}^{\substack{\text{Brønsted–}\\\text{Lowry}\\\text{base}}} \rightleftharpoons \overbrace{\mathrm{H_3O^+(aq)}}^{\substack{\text{conjugate}\\\text{acid}}} + \overbrace{\mathrm{A^-}}^{\substack{\text{conjugate}\\\text{base}}}$$

The term A⁻ refers to the anion of the acid, and the equilibrium arrow refers to a weak acid where dissociation of the proton occurs to a limited extent. A **conjugate acid** is an ion that forms when the base pair gains a proton. The **conjugate base** that pairs with an acid is the ion that is formed when an acid loses a proton. For example, the conjugate acid forms when the base (water) accepts a proton, and the conjugate base is produced when an acid (HA) donates or loses a proton. The **conjugate acid-base pair** refers to two species that are related to each other based on the transfer of a proton, i.e., HA and A^- or H^3O^+ and H_2O.

All Arrhenius acids and bases are classified as acids/bases in the Brønsted-Lowry definition, but not all Brønsted-Lowry acids/bases are considered Arrhenius acids/bases. For instance, some species such as ammonia (NH_3) do not produce hydroxide ions and may not be considered bases from the Arrhenius base point of view. However, the Brønsted-Lowry definition would classify ammonia as a base because it acts as a proton acceptor.

$$\overbrace{\mathrm{NH_3(aq)}}^{\substack{\text{Brønsted–}\\\text{Lowry}\\\text{base}}} + \overbrace{\mathrm{H_2O(l)}}^{\substack{\text{Brønsted–}\\\text{Lowry}\\\text{acid}}} \rightleftharpoons \overbrace{\mathrm{OH^-(aq)}}^{\substack{\text{conjugate}\\\text{base}}} + \overbrace{\mathrm{NH_4^+(aq)}}^{\text{conjugate acid}}$$

Water acts as an acid, and a proton is transferred to an ammonia molecule that contains lone-pair electrons, which forms a covalent bond to the hydrogen atom resulting in the formation of ammonium. Ammonia accepts a proton and acts as an electron-pair donor or proton acceptor. Ammonium and ammonia form one conjugate acid-base pair, and water and hydroxide are the second conjugate acid-base pair. If the previous reaction was reversed, the conjugate acid ammonium, NH_4-, would react with the hydroxide ion to produce ammonia, NH_3. The general formula for a weak base dissociation is

$$\overbrace{\mathrm{B(aq)}}^{\substack{\text{Brønsted–}\\\text{Lowry}\\\text{base}}} + \overbrace{\mathrm{H_2O(l)}}^{\substack{\text{Brønsted–}\\\text{Lowry}\\\text{acid}}} \rightleftharpoons \overbrace{\mathrm{OH^-(aq)}}^{\substack{\text{conjugate}\\\text{base}}} + \overbrace{\mathrm{BH^+(aq)}}^{\text{conjugate acid}}$$

The term B refers to a weak base and accepts a proton to form BH^+, the conjugate acid. In acid-base reactions, species such as water that act as acids or bases are called **amphoteric** because they can donate or accept a proton. From Table 13, we can predict the conjugate acid-base pair. For instance, NO_3- is the conjugate base of the acid HNO_3.

Strength of an Acid and Its Ionization Constant K_a

Acids and bases are characterized as strong or weak electrolytes. **Strong electrolytes** (e.g., HCl and NaOH) are species that dissociate from a molecular species to an ionic species within a solution. In a chemical equation, these types of electrolytes will be followed by a single right arrow to indicate complete ionization or dissociation. Therefore, strong acids and bases (Table 13) completely or mostly ionize in aqueous solution. The chemical reaction is driven completely forward, to the right side of the equation, where the acidic or basic ions are formed.

Because all strong acids or bases dissociate completely, if the initial concentration of the acid is known, then the proton or hydroxide concentration is also known. For instance, a 2.0 M HCl solution will have a proton or hydronium ion concentration equal to 2.0 M: $[HCl] = [H^+] = [H_3O^+] = 2.0\ M$. Similarly, a 1.5 M solution of $NaOH$ gives: $[NaOH] = [OH^-] = 1.5\ M$.

In contrast, **weak electrolytes** (e.g., $HC_2H_3O_2$, NH_3) do not completely dissociate in solution. Therefore, weak acids and bases do not completely dissociate in aqueous solution. They only partially ionize, and the solution becomes a mixture of the acid or base, water, and the acidic or basic ions. The stronger the acid, the weaker the conjugate base (HCl and Cl^-), and the weaker the acid, the stronger the conjugate base ($HC_2H_3O_2$ and $C_2H_3O_2$-). Similarly, the stronger the base, the weaker the conjugate acid ($NaOH$ and OH), and the weaker the base, the stronger the conjugate acid (NH_3 and NH_4+). The strength of the acid or base depends on the direction of equilibrium as indicated by the arrows, which refer to partial ionization. The generic formula for a weak acid-base reaction was shown above, and the direction of equilibrium (arrows) dictates the strength of the acid or base. If the equilibrium lies further to the left, toward the reactants (left arrow longer than right), the acid or base is weak. If the equilibrium lies more toward the products (right arrow longer than left), the acid-base is relatively strong.

The strength of an acid or base is given by the **acid or base ionization constant**, K_a or K_b, which is based on the following acid-base chemical dissociation equations:

$$K_a = \frac{[H^+][A^-]}{[HA]} \text{ and } K_b = \frac{[BH^+][OH^-]}{[B]}$$

The values of K_a or K_b are typically less than one, meaning that weak acids or bases only partially ionize because the equilibrium is shifted toward the reactant side. The greater the value of K_a or K_b the greater the strength of the acid or base because dissociation of the acid or base is larger. Given a K_a or K_b and the initial concentration of the acid or base (HA or B), the H^+ or OH^- concentration can be determined by setting up an ICE table (solving for $x = [H^+]$). Once the H^+ or OH^- concentration is found, the pH of the acidic or basic solution can be found.

The pH Scale

Water can act as either an acid or a base. When mixed with an acid, water can accept a proton and become an H_3O^+ ion. When mixed with a base, water can donate a proton and become an OH^- ion. Sometimes water molecules donate and accept protons from each other; this process is called **autoionization**. The chemical equation is written as follows:

$$H_2O + H_2O \rightarrow OH^- + H_3O^+$$

The term **pH** refers to the power or potential of hydrogen atoms and is used as a scale for a substance's acidity. In chemistry, pH represents the hydrogen ion concentration (written as $[H^+]$) in an aqueous, or watery, solution. The hydrogen ion concentration, $[H^+]$, is measured in moles of H^+ per liter of solution.

The **pH scale** is a logarithmic scale used to quantify how acidic or basic a substance is. The pH for a solution is the negative logarithm of its hydrogen ion concentration: $\mathrm{pH} = -\log[\mathrm{H}^+]$. A one-unit change in pH correlates with a ten-fold change in the hydrogen ion concentration. The pH scale typically ranges from zero to 14, although it is possible to have pH values outside of this range. Pure water has a pH of 7, which is considered **neutral**. Any values of pH that are less than 7 are considered **acidic**, while pH values greater than 7 are considered **basic**, or **alkaline**.

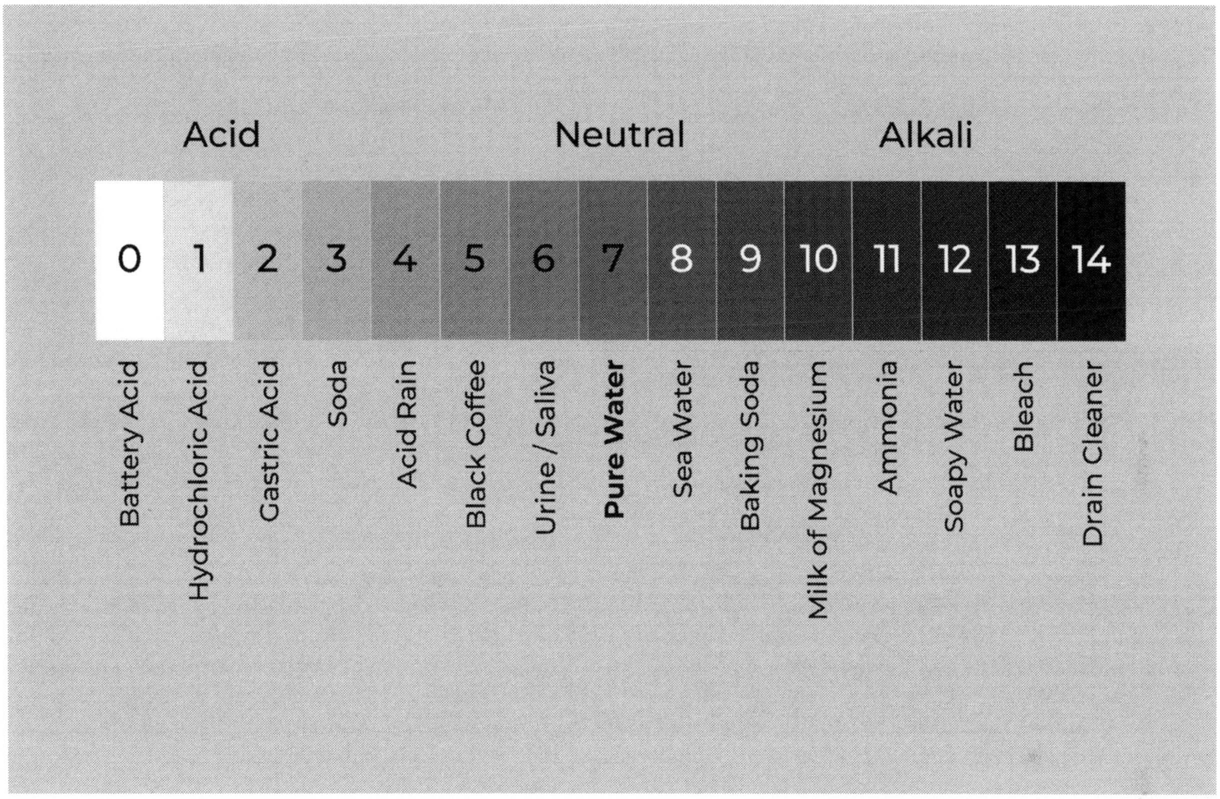

Figure 26. The pH scale showing pH values of common substances

A **buffer** is a molecule that can act as either a hydrogen ion donor or acceptor. Buffers are crucial in the blood and body fluids and prevent the body's pH from fluctuating into dangerous territory. The pH of a solution can be measured using a pH meter, test paper, or indicator sticks.

Solubility Equilibria

Solubility Product Constants and the Molar Solubility

The amount of substances that dissolve within a specific amount of liquid (e.g., water) is called **solubility**. The reaction of two ionic compounds (e.g., $Pb(NO_3)_2$ and NaCl) can result in the formation of a solid or precipitate that is insoluble ($PbCl_2$). However, these types of compounds may have a certain degree of solubility where the equilibrium is primarily toward the solid reactant. The **solubility product constant (K_{sp})** is the equilibrium constant that represents the dissociation of an ionic compound. For instance, solid lead (II) chloride will partially ionize when added to water.

$$PbCl_2(s) \rightleftharpoons Pb^{2+}(aq) + 2\,Cl^-(aq) \quad K_{sp} = 1.17 \times 10^{-5} = [Pb^{2+}][Cl^-]^2$$

The measured K_{sp} value is specific to a temperature of 25 °C. Solids are not included the constant expression, and each species represented in the constant expression has units of molarity (moles/liter). The **molar solubility, *S***, refers to the solubility for a specific ionic compound that can be determined from K_{sp}. For instance, the molar solubility of lead(II) chloride is found by setting up an ICE table:

Table 14. An ICE table showing the initial concentrations of Pb^{2+} and Cl^-

$PbCl_2(s)$ $\rightleftharpoons$	$Pb^{2+}(aq)$ +	$2\,Cl^-(aq)$
	$[Pb^{2+}]$	$[Cl^-]$
Initial	0	0
Change	$+S$	$+2S$
Equilibrium	S	$2S$

The molar solubility has units of moles per liter (moles/liter). The term S is the amount of lead(II) chloride that dissolves. Because solids are not included in the expression, there is no initial change shown in the denominator.

$$K_{sp} = 1.17 \times 10^{-5} = [Pb^{2+}][Cl^-]^2$$

$$1.17 \times 10^{-5} = (S)(2S)^2 = 4S^3$$

$$\left(\frac{1.17 \times 10^{-5}}{4}\right)^{1/3} = S = 1.43 \times 10^{-2}\ M$$

The molar solubility, S, of lead(II) chloride is 1.43×10^{-2} moles per liter. If S is given, then K_{sp} can be determined, so both terms are related to one another. The K_{sp} values of two different compounds cannot always be used to compare the solubility of one another. The connection between K_{sp} and S depends on the stoichiometry of the reaction. However, if both compounds have the same dissociation stoichiometry (e.g., CaF_2 and $PbCl_2$), then K_{sp} can be used to predict the relative solubility. For instance, consider the following compounds in Table 15.

Table 15. Comparison of K_{sp} and S for two compounds with the same dissociation stoichiometry		
Ionic compound	K_{sp}	S
CaF_2	1.46×10^{-10}	$3.32 \times 10^{-4}\ M$
$PbCl_2$	1.17×10^{-5}	$1.43 \times 10^{-2}\ M$

Because calcium fluoride has a smaller K_{sp} than lead(II) chloride, the molar solubility will be smaller.

The Common Ion Effect on Solubility

The **common ion effect** explains that the solubility of an ionic compound, in a solution containing a common ion, decreases compared to a solution without the addition or presence of a common ion. For example, consider the addition of lead(II) chloride to water:

$$\mathrm{PbCl_2(s)} \rightleftharpoons \mathrm{Pb^{2+}(aq)} + 2\ \mathrm{Cl^-(aq)}$$

This results in partial dissociation of the compound with a molar solubility of $S = 2.27 \times 10^{-2}$ M. However, what if 0.100 M of sodium chloride, NaCl, was added to the solution containing the dissociation reaction above?

$$\mathrm{NaCl(s)} \rightarrow \mathrm{Na^+(aq)} + \overbrace{\mathrm{Cl^-(aq)}}^{\text{Common ion}}$$

Based on Le Chatelier's principle, the addition of NaCl will decrease the solubility because of the existence of the chloride ion, Cl^-, which will push the equilibrium to the left, toward the solid reactant, $PbCl_2$. The actual value of S must be recalculated in the presence of a common ion, as shown in Table 16.

Table 16. An ICE table showing the effect of a common ion, Cl^-		
$\mathrm{PbCl_2(s)}$ $\rightleftharpoons$	$\mathrm{Pb^{2+}(aq)}$ +	$2\ \mathrm{Cl^-(aq)}$
	$[Pb^{2+}]$	$[Cl^-]$
Initial	0	0.100
Change	$+S$	$+2S$
Equilibrium	S	$0.100 + 2S$

The initial concentration of Cl^- will be equal to the concentration of the added salt:

$$[\mathrm{NaCl}] = [\mathrm{Cl^-}] = 0.100\ \mathrm{M}$$

The equilibrium expression for Cl^- will now be the sum of the change in Cl^- and the concentration of the added ion:

$$K_{sp} = 1.17 \times 10^{-5} = [\mathrm{Pb^{2+}}][\mathrm{Cl^-}]^2$$

$$1.17 \times 10^{-5} = (S)(0.100 + 2S)^2$$

Because the value of K_{sp} is relatively small (less than 10^{-3}), the value of S within the square can be neglected.

$$1.17 \times 10^{-5} = (S)(0.100 + \cancel{2S})^2 = (S)(0.100)^2$$

$$S = \frac{1.17 \times 10^{-5}}{(0.100)^2} = 1.17 \times 10^{-3}\ \text{M}$$

For purposes of checking, the value of S can be resubstituted into the original equation to find an approximate K_{sp}.

$$K_{sp} = 1.17 \times 10^{-5} \approx (S)(0.100 + 2S)^2 \quad S = 1.17 \times 10^{-3}\ \text{M}$$

$$1.17 \times 10^{-5} \approx (1.17 \times 10^{-3})\left(0.100 + 2(1.17 \times 10^{-3})\right)^2$$

$$1.17 \times 10^{-5} \approx 1.23 \times 10^{-5}$$

Both K_{sp} values are similar (near 5 percent error), which suggest that the calculated value of S is reasonable. Note that the percent error is given by the following equation:

$$\%\ \text{error} = \frac{|\text{True value} - \text{Approximate value}|}{\text{True value}} \times 100\%$$

$$\frac{\left|1.17 \times 10^{-5} - 1.23 \times 10^{-5}\right|}{1.17 \times 10^{-5}} \times 100\% = 5.13\%$$

The molar solubility, S, of lead(II) chloride with a common ion (Cl^-) is 1.17×10^{-3} moles per liter, which is less than the molar solubility without the common ion. From a qualitative standpoint, the value of S should be less with a common ion based on Le Chatelier's principle. If the calculated value is higher, then this suggests an algebraic or computational error.

Effect of pH with a Common Ion

Solid calcium hydroxide ($Ca(OH)_2$) has a $K_{sp} = 4.68 \times 10^{-6}$ with a dissociation stoichiometry similar to lead(II) chloride (Table 14), but results in the production of a hydroxide anion (OH^-). Determining the value of S allows for the $[OH^-]$ to be found, which can be used to find the pH ($\text{pH} + \text{pOH} = 14.00$).

$$Ca(OH)_2(s) \rightleftharpoons Ca^{2+}(aq) + 2\ OH^-(aq)$$

$$4.68 \times 10^{-6} = [Ca^{2+}][OH^-]^2$$

$$4.68 \times 10^{-6} = (S)(2S)^2 = 4S^3$$

$$\left(\frac{4.68 \times 10^{-6}}{4}\right)^{1/3} = S = 1.05 \times 10^{-2}\ \text{M}$$

Because there are two moles of hydroxide ions in the dissociation reaction, the $[OH^-]$ is twice the value of S.

$$[OH^-] = 2S$$

The pH can now be calculated as follows:

$pH = 14.00 - pOH = 14.00 - (-\log[OH^-])$

$pH = 14.00 + \log(2S) = 14.00 + \log(2 \times 1.05 \times 10^{-2}) = 12.32$

Suppose you have two beakers with one beaker containing a basic solution and another that is acidic. In both the acidic and basic solutions, you add a specific amount of solid magnesium hydroxide to each beaker. If the pH of a solution is basic or if a common ion, e.g., OH^-, is present in large amounts, the solubility of magnesium hydroxide will decrease because the equilibrium shifts to the left. However, if the solution is acidic, then H^+ will react with OH^- and the equilibrium will shift to the right, thereby increasing the solubility of magnesium hydroxide. For an ionic compound that produces either a strongly or weakly basic anion (OH^-), the solubility of that compound will increase if the solution becomes increasingly acidic. Suppose 1.00×10^{-3} M HCl is added to a solution containing a precipitate of calcium hydroxide (a saturated solution), the pH of the solution should decrease slightly.

$$[OH^-] = 2S - [H^+]$$

$$[OH^-] = 2S - 1.00 \times 10^{-3}\text{ M} = 2 \times (1.05 \times 10^{-2}\text{ M}) - 1.00 \times 10^{-3}\text{ M}$$

$$[OH^-] = 0.0200\text{ M}$$

$pH = 14.00 + \log(0.0200\text{ M}) = 10.09$

Predicting Precipitation Based on Solubility Equilibria: Q and K_{sp}

The double displacement reaction of two ionic compounds may result in the formation of a precipitate, which can have a limited degree of solubility indicated by K_{sp} values. For a slightly soluble ionic compound, the **reaction quotient, *Q*,** describes the product of the concentration of each ionic compound raised to its stoichiometric coefficient. For example:

$$PbCl_2(s) \rightleftharpoons Pb^{2+}(aq) + 2\,Cl^-(aq) \quad Q = [Pb^{2+}][Cl^-]^2$$

The reaction quotient Q is not necessarily equal to K_{sp}, which describes the value of the constant expression at equilibrium. Instead, Q refers to the value of the product expression under any condition, e.g., a value that does not reflect equilibrium. Q can be calculated for any ion concentration and then compared to K_{sp}, which contains an ion concentration at equilibrium. Suppose that a solution of lead(II) nitrate and sodium chloride are added to a beaker and the following reaction takes place:

$$Pb(NO_3)_2(aq) + 2\,NaCl(aq) \rightarrow PbCl_2(s) + 2\,NaNO_3(aq)$$

The reaction of two ionic compounds produces lead(II) chloride. If the solid was extracted using a Buchner funnel, dried, and then a small amount added to a beaker containing pure water, the solid will slightly ionize to produce lead(II) cation and the chloride anion. Suppose that the concentration of lead(II) ion and chloride are measured shortly after adding the solid to water. If Q is less than K_{sp}, the reaction will continue to move to the right toward the cation and anion products. If all of the lead(II) chloride dissolves in the solution, then the concentration of the ions, lead(II) and chloride ion, will still be less than the equilibrium concentrations of each ion. A solution where all the solid or precipitate dissolves is called an **unsaturated solution** because Q is less than K_{sp}. For example, consider a value of

Q that is less than K_{sp}, e.g., $Q = 2.00 \times 10^{-6}$, which can be substituted in place of K_{sp} in the following expression.

$$Q = [Pb^{2+}][Cl^-]^2$$

$$2.00 \times 10^{-6} = (S)(2S)^2 = 4S^3$$

$$\left(\frac{2.00 \times 10^{-6}}{4}\right)^{1/3} = S = 7.94 \times 10^{-3}\ \text{M}$$

Solving for the concentrations of each ion based on the value of S gives:

$$[Pb^{2+}] = S = 7.94 \times 10^{-3}\ \text{M} \quad [Cl^-] = 2S = 2 \times 7.94 \times 10^{-3}\ \text{M} = 1.59 \times 10^{-2}\ \text{M}$$

Now consider the equilibrium concentrations of lead(II) chloride, based on K_{sp} which was used to calculate the molar solubility, S, previously:

$$K_{sp} = [Pb^{2+}][Cl^-]^2$$

$$1.17 \times 10^{-5} = (S)(2S)^2 = 4S^3$$

$$\left(\frac{1.17 \times 10^{-5}}{4}\right)^{1/3} = S = 1.43 \times 10^{-2}\ \text{M}$$

$$[Pb^{2+}] = S = 1.43 \times 10^{-2}\ \text{M} \quad [Cl^-] = 2S = 2 \times 1.43 \times 10^{-2}\ \text{M} = 2.86 \times 10^{-2}\ \text{M}$$

The equilibrium concentrations of the lead(II) and chloride ion are greater compared to the ion concentrations given by the reaction quotient Q. If additional lead(II) chloride is added to the solution, the solid will continue to dissolve, forming lead(II) and chloride ions, provided that Q remains less than K_{sp}. Table 17 provides a comparison of Q and K_{sp}.

Table 17. Comparison of lead(II) and chloride ion concentrations

$Q < K_{sp}$ (unsaturated solution)	Q	K_{sp}
$[Pb^{2+}]$	7.94×10^{-3} M	1.43×10^{-2} M
$[Cl^-]$	1.59×10^{-2} M	2.86×10^{-2} M

If the reaction quotient Q is equal to the solubility product constant K_{sp} ($Q = K_{sp}$), then the reaction is now at equilibrium and lead(II) chloride will not continue to dissolve or move toward the product ions. The actual amount of lead(II) chloride present in the solution may be slightly visible at the bottom of the beaker. A solution where a specific amount of solid has been added such that the reaction quotient is equal to the equilibrium constant ($Q = K_{sp}$) is called a **saturated solution.** For the scenario where Q is greater than K_{sp}, meaning that the concentration of the ions is greater than the equilibrium concentrations, the reaction will move to the left to produce lead(II) chloride. In other words, a precipitate will be visible at the bottom of the beaker.

A solution where Q is greater than K_{sp} is called a **supersaturated solution.** The solution can be heated well above 25 °C, such that the precipitate completely dissolves, and then cooled back to 25 °C without any formation of a precipitate. However, the solution is unstable, and when a small crystal of lead(II) chloride is added to the solution, the lead(II) and chloride ions already present in solution are triggered and combine to form the lead(II) chloride precipitate. In any case, Q can be used to predict whether precipitation will occur when two ionic solutions are mixed. If 0.0700 M lead(II) nitrate was combined with 0.0200 M NaBr, would a precipitate form? Table 18 provides a list of the solubility rules.

Table 18. Solubility Rules

Soluble	Ions	General Statement	Exceptions
1	NH_4^+, Li^+, Na^+, K^+	Group IA and ammonium compounds are soluble	None
2	$C_2H_3O_2^-, NO_3^-$	Acetate and nitrate compounds are soluble	None
3	Cl^-, Br^-, I^-	Almost all chlorides, bromides, and iodides are soluble	$AgCl, Hg_2Cl_2, PbCl_2, AgBr, HgBr_2, Hg_2Br_2, PbBr_2, AgI, HgI_2, Hg_2I_2, PbI_2$
Insoluble			
4	SO_4^{2-}	Almost all sulfates are insoluble	$CaSO_4, SrSO_4, BaSO_4, Ag_2SO_4, Hg_2SO_4, PbSO_4$
5	CO_3^{2-}	Almost all carbonates are insoluble	Group IA carbonates; $(NH_4)_2CO_3$
6	PO_4^{3-}	Almost all phosphates are insoluble	Group IA phosphates; $(NH_4)_3PO_4$
7	S^{2-}	Almost all sulfides are insoluble	Group IA sulfides; $(NH_4)_2S$
8	OH^-	Almost all hydroxides are insoluble	Group IA hydroxides; $Ca(OH)_2, Sr(OH)_2, Ba(OH)_2$

The reaction of lead(II) nitrate and sodium bromide is:

$$\overbrace{Pb(NO_3)_2(aq)}^{0.0700\text{ M}} + \overbrace{2\,NaBr(aq)}^{0.0200\text{ M}} \rightarrow PbBr_2(s) + 2NaNO_3$$

Based on the solubility rules, lead(II) bromide is predicted to be insoluble. To determine whether the given amount will result in the formation of a precipitate, Q must be calculated based on the given concentrations and compared to K_{sp}.

$$PbBr_2(s) \rightleftharpoons Pb^{2+}(aq) + 2\,Br^-(aq)$$

$$Q = [Pb^{2+}][Br^-]^2 = (0.0700)(0.0200)^2 = 2.80 \times 10^{-5}$$

For lead(II) bromide, $K_{sp} = 4.67 \times 10^{-6}$ which is less than Q. Therefore, $Q > K_{sp}$ indicating that a precipitate will form because the solution is supersaturated. Now suppose you were asked at what ion concentration will a precipitate not form. In the scenario where $Q < K_{sp}$, lead(II) bromide will completely dissolve in solution because the ion concentrations will be below the equilibrium concentrations. The following calculation finds the molar solubility, S:

$$K_{sp} = 4.67 \times 10^{-6} = [Pb^{2+}][Br^-]^2 = (S)(2S)^2$$

$$\left(\frac{4.67 \times 10^{-6}}{4}\right)^{1/3} = S = 1.05 \times 10^{-2}\text{ M}$$

Solving for the equilibrium concentrations of each ion based on the molar solubility of lead(II) bromide, S, gives:

$$[Pb^{2+}] = S = 1.05 \times 10^{-2}\ M \quad [Br^-] = 2S = 2 \times 1.05 \times 10^{-2}\ M = 2.10 \times 10^{-2}\ M$$

Therefore, for no precipitate to form, the $[Pb^{2+}]$ and $[Br^-]$ must be less than 1.05×10^{-2} M and 2.10×10^{-2} M. If molar solubility of lead(II) bromide is less than 1.05×10^{-2} M, it will not form a precipitate. For every one liter of solution, the amount of lead(II) bromide can be quantified from S.

$$2.10 \times 10^{-2} \frac{mol}{L} \times 1\ L \times \frac{367.0\ g\ PbBr_2}{1\ mol\ PbBr_2} = 7.71\ g\ PbBr_2$$

Adding less than 7.71 g of $PbBr_2$ into a liter of water will create a situation where no precipitate will form because the reaction will push completely toward products because $Q < K_{sp}$. The solution is unsaturated.

Thermodynamics

Introduction to Entropy

Entropy Increases When Matter is Dispersed

When transitioning from the solid to liquid or liquid to gas phase, the entropy of the system will increase. In each case, the particles are spread out and further apart from one another, such that there are more ways they can move and occupy a given space. For example, water vapor has higher entropy than liquid water because the gaseous water molecules have more kinetic energy, and consequently take up more volume because the molecules are further apart. These molecules can occupy more points in space, where each point will have a different geometrical configuration. Liquid water will have higher entropy than solid water because these molecules have enough kinetic energy to slide past one another, thereby occupying another point in space within the liquid. The water molecules in ice may be further apart compared to liquid water, but these water molecules are arranged to form a solid lattice where hydrogen bonding is maximized. Consequently, solid water has the least entropy because it is more ordered compared to other phases.

$$\mathrm{H_2O(s)} < \mathrm{H_2O(l)} < \mathrm{H_2O(g)}$$

$$\rightarrow \textit{Increasing Entropy } S \rightarrow$$

When transitioning from a solid to liquid or from high to low order, the change in entropy, ΔS, will be positive: $\mathrm{H_2O(s)} \rightarrow \mathrm{H_2O(l)};\ +\Delta S$. If the phase transition goes from less to more order, the change in entropy is negative: $\mathrm{H_2O(l)} \rightarrow \mathrm{H_2O(s)};\ -\Delta S$.

In a chemical reaction, if the number of particles in the products is greater than that of the reactants, as represented by the stoichiometric coefficients in the balanced chemical equation, the entropy increases. Conversely, if the number of products is less than that of the reactants, the entropy decreases.

$$A + B \rightarrow 3C; +\Delta S$$

$$C + D \rightarrow E;\ -\Delta S$$

For gaseous particles contained in a piston at a fixed temperature, if the volume of the gas increases, then the entropy increases because the particles have more space to move around.

Entropy Increases When Energy is Dispersed

As the temperature of a collection of molecules or particles increases, the entropy increases, and the distribution of kinetic energy within those particles becomes more dispersed. For instance, the **Maxwell-Boltzmann distribution** in the image below shows that a hot gas will have more entropy compared to a cold gas because the kinetic energy has a greater spread among the fraction of gaseous particles.

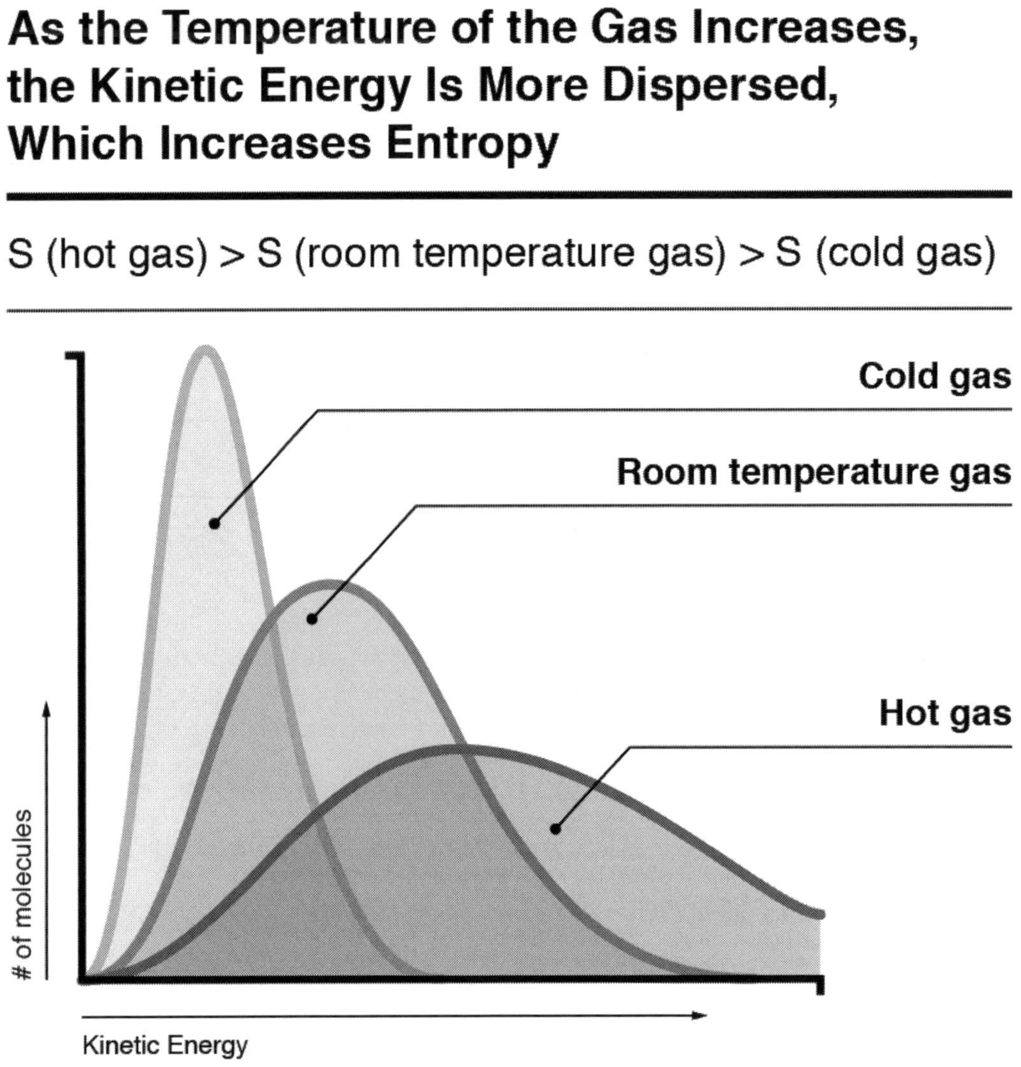

Absolute Entropy and Entropy Change

Qualitative Reasoning with Entropy

Entropy, S, is a measure of disorder in a chemical system. In physical processes, the entropy can change when a substance transitions between different phases: $Solid \leftrightarrow Liquid \leftrightarrow Gas$. In a chemical process, when reactants are converted to products, the entropy or disorder of the system can increase or decrease.

It is possible to calculate the entropy change for a process from the absolute entropies of the constituent species involved before and after the chemical process occurs:

$$\Delta S^{\circ}_{reaction} = \sum \Delta S^{\circ}_{products} - \sum \Delta S^{\circ}_{reactants}$$

Exothermic Reactions that Involve Decreases in Entropy

In nature, chemical reactions are favored toward an increase in entropy, $+\Delta S$, and a decrease in enthalpy $(-\Delta H)$ in a system. Whether a reaction occurs or not will depend on the balance of the factors that make up the **Gibbs Free energy**, ΔG. Endothermic and exothermic reactions can result in entropy changes to both the chemical system and its surroundings. In an exothermic reaction, where energy is lost to the surroundings, there is a decrease in enthalpy $(-\Delta H_{system})$. In some exothermic reactions (e.g., ammonia production), there may be a decrease in entropy $(-\Delta S_{system})$ because heat is transferred to the surroundings, thereby increasing the disorder $(+\Delta S_{surr})$. However, in an exothermic reaction, because heat is released to the surroundings, the overall entropy from both the surroundings and system can still be positive: $+\Delta S_{total} = \Delta S_{system} + \Delta S_{surroundings}$.

The equation is the **Second Law of Thermodynamics**, which says that for a process to be spontaneous, the total entropy must always increase. The second law also is written as:

$$\Delta S_{surroundings} = \frac{-\Delta H_{system}}{T}$$

and is connected to Gibbs free energy, ΔG. The value of ΔH_{system} for an exothermic reaction is negative, making the entropy of the surroundings positive $-(-\Delta H_{system})\sim + \Delta S_{surroundings}$. Substituting $\Delta S_{surroundings}$ and rearranging gives: Gibbs Free energy ΔG: $+\Delta S_{total} = \Delta S_{system} + \frac{-\Delta H_{system}}{T}$.

$$-T\Delta S_{total} = \Delta G = \Delta H_{system} - T\Delta S_{system}$$

Note that $-T\Delta S_{total}$ is called ΔG.

Gibbs Free Energy and Thermodynamic Favorability

Free Energy Change, ΔG_0

As mentioned, reactions must use energy to do work, and that available energy is called **Gibbs free energy (G)**. Gibbs free energy, or G, represents the thermodynamic work potential for a system that is at a constant temperature and pressure (it may help to know that Gibbs free energy used to be called "available energy"). Free energy can be found by identifying the changes in enthalpy and entropy of a system.

$$\Delta H_{reaction} = \Delta H_{products} - \Delta H_{reactants}$$

$$\Delta S_{reaction} = \Delta S_{products} - \Delta S_{reactants}$$

Thermodynamically Favorable Meaning

The Gibbs free energy, G, is often used to determine whether a chemical reaction is **thermodynamically favored**, which means that the reaction will proceed favorably toward the products at equilibrium.

$$A \rightleftarrows B; K > 1$$

The double-headed arrow indicates that the chemical reaction is at equilibrium, whereby the reactants are converted to products and the products to reactants. However, the reaction is favored toward the products as shown by the longer arrow, and the equilibrium constant, *K,* will be greater than one.

If a chemical reaction is **spontaneous**, meaning that it is thermodynamically favorable, the direction of the reaction will proceed toward the products (e.g., B). For a spontaneous reaction, the standard change in Gibbs free energy between the reactants and products is negative $-\Delta G^{\circ} = G_{products} - G_{reactants}$.

Determining the Signs of ΔH⁰ and ΔS⁰ for a Physical or Chemical Process

The standard (298 *K* and 1 atm) Gibbs free energy change ΔG° is given by:

$$\Delta G^{\circ} = \Delta H^{\circ} - T\Delta S^{\circ}$$

and is equal to the standard change in enthalpy (ΔH°) and the negative product of temperature and the standard change in entropy (ΔS°). The table below lists the signs of ΔG° concerning the various possible signs of ΔH° and ΔS°.

ΔG° Sign Conventions for Different Signs of ΔH° and ΔS°

Scenario	Spontaneity		K	ΔG°	ΔH°	$-T\Delta S^{\circ}$	ΔS°
1	Spontaneous		>1	$-$	$-$	$-$	$+$
2	Nonspontaneous		<1	$+$	$+$	$+$	$-$
3	Spontaneous	(low T)	>1	$-$	$-$	$+$	$-$
	Nonspontaneous	(high T)	<1	$+$			
4	Nonspontaneous	(low T)	<1	$+$	$+$	$-$	$+$
	Spontaneous	(high T)	>1	$-$			

A calculation to determine if the reaction is spontaneous is not necessary if $\Delta H^{\circ} < 0$ and $\Delta S^{\circ} > 0$ because the sum of ΔH° and $-T\Delta S^{\circ}$ will give a negative ΔG° as shown in Scenario 1 on the table.

Situations When Both Enthalpy and Entropy are Needed to Determine Favorability

In some cases, the signs and magnitudes of entropy and enthalpy must be quantified to determine the temperature conditions at which the reaction is thermodynamically favorable. In Scenario 3 from the previous table, exothermic reactions can be favorable at relatively low temperatures. However, increasing the temperature can make the reaction unfavorable, pushing it toward the reactants because $-T\Delta S > -\Delta H\ if \Delta S < 0$. For instance, the production of ammonia (Haber process) is an exothermic reaction whereby the entropy of the system decreases. As the temperature is increased, the forward reaction becomes unfavorable:

$$N_2(g) + 3H_2(g) \overset{400°C}{\rightleftarrows} 2NH_3(g);\ -\Delta H_{system} \text{ and } -\Delta S_{system}$$

The melting of ice and the dissolution of sodium nitrate in water are examples of endothermic reactions. Sodium nitrate is a common ingredient found within instant cold packs.

$$NaNO_3(s) \overset{H_2O(l)}{\rightleftarrows} Na^+(aq) + NO_3^-(aq)\,;\ +\Delta H_{system} \text{ and } + \Delta S_{system}$$

In an endothermic reaction, as the chemical system absorbs energy from the surroundings, the entropy of the system will increase ($+\Delta S_{system}$), but there will be a decrease in entropy to the surroundings ($-\Delta S_{surr}$). In Scenario 4 of the table above, endothermic reactions are not spontaneous at low temperatures given $+\Delta H_{sys}$ *and* $+\Delta S_{system}$. However, at higher temperatures, the magnitude of $-T\Delta S > \Delta H \; if \Delta S > 0$ and the combined enthalpy and entropy terms give a negative standard Gibbs free energy, $-\Delta G°$. The chemical process is thermodynamically favorable.

The Signs of ΔH^0 and ΔS^0 and the Direction of a Reaction

In Scenario 2 in the table above, $\Delta G^{\circ} > 0$ and the reaction is nonspontaneous, given that $\Delta H^{\circ} > 0$ and $\Delta S^{\circ} < 0$ where $-T\Delta S^{\circ} > 0$. Scenarios 3 and 4 are slightly more complicated and will generally require a quantitative calculation. Given Scenario 3, if the temperature is relatively small and if the ΔH° term is greater in magnitude than $-T\Delta S^{\circ}$, the reaction is spontaneous ($\Delta G^{\circ} < 0$). At equilibrium, the reaction will favor the products ($K > 1$). As the temperature increases, the magnitude of $-T\Delta S^{\circ}$ becomes more significant and more positive such that it will overtake the negative ΔH° term. As a result, the overall reaction will be nonspontaneous, where $\Delta G^{\circ} > 0$, and at equilibrium, the chemical process will favor the reactants ($K < 1$).

Thermodynamic and Kinetic Control

Thermodynamically Favorable Reactions Do Not Necessarily Proceed at a Measurable Rate

The standard free Gibbs energy, ΔG°, only indicates whether the products will be favorable or not at equilibrium, but provides no insight into the reaction rate, or how fast or slow the reaction process will occur. A thermodynamically-favorable, or spontaneous process ($-\Delta G^{\circ}$), will not necessarily occur at a measurable or observable rate. Some spontaneous processes will not happen within a person's lifetime, and some will occur in less than a second for a given set of reaction conditions (e.g., high or low temperatures). For example, the conversion of diamond (tetrahedral sp^3 carbons) to graphite (trigonal planar sp^2 carbons) is spontaneous ($\Delta G° = -2.87\ kJ/mol$) at room temperature and one atmospheric pressure. The reaction is also exothermic and increases in entropy, but the rate of reaction is extremely slow. The conversion of diamond to graphite would not occur to a great extent nor would it be noticeable in our lifetime.

Processes Under "Kinetic Control"

Chemical processes that are spontaneous but do not proceed to the products at a considerable rate will be under **kinetic control**. The conversion of diamond to graphite is under kinetic control due to the high activation barrier at moderate temperatures and pressures (e.g., 1 atm and 298K). Even though the formation of graphite is favorable ($-\Delta H$ and $+ \Delta S$) and extremely slow, it does not indicate that the chemical system will be in equilibrium. For example, suppose in one case there is one reaction mixture that contains 85 percent diamond and 15 percent graphite at one point in time. In a second case, at a much later time, let's assume that the equilibrium mixture is 0.5 percent diamond and 99.5 percent graphite.

However, in the first scenario, even though the reaction is spontaneous, the chemical system is not at equilibrium because it is under kinetic control. In the second scenario, the reaction will be closer to or at chemical equilibrium because the lowest value of ΔG° has been reached (as shown in the image below). At low temperatures, the reaction of diamond to graphite is under kinetic control; however, at higher temperatures, the reaction will be under thermodynamic control, where equilibrium can occur. For graphite formation, increasing the temperature would increase the thermodynamic favorability of the reaction (as described in Scenario 1 of the previous table titled *ΔG° Sign Conventions for Different Signs of ΔH° and ΔS°*). As seen in the image below, ΔG° decreases as the reaction proceeds to graphite. At equilibrium, ΔG° reaches a minimum, and mostly contains graphite.

ΔG° Decreases as the Reaction Proceeds to Graphite

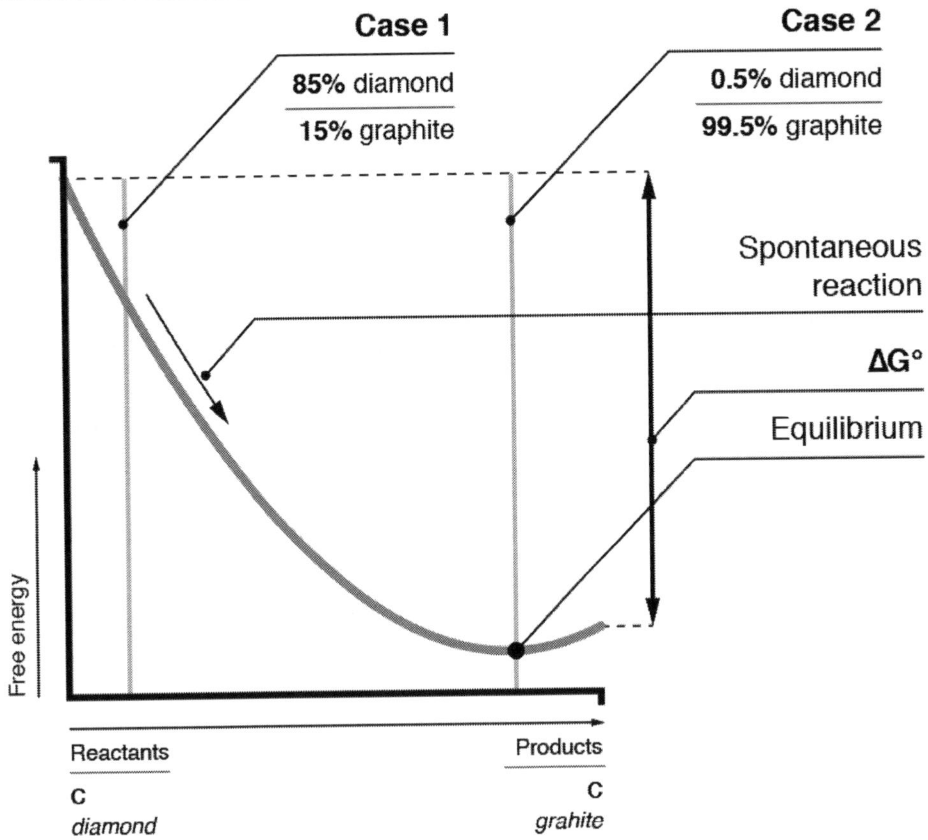

Free Energy and Equilibrium

Thermodynamically-Favorable Reactions and ΔG_0

The standard Gibbs free energy, $\Delta^{\circ}G$, determines if a chemical process is thermodynamically favorable. If $\Delta G^{\circ} < 0$, the reaction is favorable (spontaneous) and proceeds toward the products. If $\Delta G^{\circ} > 0$, the reaction is not favorable (nonspontaneous) and proceeds toward the reactants.

Using the Relationship Between K and Q to Predict the Direction of a Reaction

Standard Gibbs Free Energy Change, $\Delta G°$, and the equilibrium constant, K, of a chemical reaction are related by the following equation:

$$\Delta G° = -RT \ln K$$

In this equation, *R* is the universal gas constant and *T* is the temperature in Kelvin. This equation assumes that the reaction is happening at standard conditions of 1 M solutions and 1 atm pressure of the system. The free energy change reaction can also be rearranged to written in terms of K:

$$K = e^{-\Delta G°/RT}$$

RT, which represents the thermal energy of the system, is equal to 2.4 kJ/mol at room temperature of 298 K. When $\Delta G°$ is greater than zero, the value of K is less than one and becomes very small. The reactants are favored and are in much greater proportion to the products at equilibrium. When $\Delta G°$ is less than zero, the value of K is greater than one and the products are favored in the reaction. The change in the magnitude of K increases greatly as the value of $\Delta G°$ gets farther away from the value of RT.

Determining Whether a Reaction is Exothermic or Endothermic with Free Energy and K

Looking at the relationship between K and $\Delta G°$ elucidates information about the qualitative relationship between the thermodynamics of the system and the equilibrium of the system. Enthalpic changes increase the value of $\Delta G°$, whereas entropic changes decrease the value of $\Delta G°$. The free energy of a reaction can also qualitatively be determined by the positive or negative value of $\Delta G°$. If $\Delta G°$ is positive, the reaction is **endergonic**, which means that energy is being absorbed from the environment to run the reaction. K has a value less than one. These reactions are nonspontaneous. If $\Delta G°$ has a negative value, the reaction is **exergonic**, and the bonds that are being formed are stronger than the bonds that are being broken, so energy is released into the environment. K has a value greater than one. These reactions are mostly spontaneous, although some may require a small input of energy to start the reaction.

The Relation Between the Equilibrium Constant and Free Energy

$$N_2 + 3H_2 \leftrightarrow 2NH_3$$

The driving force of reactions is G, and if it is a very large negative number, the reaction may go almost to completion. Equilibrium, as indicated by the double arrows in equations, does not mean that the reaction has stopped, as particles are moving and dynamic. It also does not mean that there are equal amounts of products and reactants. For example, spontaneous reactions will have more products since they are so favorable. Many reactions are reversible, so learning the conditions and factors that will cause a system to reach equilibrium can be useful.

Altered conditions affect equilibrium. For example, adding more reactants yields more products. Increasing the external pressure will affect the reaction depending on where the most gas particles are (as determined by coefficients). Greater pressures will cause the side with the greatest gas particles to react faster since they will be moving faster, pushing the direction of the reaction to the other side. Increasing temperature will always change the equilibrium constant (K) because K is dependent on temperature as shown in this equation (valid with reversible reactions that are at equilibrium):

$$\Delta G = -RT\ln K$$

As previously discussed, the **equilibrium constant (K)** is a value that expresses the ratio of the products over the reactants. If K is greater than one, there are more products at equilibrium (forward reaction is favored), while a value less than one indicates that the reverse reaction is favored. The equilibrium constant can be calculated using the molarity of each product (to the power of its coefficient) divided by the molarity of each reactant (to the power of its coefficient) as shown in the equation below:

$$aA + bB \leftrightarrow cC + dD$$

$$Kc = \frac{[C]^c[D]^d}{[A]^a[B]^b}$$

While K shows the equilibrium values, the reaction quotient Q shows how far away the reaction is from equilibrium. It is the same equation but shows the ratio of products over reactants at any given time. Eventually, once a reversible reaction reaches equilibrium, Q will be equal to K.

Gas equilibrium constants are measured in terms of **partial pressure**, rather than concentration, and the equation is:

$$Kp = \frac{[PC]^c[PD]^d}{[PA]^a[PB]^b}$$

The equilibrium constant for heterogeneous solutions is the same except no substances other than gases are included.

Catalysis describes the increase in the rate of a reaction caused by the addition of a catalyst. The addition of a catalyst causes reactions to speed up and require less activation energy. Only small amounts of catalysts are required, and they are not consumed by the reaction. Catalytic activity is indicated using the symbol *z*, and it is measured in mol/s. Catalysts usually react with one—or sometimes more than one—reactant, forming intermediates. Catalysts provide alternative mechanisms for chemical reactions that involve different transition states and lower activation energy.

Electrochemistry

Balancing Oxidation-Reduction Reactions

When two chemical species react with one another in solution, one species may lose electrons while the other gains electrons. **Oxidation-reduction** or **redox chemical reactions** involve the loss and gaining of electrons between two different reactants or reacting species. Therefore, a change in oxidation state for a particular ion within the chemical species will change when transitioning from a reactant to a product. For a given species or ion, **oxidation** refers to the loss of electrons or an increase in oxidation number (e.g., Fe^{2+} to Fe^{3+}), and **reduction** refers to gaining of electrons or decrease in oxidation state or number (e.g., Fe^{2+} to Fe^{3+}). Chemical reactions can occur in either an acidic or basic solution. The **half-reaction method** of balancing requires that a redox reaction be separated into two half-reactions, an oxidation half and a reduction half, to help balance the charge using electrons. Hydronium ions and water are used to balance an acidic reaction, and hydroxide ions are used to balance a reaction in basic solution. The half-reactions are then combined to give the overall reaction equation. For example, consider the following reaction that occurs in an acidic solution. First, identify the oxidation states for each species.

$$\text{Step 1: } \mathrm{Cu(s) + NO_3^-(aq) \rightarrow Cu^{2+}(aq) + NO_2(g)}$$

Solid copper is oxidized because it loses electrons and increases in oxidation state (Cu to Cu^{2+}). The nitrate ion is the reactant species that is reduced because the gaseous nitrogen dioxide product has a charge of zero. Specifically, it is the nitrogen atom that changes or reduces in oxidation state because:

$$\overbrace{\mathrm{NO_3^-}}^{x+3(-2)=-1} \quad \rightarrow \quad \overbrace{\mathrm{NO_2}}^{x+2(-2)=0}$$

The x term refers to the oxidation number of nitrogen, and –2 is the known/standard oxidation number of oxygen. For the nitrate ion, the term x must be five ($x = +5$) because $5 + 3(-2) = -1$ and for nitrogen dioxide, x must be four ($x = +4$) because $4 + 2(-2) = 0$. The change in oxidation number for nitrogen is N^{5+} to N^{4+}. The reaction can now be separated into an oxidizing and reducing half as follows:

$$\text{Step 2: } \mathrm{Cu(s) \rightarrow Cu^{2+}(aq)} \quad \text{Oxidation}$$

$$\mathrm{NO_3^-(aq) \rightarrow NO_2(g)} \quad \text{Reduction}$$

Now balance each half-reaction based on the mass, if needed, using water molecules and hydronium ions, because the reaction occurs in aqueous solution. The copper half-reaction does not need mass balancing, but the second half-reaction does.

$$\text{Step 3: } \mathrm{Cu(s) \rightarrow Cu^{2+}(aq)}$$

$$\mathrm{2\ H^+(aq) + NO_3^-(aq) \rightarrow NO_2(g) + H_2O(l)}$$

Note that one water molecule is added first on the product side to balance the oxygen atoms, followed by the addition of hydronium ions on the reactant side to balance hydrogen. Next balance each half-reaction based on charge by adding negatively charged electrons either to the reactant or product's side.

$$\text{Step 4: Cu(s)} \rightarrow \text{Cu}^{2+}\text{(aq)} + 2\ \text{e}^-$$

$$\text{e}^- + 2\ \text{H}^+\text{(aq)} + \text{NO}_3^-\text{(aq)} \rightarrow \text{NO}_2\text{(g)} + \text{H}_2\text{O(l)}$$

For the copper half-reaction, two electrons are added to the product side because oxidation results in the loss of electrons. The reactants side has an overall charge of zero, and the products side is also neutral because two electrons are needed to make the copper(II) ion neutral. For the second half-reaction containing nitrogen, the product side is neutral in charge. So, one electron must be added to make the reactant side neutral in charge: −1 from the electron, +2 from two protons, and −1 from the nitrate ion give $-1 + 2 - 1 = 0$. Before the half-reactions are combined, each half-reaction must be multiplied by a small whole number such that each half-reaction has an equal number of electrons. The second half-reaction must be multiplied by two.

$$\text{Step 5: Cu(s)} \rightarrow \text{Cu}^{2+}\text{(aq)} + 2\ \text{e}^-$$

$$2\left(\text{e}^- + 2\ \text{H}^+\text{(aq)} + \text{NO}_3^-\text{(aq)} \rightarrow \text{NO}_2\text{(g)} + \text{H}_2\text{O(l)}\right)$$

In the last step, the half-reactions can now be combined.

$$\text{Step 6: Cu(s)} \rightarrow \text{Cu}^{2+}\text{(aq)} + 2\ \text{e}^-$$

$$2\ \text{e}^- + 4\ \text{H}^+\text{(aq)} + 2\ \text{NO}_3^-\text{(aq)} \rightarrow 2\ \text{NO}_2\text{(g)} + 2\ \text{H}_2\text{O(l)}$$

$$\text{Cu(s)} + \cancel{2\ \text{e}^-} + 4\ \text{H}^+\text{(aq)} + 2\ \text{NO}_3^-\text{(aq)} \rightarrow \text{Cu}^{2+}\text{(aq)} + \cancel{2\ \text{e}^-} + 2\ \text{NO}_2\text{(g)} + 2\ \text{H}_2\text{O(l)}$$

The final balanced equation is:

$$\text{Cu(s)} + 4\ \text{H}^+\text{(aq)} + 2\ \text{NO}_3^-\text{(aq)} \rightarrow \text{Cu}^{2+}\text{(aq)} + 2\ \text{NO}_2\text{(g)} + 2\ \text{H}_2\text{O(l)}$$

Each side of the equation has a total charge of +2, and all elements are balanced according to mass. Copper is oxidized and acts as a **reducing agent**, which is a species that reduces another substance, thereby losing its electrons to that substance. The nitrate ion acts as the **oxidizing agent** because it is the species that oxidizes another substance and gains electrons from that substance.

Voltaic Cells

Voltaic cells are electrochemical cells that can be used to generate electricity through a spontaneous reaction. An electrical current or flow of electrical charge, created by the movement of electrons, is created. Figure 27 shows a schematic of a typical voltaic cell, which consists of two **half-cells**, with each half-cell containing an electrode (e.g., a metal plate) and an ionic solution where oxidation and reduction occur.

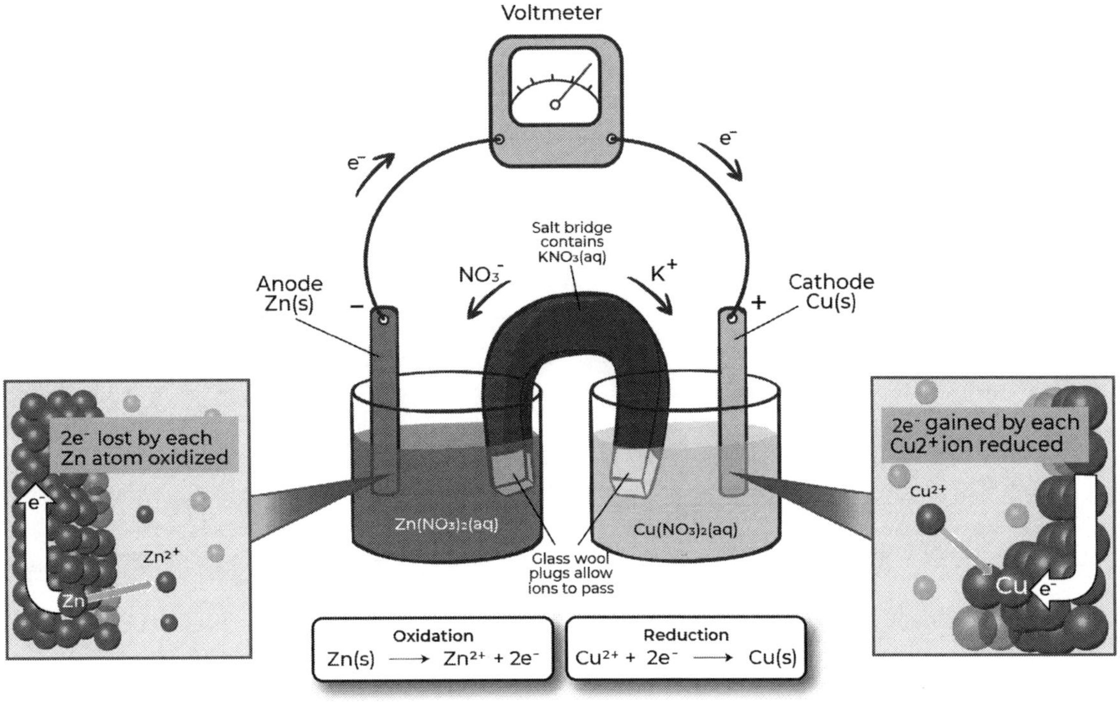

Figure 27. A galvanic or voltaic cell

Electrodes or conductive surfaces, e.g., metal strips, allow the flow of electrons and either undergo oxidation or reduction. The **anode** is the electrode or metal plate that undergoes oxidation, and the **cathode** is the electrode where reduction occurs. The anode carries a negative charge and the cathode a positive charge. An electrical wire connects the anode and cathode. Based on Le Chatelier's principle, solid zinc converts to zinc(II) ions, which increase in concentration over time. Likewise, in the reduction cell, copper(II) ions are converted to solid copper, which will collect around the plate over time. Electrons flow from the anode to the cathode (along a wire), which spontaneously creates a current that is opposite to electron flow. A **salt bridge** containing a strong electrolyte (e.g., potassium nitrate) is found in a U-shaped tube, with a permeable stopper at the end of each tube and allows for the passage of positive ions to the cathode and negative ions to the anode. The salt bridge prevents a buildup of charge through charge neutralization and therefore balances the charge of the cell, allowing the redox reaction to continue. The reaction is described as follows:

$$Zn(s) \rightarrow 2\ e^- + Zn^{2+}(aq) \quad \text{Oxidation}$$

$$Cu^{2+}(aq) + 2\ e^- \rightarrow Cu(s) \quad \text{Reduction}$$

$$Zn(s) + Cu^{2+}(aq) \rightarrow Cu(s) + Zn^{2+}(aq)$$

The reaction lies mostly to the right because zinc has a greater tendency to ionize or lose electrons than copper, which causes the zinc electrode to become negatively charged. The reaction may take on the following electrochemical cell notation:

$$\mathrm{Zn(s)|Zn^{2+}(aq)||Cu(s)|Cu^{2+}(aq)}$$

The salt bridge is indicated by | |, which separates the two half-reactions. The anode is to the left of the salt bridge where the oxidation half takes place, and the cathode is on the right side where the reduction process takes place. The vertical line | separates the different phases for a particular species.

Stoichiometry of Redox Reactions

The electrical current is measured in **amperes** or **amps (A)**, which has units of coulombs per second ($1\ \mathrm{A} = 1\ \ \mathrm{C/s}$). An electron has a charge of:

$$1.602 \times 10^{-19}\ \mathrm{C}$$

For the reduction of Cu^{2+}(aq) to Cu(s), which occurs at the cathode in Figure 27, if there is a constant current of 1.50 A (flowing through the circuit), how long will it take for 1.00 g of Cu(s) to accumulate on the copper plate (cathode)? To solve this problem, consider the following roadmap or relationship regarding unit conversions:

$$\text{grams of Cu} \rightarrow \text{moles of Cu} \rightarrow \text{moles of e}^- \rightarrow \text{coulombs} \rightarrow \text{time in minutes}$$

The moles of copper are related to the moles of electrons needed for reduction, which is two moles.

$$\mathrm{Cu^{2+}(aq) + 2\ e^- \rightarrow Cu(s)}$$

One mole of electrons has a specific charge of 96,485 C or 1 faraday (C/mol) because:

$$\frac{1\ \text{mole of electrons}}{6.022 \times 10^{23}\ \text{electrons}} \times \frac{1\ \text{electron}}{1.602 \times 10^{-19}\ \mathrm{C}} \approx \frac{1\ \text{mole of electrons}}{96{,}485\ \mathrm{C}}$$

From the definition of an amp, 1.50 A is equivalent to 1.50 C/s. Therefore, the amount of time it takes for 1.00 g of Cu(s) to collect on the cathode is given by the following calculation:

$$1.00\ \text{g of Cu} \times \frac{1\ \text{mol Cu}}{63.55\ \text{g}} \times \frac{2\ \text{mol e}^-}{1\ \text{mol Cu}} \times \frac{96{,}485\ \mathrm{C}}{1\ \text{mol e}^-} \times \frac{1\ \mathrm{s}}{1.50\ \mathrm{C}} \times \frac{1\ \text{min}}{60\ \mathrm{s}} = 33.7\ \text{min}$$

Predicting the Spontaneous Direction of a Redox Reaction Using Standard Electrode Potentials

In a redox reaction, the **potential difference** (in units of volts, V), refers to an electrical current that is created by a difference in potential energy, in joules per coulomb: $1\ \mathrm{V} = 1\ \mathrm{J/C}$. The force created by this potential difference is called the **electromotive force (emf)** or **cell potential (E_{cell})**. The **standard emf** or **standard cell potential (E°_{cell})** refers to the standard cell potential at 25 °C and 1 M concentration for any reaction in solution or at 1 atm for a gaseous substance. The greater the value of E°_{cell} the more likely the reaction will occur. A **positive** E°_{cell} indicates a spontaneous forward reaction and a **negative** E°_{cell} refers to a nonspontaneous forward reaction. The E°_{cell} is also the difference between two standard electrode potentials or the standard half-cell potentials (E°_{anode} and E°_{cathode}).

The E°_{cell} for the copper and zinc reaction (Figure 27) is 1.10 V and is the difference of each half-cell potential between the cathode (final state) and anode (initial state). To find E°_{cell}, one must consult a table of standard electrode potentials (given at 25.0 °C), which lists several half-cell reduction reactions with corresponding half-cell potential (E°) values. Values for the half-cell potentials will range from 3.00 V to −3.00 V. The more positive the half-cell potential is for the reduction of a species, the greater the oxidation strength (stronger oxidizing agent), and the more negative the half-cell potential, the greater the reducing strength (stronger reducing agent). The greater the negativity of an electrode potential, the more likely that the electrode will repel electrons and undergo oxidation. In other words, electrons will spontaneously flow from the negative electrode (anode) to the positive electrode (cathode).

Conversely, the more positive the electrode potential (e.g., $E^\circ_{cathode}$) is, the more likely that the electrode will attract electrons to undergo reduction. A useful mnemonic is: more Negative Is Oxidation (NIO), and more Positive Is Reduction (PIR). The standard half-cell potentials for zinc and copper, from positive to negative E° are listed below.

$$\mathrm{Cu^{2+}(aq)} + 2\,\mathrm{e^-} \rightarrow \mathrm{Cu(s)} \quad E^\circ = +0.34\ \mathrm{V}$$

$$\mathrm{Zn^{2+}(aq)} + 2\,\mathrm{e^-} \rightarrow \mathrm{Zn(s)} \quad E^\circ = -0.76\ \mathrm{V}$$

Because copper has a greater half-cell potential, it is more likely to be reduced at the electrode (as the stronger oxidizing agent), meaning that the copper electrode will be the cathode or the positively charged electrode. Zinc has a more negative half-cell potential and is more easily oxidized (as the stronger reducing agent). When combining the half-cell reactions, the zinc reaction must be written to indicate that oxidation is occurring. The value of the half-cell potential will also change sign.

$$\text{Oxidation: } \mathrm{Zn(s)} \rightarrow 2\,\mathrm{e^-} + \mathrm{Zn^{2+}(aq)}$$

Electrons flow from the anode (initial) to the cathode (final), so E°_{cell} is:

$$E^\circ_{cell} = E^\circ_{final} - E^\circ_{initial} = E^\circ_{cathode} - E^\circ_{anode} = 0.34\ \mathrm{V} - (-0.76\ \mathrm{V}) = 1.10\ \mathrm{V}$$

Note that the half-cell potential value of copper changes sign, which is consistent with the new half-cell potential for zinc. For a standard reduction table, half-reactions at the top (positive electrode potentials) attract electrons and tend to proceed in the forward direction. Half-reactions at the bottom (negative electrode potentials) repel electrons and will move in the reverse direction. A reduction reaction is spontaneous if it's paired with the reverse of any reaction listed below it in a standard reduction table. For example, consider the following reaction:

$$\mathrm{Zn(s)} + \mathrm{Ni^{2+}(aq)} \rightarrow \mathrm{Zn^{2+}(aq)} + \mathrm{Ni(s)}$$

The standard half-cell potentials, from positive to negative, are:

$$\mathrm{Ni^{2+}(aq)} + 2\,\mathrm{e^-} \rightarrow \mathrm{Ni(s)} \quad E^\circ = -0.23$$

$$\mathrm{Zn^{2+}(aq)} + 2\,\mathrm{e^-} \rightarrow \mathrm{Zn(s)} \quad E^\circ = -0.76$$

The half-cell reaction for zinc is listed below nickel, so reversing the zinc reaction ($E^\circ = +0.76\text{ V}$) and pairing it with the forward reaction for nickel, will make the reaction spontaneous.

$$\text{Reduction: } Ni^{2+}(aq) + 2\,e^- \rightarrow Ni(s)$$

$$\text{Oxidation: } Zn(s) \rightarrow Zn^{2+}(aq) + 2\,e^-$$

$$Ni^{2+}(aq) + \cancel{2\,e^-} + Zn(s) \rightarrow Ni(s) + Zn^{2+}(aq) + \cancel{2\,e^-}$$

The resulting cell potential (E°_{cell}) is calculated the same way as before:

$$E^\circ_{\text{cell}} = E^\circ_{\text{final}} - E^\circ_{\text{initial}} = E^\circ_{\text{cathode}} - E^\circ_{\text{anode}} = -0.23\text{ V} - (-0.76\text{ V}) = 0.53\text{ V}$$

The Gibbs Standard Free Energy Change ΔG° and E°_{cell}

The relation between the standard cell potential, E°_{cell}, and the **Gibbs standard change in free energy (ΔG°)** is given by the following equation:

$$\Delta G^\circ = nFE^\circ_{\text{cell}}$$

The term n refers to the number of mole electrons that are transferred in the redox reaction. The term F is **Faraday's constant**, which is equal to $96{,}485\text{ C/(mol e}^-)$. E°_{cell} is also related to the equilibrium constant, K, through the following equation:

$$E^\circ_{\text{cell}} = \frac{0.0592\text{ V}}{n}\log K$$

For a spontaneous redox reaction where the products are favored in the standard state, ΔG° is negative (< 0), E°_{cell} is positive (> 0), and K is greater than one (> 1). In contrast, for a nonspontaneous reaction, where the reactants are favored in their standard states, ΔG° is positive (> 0), E°_{cell} is negative (< 0), and K is less than one (< 1). For nonstandard or nonequilibrium conditions, the relationship between E_{cell} and the reaction quotient, Q, is given by the **Nernst equation**:

$$E_{\text{cell}} = E^\circ_{\text{cell}} - \frac{0.0592\text{ V}}{n}\log Q$$

Under standard conditions, if Q is equal to one ($Q = 1$) then $E_{\text{cell}} = E^\circ_{\text{cell}}$ because $\log 1 = 0$. If $Q < 1$, then the concentrations of the reactants are greater than the products, so the reaction proceeds to the right and $E_{\text{cell}} > E^\circ_{\text{cell}}$. If $Q > 1$, then the concentrations of the products are greater than the reactants, so the reaction proceeds to the left and $E_{\text{cell}} < E^\circ_{\text{cell}}$. At equilibrium, $Q = K$, the reaction will not move in any particular direction, so $E_{\text{cell}} = 0$. When a battery discharges and becomes depleted, it's because the reaction proceeds toward equilibrium such that the reactants are depleted and $Q = K$. The cell potential becomes zero.

Nuclear Chemistry

Nuclear Chemistry

Radioactivity describes the emission of subatomic particles (e.g., nuclei, protons, electrons) that can occur for specific atoms. The French scientist **A. H. Becquerel** discovered radioactivity in 1896 when he exposed a photographic plate to sunlight containing uranium. He hypothesized that the plate emitted X-rays and exhibited **phosphorescence**, which is the emission of light due to light absorption. The plate was shown to glow in the dark. However, when Becquerel repeated the results without exposing the plate to light, he discovered that the uranium crystals were emitting uranic rays even without phosphorescence. Shortly after, a doctoral student by the name of **Marie Curie** discovered that the elements polonium (named after Curie's home country Poland) and radium also emitted uranic rays.

The term "uranic rays" was eventually referred to as radiation or radioactivity because other elements besides uranium also emitted these rays. In 1903, Marie Curie, Pierre Curie, and Becquerel were awarded the Nobel Prize in physics for the discovery of radioactivity. In 1911, Marie Curie received the Nobel Prize in chemistry for her discovery of polonium and radium. Since the discovery of radioactive atoms, many scientists such as **Ernest Rutherford** focused on nuclear chemistry and radioactivity. **Nuclear chemistry** is the study of reactions in which the nuclei of atoms are transformed whereby the identities of the elements are changed. The unstable nuclei spontaneously decompose, emitting certain sub-particles, in order to become more stable. These reactions can involve large changes in energy—much larger than the energy changes that occur when chemical bonds between atoms are made or broken. Nuclear chemistry is also used to create electricity.

Radioactivity Types: Alpha, Beta, and Gamma Radiation

In some cases, and for specific atoms, the nucleus of an atom constantly emits particles due to its instability. These atoms are described as radioactive, and the isotopes are referred to as **radioisotopes.** Specific isotopes of an element are called **nuclides**. Recall that the atomic number (Z) refers to the number of protons and that the mass number (A) indicates the number of protons and neutrons for an element, X. The atomic number is shown as a subscript and the mass number as a superscript, which is both placed to the left of the chemical symbol, X. Argon has three stable isotopes (Ar-36, Ar-38, and Ar-40), which have a different number of neutrons with respect to one another:

$$^{A}_{Z}\mathrm{X} \quad ^{36}_{18}\mathrm{Ar} \quad ^{38}_{18}\mathrm{Ar} \quad ^{40}_{18}\mathrm{Ar}$$

The equation $N = A - Z$ gives the number of neutrons (N). The number of neutrons for each nuclide is $N = 36 - 18 = 18$ (Ar-36), $N = 38 - 18 = 20$ (Ar-38), and $N = 40 - 18 = 22$ (Ar-40). The notation for sub-particles such as the proton, neutron, and electron is:

$$^{1}_{1}\mathrm{p}\ (\mathrm{proton}) \quad ^{1}_{0}\mathrm{n}\ (\mathrm{neutron}) \quad ^{0}_{-1}\mathrm{e}\ (\mathrm{electron})$$

The proton and neutron have a mass number (A) of one, whereas the electron is given a value of zero. The subscripts for the proton and neutron indicate one and zero protons. A value of −1 is given to the electron and reflects the charge of the electron. The notation doesn't follow the naming convention for an atomic number, although it's useful to note the atomic number is typically equal to the number of electrons.

Several types of natural radioactive decay occur and include alpha (α), beta (β), and gamma (γ) ray emission, and positron emission. Certain unstable nuclei will even absorb an electron from one of its orbitals to become more stable, a process called **electron capture**. **Alpha radiation** is emitted or released when a nucleus decomposes to produce two protons and two neutrons, which are collectively called an **alpha (α) particle**. Helium-4 nuclei contain two protons and two neutrons, so an alpha particle also takes the same symbol: ${}^{4}_{2}\mathrm{He}$. **Nuclear equations**, a type of equation showing a nuclear reaction or process such as radioactivity, can be used to show how specific elements emit an alpha particle, which shows how the number of protons within a nucleus changes. Nuclear equations have different notations than regular chemical equations. For example, consider the alpha decay of uranium (U-238). The nuclear equations are written as follows, where the top number or superscript is the atomic mass number (A), and the bottom number or subscript is the atomic number (Z) for each element:

$$\overbrace{{}^{238}_{92}\mathrm{U}}^{\text{parent nuclide}} \rightarrow \overbrace{{}^{234}_{90}\mathrm{Th}}^{\text{daughter nuclide}} + \overbrace{{}^{4}_{2}\mathrm{He}}^{\text{alpha particle}}$$

The equation describes the spontaneous decomposition of uranium-238 (U-238) into thorium-234 (Th-234) and helium-4 (He-4) via alpha decay. When this happens, the process is referred to as **nuclear decay**, and results in a change in chemical identity, unlike chemical reactions which retain their identity. However, similar to chemical equations, nuclear equations must be balanced on each side; the sum of the mass numbers and the sum of the atomic numbers should be equal on both sides of the equation. Table 12 shows how the mass number A decreases by four, and how the atomic number Z lowers to two with respect to the conversion of Uranium to Thorium.

Table 19. Decomposition of U-238 to Th-234 and He-4	
Reactants: Uranium	Products: Thorium and Helium
$A = 238$	$A = 234 + 4 = 238$
$Z = 92$	$Z = 90 + 2 = 92$

Based on the law of conservation of mass, the nuclear equation is balanced. Alpha particles have relatively low penetrating power, or the ability to move through or penetrate matter. For example, a substance that emits alpha particles will not go through a piece of paper and will even have trouble moving through air.

Beta radiation or **Beta (β) decay** occurs when an unstable nucleus emits a stream of high-speed electrons. The beta particles are often noted as β^-. Specifically, a neutron will transform into a proton as an electron is emitted. The general reaction is:

$$\text{Beta }(\beta)\text{ decay: neutron }({}^{1}_{0}\mathrm{n}) \rightarrow \text{proton }({}^{1}_{1}\mathrm{p}) + \overbrace{\text{electron }({}^{0}_{-1}\mathrm{e})}^{\text{beta particle}}$$

In a beta reaction, the parent nuclide will change its atomic number by one due to the addition of a proton. For example, consider the following beta reaction:

$$\overbrace{{}^{249}_{97}\mathrm{Bk}}^{\text{parent nuclide}} \rightarrow \overbrace{{}^{249}_{98}\mathrm{Cf}}^{\text{daughter nuclide}} + \overbrace{{}^{0}_{-1}\mathrm{e}}^{\text{beta particle}}$$

A neutron from berkelium-249 (Bk-249) transforms into a proton to form californium-249 (Cf-249), which has one extra proton. One beta particle is emitted in the process. A beta particle will have less ionizing power because it is much smaller than an alpha particle but will have more penetrating power. A sheet of metal can be used to stop a beta particle.

Gamma (γ) radiation is a form of electromagnetic radiation and occurs when the nucleus emits high-energy or short-wavelength photons. The following notation represents gamma rays:

$$\text{Gamma } (\gamma) \text{ ray: } {}^{0}_{0}\gamma$$

Because gamma rays have no mass or charge, both the superscript and subscript have a value of zero. Consequently, the parent nuclide will not change in mass or atomic number during gamma ray emission. This type of radiation represents a rearrangement of an unstable nucleus into a more stable one and often accompanies other types of radioactive emissions. For example, the alpha decay of U-238 to Th-234 and He-4 additionally produces a gamma ray. Gamma rays have the highest penetrating power but the lowest ionizing power. Biologically, gamma rays are hazardous because they can pass through the body. Thick slabs of concrete or lead can serve as a shield against gamma radiation, which can be produced from nuclear explosions or nuclear reactors (e.g., decomposition of U-235 to U-236).

In **positron (β+) emission**, a proton is converted to a neutron within an unstable nucleus, and a positron is emitted. The **positron** is referred to as the antiparticle with respect to an electron (i.e., an antielectron) because it has the same mass as an electron but with a +1 charge. If an electron and positron collide with one another, each particle is annihilated, and energy is released in the form of a gamma ray. The general nuclear mechanism is:

$$\text{Positron emission: proton } ({}^{1}_{1}\text{p}) \rightarrow \text{neutron } ({}^{1}_{0}\text{n}) + \text{positron } ({}^{0}_{+1}\text{e})$$

During positron emission, the atomic number (Z) for the parent nuclide will decrease by one. The daughter nuclide will have one less proton compared to the parent nuclide. For instance, consider the decomposition of carbon-10 to boron-10 in the following nuclear reaction:

$$\overbrace{{}^{10}_{6}\text{C}}^{\substack{\text{parent}\\ \text{nuclide}}} \rightarrow \overbrace{{}^{10}_{5}\text{B}}^{\substack{\text{daughter}\\ \text{nuclide}}} + \overbrace{{}^{0}_{+1}\text{e}}^{\text{positron}}$$

The mass number remains the same because a proton is converted to a neutron. Positrons (β^+) have similar penetrating and ionizing power like beta (β^-) particles.

Electron capture differs from other types of radioactive decay, and instead of emitting a particle or radiation, the process involves the absorption of a particle. Specifically, when a nucleus acquires an electron from one of its inner orbitals within its electron cloud, the process is called **electron capture**. The process is similar to positron emission and involves the conversion of a proton to a neutron.

$$\text{Electron capture: } {}^{1}_{1}\text{p} + {}^{0}_{-1}\text{e} \rightarrow {}^{1}_{0}\text{n}$$

Notice how the subscripts will denote the charge, which is conserved on both sides of the equation. For an atom that undergoes electron capture, its atomic number (Z) will decrease by one with its mass number (A) remaining the same. Consider the following example where iodine-111 decomposes to tellurium-111:

$$^{111}_{53}\text{I} + {}^{0}_{-1}\text{e} \rightarrow {}^{111}_{52}\text{Te}$$

Determining Radioactivity Type

Protons and neutrons, called **nucleons**, are attracted to each other by the **strong force**, a force that acts at short distances and keeps the positively charged protons in the nucleus together. The nuclear stability of an isotope is determined by the ratio of neutrons to protons (N/Z). If the number of neutrons was plotted as a function of the atomic number, it would allow one to determine which isotopes are stable and which ones would undergo decay. Figure 28 shows a number of stable isotopes.

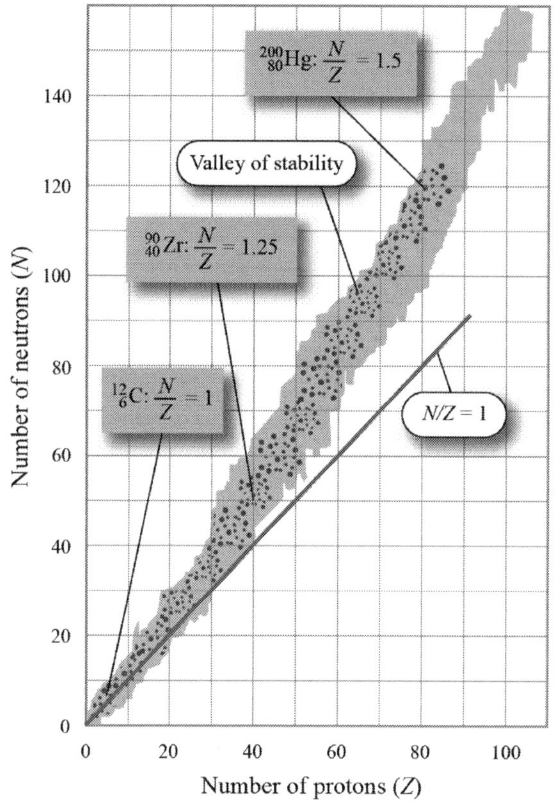

Figure 28. Valley of stability

The isotopes carbon-12, zirconium-90, and mercury-200 are among many stable isotopes that are found in the valley or island of stability (scattered dots). The neutron to proton ratio for these elements is between 1 and 1.5. If the N/Z ratio is too high (i.e., lies above the shaded region) or over 1.5, then that nuclide/isotope has too many neutrons and will tend to beta decay. In other words, that nuclide will undergo beta decay where a neutron is transformed into a proton, thereby reducing the number of neutrons in the daughter nuclide. The daughter nuclide will be closer to the valley of stability. For example, consider the following reaction:

$$\overbrace{{}^{249}_{97}\text{Bk}}^{\text{parent nuclide}} \rightarrow \overbrace{{}^{249}_{98}\text{Cf}}^{\text{daughter nuclide}} + \overbrace{{}^{0}_{-1}\text{e}}^{\text{beta particle}}$$

In this example, Bk-249 has an N/Z ratio of 1.6, and Cf-249 has an N/Z ratio of 1.5. If the N/Z ratio is too low, then there are too many protons, and some of these protons will convert to neutrons either through electron capture or positron emission. For example, consider the positron emission of C-10 to B-10, shown previously. The N/Z ratio for C-10 is 0.67, but for B-10, it's 1.0. The new nuclide moves up or closer to the valley of stability. To determine whether a given nuclide is stable, it's best to find its N/Z value, and see if it lies along the valley of stability. For example, magnesium-28 or ${}^{28}_{12}\text{Mg}$ has 12 protons and 16 neutrons. Its N/Z ratio is $16/12 = 1.3$. Based on Figure 28, this value is not between 1 and 1.25. The N/Z ratio is too high, meaning that there are too many neutrons, and it will undergo beta decay:

$$ {}^{28}_{12}\text{Mg} \rightarrow {}^{28}_{13}\text{Al} + \overbrace{{}^{0}_{-1}\text{e}}^{\text{beta particle}}$$

A neutron is converted to a proton, and an electron or beta particle is emitted. The N/Z ratio for aluminum-28 is 1.2.

Atoms that have an atomic number greater than 83 ($Z > 83$) are **radioactive** and can decay in one or multiple steps either through alpha, beta, or gamma decay, such as the alpha decay of uranium-238 to thorium-234. The daughter nuclide, thorium-234, can also decay to protactinium-234 via beta decay.

Kinetics of Radioactive Decay

Radioactive decay is often described in terms of its **half-life ($t_{1/2}$)**, which is the time that it takes for half of the radioactive substance to react. Radioactive decay follows first-order kinetics and is similar to chemical reactions. The relationship between the half-life of a nuclide and its rate constant (k) is given by:

$$t_{1/2} = \frac{0.693}{k}$$

The larger the rate constant is for the nuclide, the shorter the half-life is.

For example, the radioisotope strontium-90 has a half-life of 28.8 years. If there are 10 grams of strontium-90 to start with, after 28.8 years, there would be 5 grams left. If you were only given the initial amount (10 g) and a final amount at time t (5 grams) and were asked to find the half-life at time t, then you would need to find the rate constant.

$$k = \frac{0.693}{t_{1/2}} = \frac{0.693}{28.8 \text{ years}} = 0.02406 \text{ years}^{-1}$$

Now solve for t using the following equation below:

$$\ln[\mathrm{B}]_t = -kt + \ln[\mathrm{B}]_0$$

$$\ln[\mathrm{B}]_t - \ln[\mathrm{B}]_0 = -kt$$

$$t = -\ln\left(\frac{[\mathrm{B}]_t}{[\mathrm{B}]_0}\right)\frac{1}{k}$$

The term $[B]_t$ is the amount at a time which happens to be the half-life because 5 g is 50 percent of the initial amount (10 g). $[\mathrm{B}]_0$ represents the initial amount at time zero. Therefore, $[\mathrm{B}]_0 = 10\ \mathrm{g}$, so $[\mathrm{B}]_\mathrm{t} = 0.50(10\ \mathrm{g}) = 5\ \mathrm{g}$. The half-life is:

$$t = t_{1/2} = -\ln\left(\frac{5\ \mathrm{g}}{10\ \mathrm{g}}\right)\frac{1}{0.02406\ \mathrm{years}^{-1}} = 28.8\ \mathrm{years}$$

If asked to calculate the time given the half-life, where the final amount is half the initial amount, the answer will be the half-life (28.8 years). However, suppose you were asked to find the time at which strontium-90 decayed to 40 percent of its initial amount (4.0 g), then the time would be:

$$t = -\ln\left(\frac{0.40(\cancel{[\mathrm{B}]_0})}{\cancel{[\mathrm{B}]_0}}\right)\frac{1}{0.02406\ \mathrm{days}^{-1}} = 38.1\ \mathrm{days}$$

Note that 40 percent in decimal form is just $40/100 = 0.40$ and that the final time is now longer than the half-life. It's also important to recognize how to rearrange the previous equation if asked to calculate the amount of substance at a time t, given the initial amount and the half-life:

$$[\mathrm{B}]_t = [\mathrm{B}]_0 e^{-kt}$$

For instance, how much of strontium-90 is left after $t = 38.1$ days if it has $t_{1/2} = 28.8$ days and an initial starting amount of 10 g? Solving for $[\mathrm{B}]_t$ gives:

$$[\mathrm{B}]_t = [\mathrm{B}]_0 e^{-kt} = (10\ \mathrm{g})e^{-0.02406\ \mathrm{days}^{-1}\times 38.1\ \mathrm{days}} = 4.0\ \mathrm{g}$$

Note that half-life was given to solve for k, which was shown above.

Fission and Fusion

There are two distinct types of nuclear reactions: fission and fusion reactions. Both involve a large energy release. In **fission** reactions, a large atom is split into two or more smaller atoms. The nucleus absorbs slow-moving neutrons, resulting in a larger nucleus that is unstable. The unstable nucleus then undergoes fission. Nuclear power plants depend on nuclear fission reactions for energy. The bombardment of neutrons toward uranium-235 atoms results in the formation of barium-140 and krypton-93 in addition to several neutrons.

$${}^{235}_{92}\mathrm{U} + {}^{1}_{0}\mathrm{n} \rightarrow {}^{140}_{56}\mathrm{Ba} + {}^{93}_{36}\mathrm{Kr} + 3\ {}^{1}_{0}\mathrm{n} + \mathrm{energy}$$

Scientists later realized that this reaction could undergo a **chain reaction**, a process where neutrons produced from one fission reaction induce a fission reaction in other uranium nuclei. The energy produced is the basis for how atomic bombs work.

Fusion reactions involve the combination of two or more lighter atoms into a larger atom. Fusion reactions do not occur on Earth naturally due to the extreme temperature and pressure conditions required to make them happen. Fusion products are generally not radioactive. Fusion reactions are responsible for the energy that is created by the sun. Nuclear fusion, the basis of modern nuclear bombs, employs the following type of reaction:

$$^{2}_{1}\mathrm{H} + ^{3}_{1}\mathrm{H} \rightarrow ^{4}_{2}\mathrm{He} + ^{1}_{0}\mathrm{n}$$

Hydrogen bombs are created by first detonating a fission bomb, which creates temperatures high enough to allow fusion to occur whereby deuterium (hydrogen-2) and tritium (hydrogen-3) combine.

Practice Test #1

1. Which of the following is an example of a Brønsted-Lowry base in water?
   a. H_3O^+
   b. CO_2
   c. NH_3
   d. HCl

2. Bromine exists naturally as a mixture of two isotopes that have atomic masses of 78.918 amu and 80.916 amu. Determine the % relative abundance for Br-79 and Br-81, respectively, given that the average atomic mass of bromine is 79.904 amu.
   a. 51% and 49%
   b. 49% and 51%
   c. 46% and 54%
   d. 54% and 46%

3. What is the temperature in Fahrenheit when it is 35 °C outside?
   a. 67 °F
   b. 95 °F
   c. 63 °F
   d. 75 °F

4. If an electronic transition from $n = 5$ to $n = 2$ occurs for the hydrogen atom, what is the wavelength of emitted light in nanometers (nm)?
   a. 345 nm
   b. 226 nm
   c. 434 nm
   d. 541 nm

5. Which of the following set of quantum numbers corresponds to the 4f orbital?
   a. $l = 4$, $m_l = -3$, and $m_s = -1/2$
   b. $l = 3$, $m_l = -3$, and $m_s = +1/2$
   c. $l = 3$, $m_l = +4$, and $m_s = -1/2$
   d. $l = 2$, $m_l = +2$, and $m_s = +1/2$

6. Which of the following substances contains the greatest number of atoms?
   a. 2.00 g C
   b. 2.00 g N_2
   c. 2.00 g Cr
   d. 2.00 g Na

7. How many grams of iron (VI) oxide is produced when 5.50 mol of iron reacts with excess oxygen?

$$4\ Fe(s) + 3\ O_2(g) \rightarrow 2\ FeO_3(s)$$

a. $1142.35\ g\ FeO_3$
b. $285.59\ g\ FeO_3$
c. $2.75\ g\ FeO_3$
d. $380.78\ g\ FeO_3$

8. Which of the following is the net ionic equation for the reaction between K_2S(aq) and $Pb(C_2H_3O_2)_2$(aq)?

a. $2\ K^+(aq) + S^{2-}(aq) + Pb^{2+}(aq) + 2\ C_2H_3O_2^-(aq) \rightarrow 2\ K^+(aq) + 2\ C_2H_3O_2^-(aq) + PbS(s)$
b. $S^{2-}(aq) + Pb^{2+}(aq) + 2\ C_2H_3O_2^-(aq) \rightarrow 2\ C_2H_3O_2^-(aq) + PbS(s)$
c. $K_2S(aq) + Pb(C_2H_3O_2)_2\ (aq) \rightarrow 2\ KC_2H_3O_2(aq) + PbS(s)$
d. $Pb^{2+}(aq) + S^{2-}(aq) \rightarrow PbS(s)$

9. Determine the mass of carbon needed to release 25.5 kJ of heat for the reaction shown below.

$$C(s) + 2H_2(g) \rightarrow CH_4(g); \qquad \Delta H^\circ_{rxn} = -74.8 \frac{kJ}{mol}$$

a. 1.37 g
b. 0.34 g
c. 0.68 g
d. 4.09 g

10. Determine the number of sigma (σ) bonds, pi (π) bonds, and lone electron pairs in the chemical structure below.

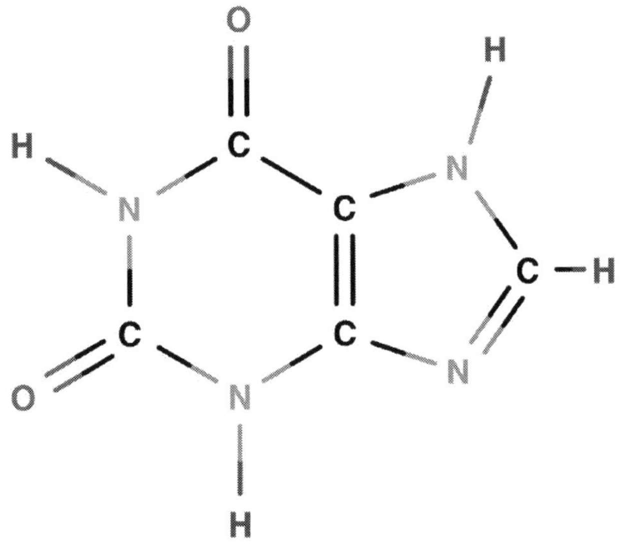

a. 16 σ bonds, 4 π bonds, and 8 lone pair electrons
b. 12 σ bonds, 4 π bonds, and 8 lone pair electrons
c. 12 σ bonds, 8 π bonds, and 4 lone pair electrons
d. 16 σ bonds, 4 π bonds, and 4 lone pair electrons

11. The graphs below represent two vapor pressure curves, which are labeled as A and B. One curve is for ethanol CH_3CH_2OH, and another is for 1-pentanol $CH_3CH_2CH_2CH_2CH_2OH$.

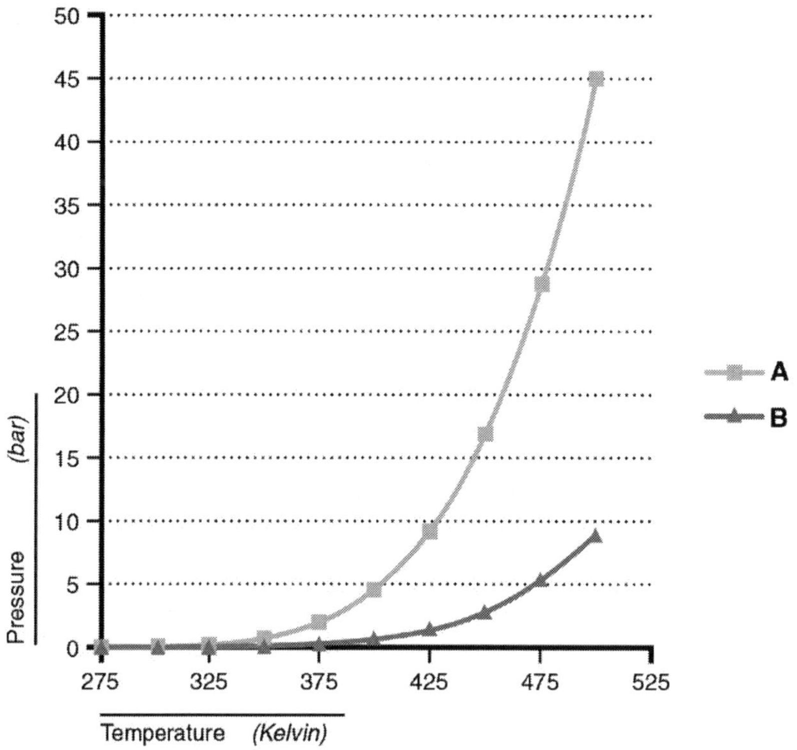

If the temperature is equal to 475 K, which of the following sentences is accurate?

a. Curve B represents 1-pentanol since 1-pentanol has weaker intermolecular forces than ethanol.
b. Curve B represents 1-pentanol since 1-pentanol has stronger intermolecular forces than ethanol.
c. Curve B represents ethanol since ethanol has weaker intermolecular forces than 1-pentanol.
d. Curve B represents ethanol since ethanol has stronger intermolecular forces than 1-pentanol.

12. Which factors decrease solubility of solids?

a. Heating
b. Agitation
c. Large surface area
d. Decreasing solvent

13. What information is used to calculate the quantity of solute in a solution?

a. Molarity of the solution
b. Equivalence point
c. Limiting reactant
d. Theoretical yield

14. Which of the 0.5 molal aqueous solutions will have the highest boiling point?
   a. CH_3CH_2OH
   b. KNO_3
   c. $Al(C_2H_3O_2)_3$
   d. $BaCl_2$

15. Consider the following equilibrium reaction:

$$2\ NO_2F(g) \rightleftarrows F_2(g) + 2\ NO_2(g)$$

The forward reaction occurs at a specific rate, temperature, and pressure. If the pressure of the reaction is decreased, how will the forward reaction change at equilibrium?
   a. a lesser reaction rate and greater yield of $F_2(g) + 2NO_2(g)$
   b. a greater reaction rate with the same yield of $F_2(g) + 2NO_2(g)$
   c. a lesser reaction rate and smaller yield of $F_2(g) + 2NO_2(g)$
   d. a greater reaction rate and greater yield of $F_2(g) + 2NO_2(g)$

16. 2.0 L flask is filled with 0.40 mol of N_2 and 0.40 mol of O_2 at 2000°C. What is the concentration of nitric oxide (NO) when the chemical reaction reaches equilibrium? The equilibrium constant $K_c = 0.10$ at 2000°C.

$$N_2(g) + O_2(g) \rightleftarrows 2\ NO(g)$$

   a. 0.11 M
   b. 0.096 M
   c. 0.027 M
   d. 0.055 M

17. Determine the pH of the solution that results when mixing 25.0 mL of 0.500 M NaOH and 50.0 mL of 0.250 M $HC_2H_3O_2$. Note that $K_a = 1.8 \times 10^{-5}$ for acetic acid.
   a. 8.98
   b. 5.016
   c. 2.76
   d. 11.23

18. If sodium hydroxide (NaOH) is added to a dilute solution of potassium hydroxide (KOH), how will the NaOH equilibrium be affected, compared to NaOH dissolved in pure water?
   a. Sodium hydroxide always dissociates completely to form more ions.
   b. The equilibrium of sodium hydroxide is unaffected by KOH.
   c. The equilibrium of the reaction favors sodium hydroxide.
   d. Sodium hydroxide does not dissociate in the KOH solution.

19. What coefficients are needed to balance the following combustion equation?

$$\_\ C_2H_{10} + \_\ O_2 \rightarrow \_\ H_2O + \_\ CO_2$$

   a. 1:5:5:2
   b. 1:9:5:2
   c. 2:9:10:4
   d. 2:5:10:4

20. saturated solution of salt, MX_2 (where M is a metal and X is a halide), contains 2.00×10^{-3} mol of MX_2 per 2.00 L at 25°C. What is the K_{sp} at that temperature?

a. 4.00×10^{-9}
b. 1.00×10^{-9}
c. 1.00×10^{-6}
d. 4.00×10^{-6}

21. Which substance is oxidized in the following reaction?

$$4\ Fe + 3\ O_2 \rightarrow 2\ Fe_2O_3$$

a. Fe
b. O
c. O_2
d. Fe_2O_3

22. Which statements are true regarding nuclear fission?

I. It splits heavy nuclei.
II. It is utilized in power plants.
III. It occurs on the sun.

a. Choice I only
b. Choices II and III
c. Choices I and II
d. Choice III only

23. The ionization of aqueous nitrous acid has an equilibrium constant, K, equal to 4.50×10^{-4} at 25°C. Determine the value of the standard Gibbs free energy, ΔG°_{rxn}, for the reaction.

a. $-19.1\ kJ \cdot mol^{-1}$
b. $19.1\ kJ \cdot mol^{-1}$
c. $-1.60\ kJ \cdot mol^{-1}$
d. $1.60\ kJ \cdot mol^{-1}$

24. Which statement below is correct for the combustion of butane under standard conditions?

$$C_4H_{10}(g) + \frac{13}{2}O_2(g) \rightarrow 4\ CO_2(g) + 5\ H_2O(g),\quad \Delta H^{\circ}_{comb} = -2658\ kJ \cdot mol^{-1}$$

a. At high temperatures, the reaction is spontaneous.
b. At any temperature, the reaction is not spontaneous.
c. At low temperatures, the reaction is spontaneous.
d. At all temperatures, the reaction is spontaneous.

25. An oxidation-reduction reaction has a $\Delta G^{\circ} = 15.75\ kJ \cdot mol^{-1}$ at 25°C. What is the value of E° if two electrons are transferred in the reaction?

a. -0.08162 V
b. -0.1632 V
c. 0.08162 V
d. -8.16×10^{-5} V

26. An atom of radium-226, $^{226}_{88}\mathrm{Ra}$, contains:
   a. 88 neutrons, 138 protons, and 226 electrons
   b. 88 protons, 138 electrons, and 226 neutrons
   c. 88 protons, 88 electrons, and 138 neutrons
   d. 88 electrons, 88 protons, and 226 neutrons

27. Which of the following sets of quantum numbers is INCORRECT?
   a. $n = 2, l = 1, m_l = +1$
   b. $n = 2, l = 1, m_l = 0$
   c. $n = 1, l = 0, m_l = 0$
   d. $n = 3, l = 1, m_l = -2$

28. Suppose that you exhale half a liter (0.500 L) of carbon dioxide (CO_2) gas into a balloon. How many oxygen atoms are present inside the balloon if the oxygen atoms come from carbon dioxide? The molar volume of carbon dioxide is 22.4 L/mol.
   a. 1.34×10^{22} O atoms
   b. 2.69×10^{22} O_2 atoms
   c. 2.69×10^{22} O atoms
   d. 1.34×10^{22} O_2 atoms

29. The caffeine molecule, found in coffee and tea, has a molecular formula of $C_8H_{10}N_4O_2$. What is the mass in kilograms for one molecule of caffeine?
   a. 3×10^{-25} kg
   b. 4×10^{-25} kg
   c. 3×10^{-22} kg
   d. 1×10^{-22} kg

30. If a compound containing nitrogen and oxygen weighs a total of 2.04 g, what is the empirical formula if the substance contains 1.51 g of oxygen?
   a. N_2O_5
   b. N_2O
   c. NO
   d. NO_2

31. A compound containing sulfur and oxygen has the empirical formula of SO_2. If 0.162 grams of the actual compound, $(SO_2)_n$, contains 7.61×10^{20} molecules, what must the value of n be?
   a. 4
   b. 3
   c. 2
   d. 1

32. Find the mass of oxygen present in 1.50 mole of sucrose ($C_{12}H_{22}O_{11}$).
   a. 195 g
   b. 200 g
   c. 245 g
   d. 264 g

33. Carbon dioxide can be prepared by the reaction or combustion of carbon monoxide and oxygen:

$$2\ CO(g) + O_2(g) \rightarrow 2\ CO_2$$

If three moles of carbon monoxide react with one mole of oxygen gas, the amount of carbon dioxide that is produced is called the:

a. Product yield
b. Theoretical yield
c. Limiting reactant
d. Excess reactant

34. If carbon dioxide is passed over charcoal, it will produce carbon monoxide:

$$CO_2(g) + C(s) \rightarrow 2\ CO(g)$$

Suppose two moles of carbon dioxide react with three moles of carbon to produce a theoretical amount of carbon monoxide. If the excess reactant is consumed or depleted, how many more moles of carbon monoxide could be produced?

a. 2 moles
b. 3 moles
c. 4 moles
d. 5 moles

35. If 3.52 g of aluminum sulfate is mixed with 4.06 g of barium chloride in solution, what is the theoretical yield of barium sulfate (molar mass is 233.40 g/mol)?

$$Al_2(SO_4)_3(aq) + 3\ BaCl_2(aq) \rightarrow 3\ BaSO_4(s) + 2\ AlCl_3(aq)$$

a. 3.15 g $BaSO_4$
b. 1.95 g $BaSO_4$
c. 3.09 g $BaSO_4$
d. 4.55 g $BaSO_4$

36. If 3.96 grams of barium sulfate is collected through a separate filtration process, what is the percent yield for a mixture of aluminum sulfate and barium chloride that had a theoretical yield of 4.21 g?

a. 106%
b. 0.94
c. 94%
d. 1.06

37. How many grams of excess reactant is present if 3.52 g of aluminum sulfate is mixed with 4.06 grams of barium chloride?

a. 2.00 g $Al^2(SO^4)^3$
b. 0.50 g $Al^2(SO^4)^3$
c. 1.30 g $Al^2(SO^4)^3$
d. 2.50 g $Al^2(SO^4)^3$

38. If 100 mL of 0.050 M $AgNO_3$ is added to 50.0 mL of 0.050 M Na_2SO_4, which of the following choices is true? Note that K_{sp} of Ag_2SO_4 is 6.9×10^{-15}.
   a. A precipitate will form without any excess ions.
   b. A precipitate will form with excess Ag^{+}.
   c. There will be no precipitate.
   d. A precipitate will form with an excess of Ag^{+} and $SO_4{}^{2-}$

39. Determine the balanced half-reaction for the formation of nitrogen monoxide from nitrate ion in a basic solution.

$$NO_3^-(aq) \rightarrow NO(g)$$

   a. $NO_3^-(aq) + 2\,H_2O(l) \rightarrow NO\,(g) + 4\,H^+ + 3\,e^-$
   b. $4\,H^+ + 3\,e^- + NO_3^-(aq) \rightarrow NO\,(g) + 2\,H_2O(l)$
   c. $2\,H_2O(l) + 3\,e^- + NO_3^-(aq) \rightarrow NO\,(g) + 4\,OH^-$
   d. $4\,OH^- + NO_3^-(aq) \rightarrow NO\,(g) + 2\,H_2O(l) + 3\,e^-$

40. What mass of water is needed to dissolve 250.0 g of AgCl to make a 0.35 mol/kg AgCl aqueous solution?
   a. 5.0 kg
   b. 1.7 moles per liter
   c. 5.0 moles per liter
   d. 1.7 kg

41. What volume of a 5.00 M HNO_3 solution should be added to water to make a 2.00 M HNO_3 solution?
   a. Take 350 mL of water and add 140 mL the concentrated acid.
   b. Take 210 mL of water and add 140 mL the concentrated acid.
   c. Take 350 L of water and add 140 L the concentrated acid.
   d. Take 210 L of water and add 140 L the concentrated acid.

42. During an acid-base titration experiment, the endpoint was reached when 35.00 mL of a standardized 1.500 M potassium hydroxide was added to a 15.00 mL solution of sulfuric acid. What is the concentration of the acid assuming that the endpoint is near the equivalence point? The reaction of sulfuric acid and potassium hydroxide is shown below:

$$H_2SO_4(aq) + 2\,KOH(aq) \rightarrow K_2SO_4(aq) + 2\,H_2O(l)$$

   a. 0.5250 M H_2SO_4
   b. 0.750 M H_2SO_4
   c. 1.750 M H_2SO_4
   d. 3.500 M H_2SO_4

43. In anticipation of freezing weather, farmers may spray water over their plants and cover them with large plastic materials. As the temperature drops below 0 °C (32 °F), the following physical process will occur for the water found on the plants:

$$H_2O(l) \rightarrow H_2O(s)$$

If water is treated as the chemical system, which of the following is correct?

a. The process is exothermic and $+q_{\text{system}} = -q_{\text{surroundings}}$.
b. The process is endothermic and $+q_{\text{system}} = +q_{\text{surroundings}}$.
c. The process is exothermic and $-q_{\text{system}} = +q_{\text{surroundings}}$.
d. The process is endothermic and $-q_{\text{system}} = +q_{\text{surroundings}}$.

44. The standard enthalpies of formation for lithium bromide and lithium chloride are shown below.

Standard enthalpies of formation at 298K, ΔH_f° (kJ/mol)	
LiBr	-351.2
LiCl	-408.6

Which of the following statements is true?

a. ΔH_f° for LiCl is less exothermic than ΔH_f° for LiBr
b. ΔH_f° for LiCl is more exothermic than ΔH_f° for LiBr
c. ΔH_f° for LiCl is more endothermic than ΔH_f° for LiBr
d. ΔH_f° for LiCl is less endothermic than ΔH_f° for LiBr

45. The combustion of one mole of methane produces carbon dioxide and water with an amount of heat (in kJ) shown in the following thermochemical equation:

$$CH_4(g) + 2\,O_2(g) \rightarrow CO_2(g) + 2\,H_2O(g) \quad \Delta H_{\text{rxn}}^{\circ} = -802.3 \text{ kJ}$$

How much heat is produced if 1.5 kg of methane is combusted in oxygen gas?

a. -7.50×10^4 kJ/mol
b. $+7.50 \times 10^4$ kJ/mol
c. $+7.50 \times 10^4$ kJ
d. -7.50×10^4 kJ

46. For the reaction shown below, calculate the standard enthalpy of reaction $\Delta H_{\text{rxn}}^{\circ}$ using the standard enthalpies of formation shown in the table below.

$$2\,Al(s) + Fe_2O_3(s) \rightarrow Al_2O_3(s) + 2\,Fe(s) \quad \Delta H_{\text{rxn}}^{\circ} = ?$$

Standard enthalpies of formation at 298K, ΔH_f° (kJ/mol)	
Al(s)	0
$Fe_2O_3(s)$	-824.2
$Al_2O_3(s)$	-1675.7
Fe(s)	0

a. -851.5 kJ
b. -2499.9 kJ
c. +851.5 kJ
d. +2499.9 kJ

47. A 43.0 g metal sample at a temperature of 100.0 °C is dropped into a 100.0 mL water bath with an initial temperature of 25.0 °C. The temperature of the water bath increased to a final temperature of 37.0 °C. What is the specific heat of the metal if the specific heat capacity of water is 4.184 J/(g °C)? The density of water is about 1 g/mL.
   a. 2.95 J/(g °C)
   b. 0.87 J/(g °C)
   c. 1.85 J/(g °C)
   d. 4.25 J/(g °C)

48. Which of the following processes involves an increase in entropy?
   a. The contraction of a gas
   b. The freezing of water: $H_2O(l) \rightarrow H_2O(s)$
   c. $CaO(s) + CO_2(g) \rightarrow CaCO_3(s)$
   d. Adding sugar to water: $C_{12}H_{22}O_{11}(s) \xrightarrow{H_2O(l)} C_{12}H_{22}O_{11}(aq)$

49. The following equation gives the Gibbs free energy ΔG for a chemical reaction:

$$\Delta G = \Delta H - T\Delta S$$

If the Gibbs free energy of the system is negative, the reaction is spontaneous. If it is positive, the reaction is not spontaneous and will occur. If the free energy is zero, then the reaction is at equilibrium. Which of the following is true if both ΔH and ΔS are positive?
   a. The reaction is spontaneous when the temperature is increased.
   b. The reaction is spontaneous at any temperature.
   c. The reaction is spontaneous when the temperature is decreased.
   d. The reaction is nonspontaneous at any temperature.

50. Consider the following hypothetical reaction:

$$2\ A(g) \rightarrow A_2(g) \quad \Delta H^{\circ} = -300\ kJ$$

At what conditions would this reaction be spontaneous? What is the sign of ΔS°_{rxn}?
   a. Spontaneous at low temperatures and $+\Delta S^{\circ}_{rxn}$
   b. Spontaneous at high temperatures and $+\Delta S^{\circ}_{rxn}$
   c. Spontaneous at low temperatures and $-\Delta S_{rxn}$
   d. Spontaneous at high temperatures and $+\Delta S_{rxn}$

51. How many electrons are in the p subshell for the nitrogen atom?
   a. 2
   b. 3
   c. 4
   d. 5

52. Based on the Aufbau principle, which of the following choices most likely represents the set of quantum numbers corresponding to the eighth electron in the oxygen atom?
   a. $n = 2, l = 0, m_l = 0, m_s = +\frac{1}{2}$
   b. $n = 2, l = 1, m_l = -1, m_s = +\frac{1}{2}$
   c. $n = 2, l = 0, m_l = 0, m_s = -\frac{1}{2}$
   d. $n = 2, l = 1, m_l = -1, m_s = -\frac{1}{2}$

53. Which of the following quantum numbers does not represent an electron in the nitrogen atom?
   a. $n = 2, l = 1, m_l = -2, m_s = -\frac{1}{2}$
   b. $n = 1, l = 0, m_l = 0, m_s = -\frac{1}{2}$
   c. $n = 2, l = 0, m_l = 0, m_s = -\frac{1}{2}$
   d. $n = 2, l = 1, m_l = -1, m_s = +\frac{1}{2}$

54. What is the electron group geometry of the NF_3 molecule?
   a. Trigonal planar
   b. Tetrahedral
   c. Trigonal bipyramidal
   d. Octahedral

55. For the three structures below, which Lewis structure for nitrous oxide (N_2O) is the most likely the correct structure? Choose the right answer choice below which has the correct corresponding formal charges for the N, N, and O atoms.

I II III

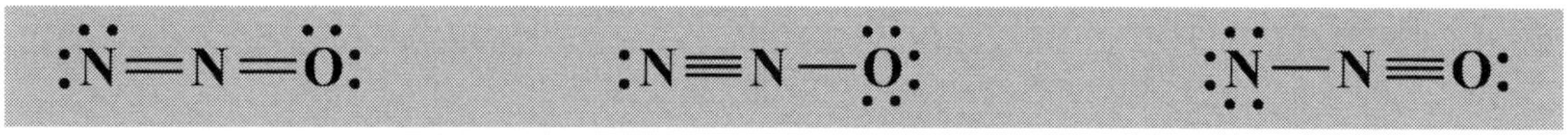

   a. Structure 1, formal charges are −1, +1, 0
   b. Structure 2, formal charges are 0, +1, −1
   c. Structure 3, formal charges are −2, +1, +1
   d. Structure 1, formal charges are +2. +1, 0

56. Which of the following statements is NOT true regarding the phase diagram below.

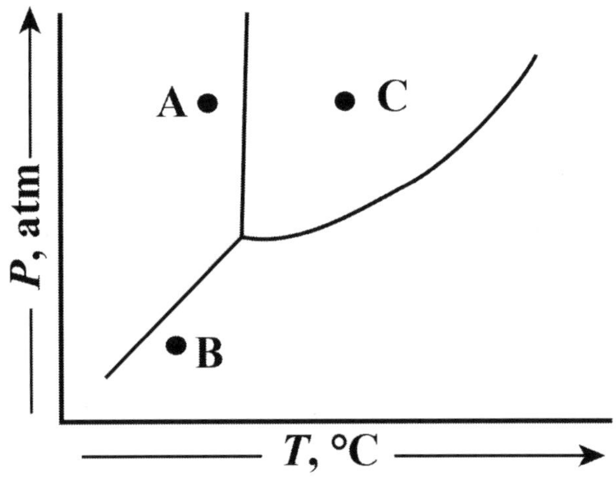

a. If a compound is in state A, with the temperature held constant, reducing the pressure will cause it to sublime.
b. Decreasing the pressure and temperature from point C to point B represents evaporation.
c. The slope of the solid and liquid equilibrium line is positive, similar to the phase diagram of water.
d. Increasing the temperature from point A to point C represents melting.

57. The vapor pressure of a solution is lowered when a nonvolatile solute is added to a pure solvent. As a result, the freezing point for the solution decreases, and the boiling point increases. The following equation gives the freezing point depression:

$$\Delta T_f = m \times K_f$$

The term $\Delta T_f = T_{solvent} - T_{solution}$ represents the temperature change or freezing point depression in degrees Celsius, and the terms m and K_f are the molality (units of molal or mol/kg) and freezing point depression constant for the solvent (units of $\frac{°C}{mol\ kg^{-1}}$). If 1.00×10^3 g of ethylene glycol ($C_2H_6O_2$, molar mass $= 62.07$ g/mol) is added to a radiator that contains 5.00×10^3 g of water, how much would the freezing point lower? Note that $K_f = 1.86\ °C/(mol\ kg^{-1})$.

a. −5.99 °C
b. +5.99 °C
c. −3.22 °C
d. +3.22 °C

58. The activation energy for a chemical reaction involving the breakage of a carbon-oxygen single bond was estimated at 125 kJ/mol at 25.0 °C. If the temperature is increased to about 50.0 °C, by what factor does the rate constant increase?

a. 10.5
b. 32.1
c. 49.5
d. 29.6

59. The half-life for an unknown element called X is 7.95 days How many days would this sample need to reach 35.0 percent of its original amount?

a. 19.5 days
b. 12.0 days
c. 11.5 days
d. 15.0 days

60. Consider the following two-step reaction below:

$$2\ CO(g) + O_2(g) \rightleftharpoons 2\ CO_2(g)$$

$$CO_2(g) + C(s) \rightleftharpoons 2\ CO(g)$$

What is the overall equilibrium expression?

a. $K_{overall} = \frac{[CO_2]^2}{[CO]^2[O_2]}$
b. $K_{overall} = \frac{[CO]^2}{[CO_2]}$
c. $K_{overall} = \frac{[CO_2]^2}{[O_2]}$
d. $K_{overall} = \frac{[CO_2]}{[O_2]}$

61. Consider the following exothermic reaction:

$$SO_2(g) + CaO(s) \rightleftharpoons CaSO_3(s) + \text{heat}$$

Which of the following changes will result in a decrease in pressure of $SO_2(g)$ at equilibrium?

a. Addition of CaO(s)
b. Removal of $CaSO_3$(s)
c. Increasing the volume of the reaction vessel
d. Decreasing the temperature of the chemical reaction system

62. What is the pH of a 0.35 M solution of ammonia in water? Note that $K_b = 1.8 \times 10^{-5}$

a. 10.20
b. 8.01
c. 11.40
d. 8.96

63. What is the equilibrium concentration of a reaction mixture that initially had 1.00 mol H_2 and 1.00 mol I_2 in a 1.0 L vessel?

$$H_2(g) + I_2(g) \rightleftharpoons 2HI(g) \quad K_c = 49.7 \text{ at } 458\ °C$$

a. $[H_2] = [I_2] = 0.22\ M, [HI] = 1.6\ M$
b. $[H_2] = [I_2] = 0.33\ M, [HI] = 1.8\ M$
c. $[H_2] = [I_2] = 0.44\ M, [HI] = 2.0\ M$
d. $[H_2] = [I_2] = 0.55\ M, [HI] = 2.2\ M$

64. For the following radioactive decay process, which of the following is the correct product shown in the nuclear equation below?

$$^{92}_{44}Ru + {}^{0}_{-1}e \rightarrow ?$$

a. $^{92}_{45}Rh$
b. $^{92}_{43}Rh$
c. $^{92}_{43}Tc$
d. $^{4}_{2}He + {}^{92}_{43}Tc$

65. Find the N/Z ratio of Pb-212 to predict whether beta decay or positron emission will occur, and then determine which choice below represents the N/Z ratio of the daughter nuclide.

a. 1.59
b. 1.55
c. 1.41
d. 1.37

66. For the following redox reaction, which of the following statements is true?

$$6\ I^-(aq) + 4\ H_2O(l) + 2\ MnO_4^-(aq) \rightarrow 3\ I_2(aq) + 2\ MnO_2(s) + 8\ OH^-(aq)$$

a. MnO_4- is oxidized in the reaction.
b. MnO_4- is the oxidizing agent.
c. I^- is reduced in the reaction.
d. I^- is the oxidizing agent.

67. Consider the standard reduction potentials for the reactions shown below. Calculate *the* standard cell potential, E°_{cell}, for the spontaneous reaction.

$$Ni^{2+}(aq) + 2\ e^- \rightarrow Ni(s) \quad E^{\circ} = -0.23\ V$$

$$Al^{3+}(aq) + 3\ e^- \rightarrow Al(s) \quad E^{\circ} = -1.66\ V$$

a. $E^{\circ}_{cell} = -1.43\ V$
b. $E^{\circ}_{cell} = +1.43\ V$
c. $E^{\circ}_{cell} = -2.63\ V$
d. $E^{\circ}_{cell} = +2.63\ V$

68. The solubility of silver chloride ($AgCl$) is approximately 1.9×10^{-3} g/L in water. Which of the following choices below most closely corresponds to the correct solubility product constant (K_{sp})?
  a. 1.6×10^{-10}
  b. 1.8×10^{-10}
  c. 2.0×10^{-10}
  d. 3.6×10^{-10}

69. Which of the following choices is NOT true regarding the equilibrium constant?
  a. It can be used to predict the extent of the reaction.
  b. It gives information on the direction of the reaction.
  c. It can be used to determine the time needed to reach equilibrium.
  d. It can be used to help calculate equilibrium concentrations.

70. In 1939, Lise Meitner submitted a letter to the editor of *Nature* and described the process of fission using a liquid droplet model. According to her model, when a neutron bombards uranium, $^{235}_{92}U$, the fission reaction produces a total of two neutrons, a $^{95}_{36}Kr$ atom, and ______.

  a. $^{226}_{88}Ra$
  b. $^{139}_{56}Ba$
  c. $^{235}_{92}U$
  d. $^{92}_{37}Rb$

Answer Explanations

1. C: A Brønsted-Lowry base is any substance capable of accepting a proton, or H^+. Choices *A* and *D* are incorrect because they both have dissociable hydrogens, meaning they would likely donate a hydrogen in an aqueous solution. Choice *B*, carbon dioxide (CO_2), would not be considered a base on its own because it is nonpolar and does not normally accept a proton in the presence of water. Choice *C*, ammonia (NH_3) is the only choice that acts as a base in aqueous solution, since it is more likely to accept a proton from water, forming ammonium ($NH_4{}^+$) and hydroxide ions.

2. A: Choice *A* is the correct answer. The isotopes of bromine are represented as Br-79 (78.918 amu) and Br-81 (80.916 amu). The mass of bromine in the periodic table is the average atomic mass (a weighted average of the isotopes), which is 79.904. There are two stable or naturally occurring isotopes of bromine, so the average atomic mass is a weighted average of ^{79}Br and ^{81}Br. The following general equations will be required:

$$Average\ atomic\ mass = \left[(mass\ of\ isotope\ 1)\frac{\%\ isotope\ 1}{100\%}\right] + \left[(mass\ of\ isotope\ 2)\frac{\%\ isotope\ 2}{100\%}\right]$$

$$100\%\ \text{abundance of stable isotopes} = \%\ \text{isotope } 1 + \%\ \text{isotope } 2$$

Step 1: substitute the correct isotope name into each equation below.

$$\text{Equation 1a:}\quad Average\ atomic\ mass_{\text{Br}} = \left[(mass\ ^{79}\text{Br})\frac{\%^{79}\text{Br}}{100\%}\right] + \left[(mass\ ^{81}\text{Br})\frac{\%^{81}\text{Br}}{100\%}\right]$$

$$\text{Equation 2a:}\quad 100\% = \%^{79}\text{Br} + \%^{81}\text{Br}$$

Step 2: First solve for $\%^{79}$Br by subtracting $\%^{81}$Br on both sides of equation 2a.

$$100\% = \%^{79}\text{Br} + \%^{81}\text{Br}$$

$$100\% - \%^{81}\text{Br} = \%^{79}\text{Br} + \%^{81}\text{Br} - \%^{81}\text{Br}$$

$$\text{Equation 2b:}\quad 100\% - \%^{81}\text{Br} = \%^{79}\text{Br}$$

Step 3: Now substitute equation 2b into the first term of Equation 1a.

Note that $\%^{79}\text{Br} = 100\% - \%^{81}\text{Br}$:

$$\text{Equation 1b:}\quad Average\ atomic\ mass_{\text{Br}} = \left[(mass\ ^{79}\text{Br})\frac{100\% - \%^{81}\text{Br}}{100\%}\right] + \left[(mass\ ^{81}\text{Br})\frac{\%^{81}\text{Br}}{100\%}\right]$$

In equation 1b, rearrange the equation in terms of $\%^{81}$Br.

$$\%^{81}\text{Br} = \left(\frac{Average\ atomic\ mass_{\text{Br}} - mass\ ^{79}\text{Br}}{mass\ ^{81}\text{Br} - mass\ ^{79}\text{Br}}\right) \times 100\%$$

Now substitute into the equation the average atomic mass (79.904 amu), the isotope mass of $^{79}\mathrm{Br}$ (78.918 amu), and the isotope mass of $^{81}\mathrm{Br}$ (80.916 amu).

$$\%^{81}\mathrm{Br} = \left(\frac{79.904 - 78.918}{80.916 - 78.918}\right) \times 100\% = 49.349\%$$

Step 4: Given the % abundance of $^{81}\mathrm{Br}$, equation 2b can be used to solve for % $^{79}\mathrm{Br}$.

$$\%^{79}\mathrm{Br} = 100\% - \%^{81}\mathrm{Br}$$

$$\%^{79}\mathrm{Br} = 100\% - 49.349\% = 50.651\%$$

The % relative abundance is $\%^{79}\mathrm{Br} = 50.651\%$ and $\%^{81}\mathrm{Br} = 49.349\%$. Choice *A* is the correct answer. Choice *B* is incorrect since the answers are reversed.

3. B: The conversion from Celsius to Fahrenheit is $°\mathrm{F} = \frac{9}{5}(°\mathrm{C}) + 32$. Substituting the value for °C gives $°\mathrm{F} = \frac{9}{5}(35) + 32$, which yields 95 °F. The other choices do not apply the formula correctly and completely.

4. C: Choice *C* is the correct answer. To solve the problem, the Rydberg formula is used to calculate the change in energy as an electron moves from the $n = 5$ orbital to the $n = 2$ orbital. To find the wavelength of the electronic transition, use Planck's equation, which relates the energy to the frequency of light. The wavelength of emitted radiation is inversely proportional to the frequency.

Step 1: Use the Rydberg formula.

$$\Delta E = R_H\left(\frac{1}{n_\mathrm{i}^2} - \frac{1}{n_\mathrm{f}^2}\right); \qquad R_H = 2.18 \times 10^{-18}\ \mathrm{J}; \qquad n_i = 5\ and\ n_f = 2$$

$$i = \text{initial orbital} \qquad \text{and} \qquad f = \text{final orbital}$$

$$\Delta E = R_H\left(\frac{1}{5^2} - \frac{1}{2^2}\right) = (2.18 \times 10^{-18}\ J)\left(\frac{1}{25} - \frac{1}{4}\right) = -4.578 \times 10^{-19}\ \mathrm{J}$$

The negative sign corresponds to the loss of energy in an atom because a photon is produced. The energy of the photon is the absolute value of the energy transition.

$$|\Delta E_{transition}| = E_{photon} = 4.578 \times 10^{-19}\ J$$

Step 2: Rearrange Planck's equation to find the wavelength.

$$E = h\nu \text{ or } E = \frac{hc}{\lambda}; \qquad h = 6.626 \times 10^{-34}\ \mathrm{J \cdot s}; \qquad c = 3.00 \times 10^8\ \frac{\mathrm{m}}{\mathrm{s}}$$

$$\lambda = \frac{hc}{E} = \frac{(6.626 \times 10^{-34}\ \mathrm{J \cdot s})\left(3.00 \times 10^8\ \frac{\mathrm{m}}{\mathrm{s}}\right)}{4.578 \times 10^{-19}\ \mathrm{J}} = 4.342 \times 10^{-7}\mathrm{m}$$

Step 3: Convert meters into nanometers using the conversion factor below.

$$1 \text{ meter} = 1 \times 10^9 \text{ nanometer (equivalency equation)}$$

$$4.342 \times 10^{-7}\text{m} \times \left(\frac{1 \times 10^9 \text{ nm}}{1 \text{ m}}\right) = 434 \text{ nm}$$

5. B: Choice *B* is the correct answer. The correct set of quantum numbers will first be determined by the principal quantum number (n). The 4f orbital has the leading coefficient of 4. Therefore, the principal quantum number will be $n = 4$. Since $n = 4$, then the value of the angular quantum number, l, must be less than the principal quantum number (n) and is given by the formula:

$$l = n - 1 = 4 - 1 = 3$$

The value of l designates the shape. For example, if $l = 0$, the orbital is s shaped. If $l = 3$, the orbital is f shaped. The table below lists the value of each quantum number for $n = 4$.

Quantum Numbers for 4f

Principal Quantum Number (n)	Angular quantum number (l)	Magnetic Quantum Number (m_l)	Orbitals (combination of n and l):
4	$0\ (n = 0, s)$	$0\ (l = 0; s)$	$4s$
	$1\ (n = 1, p)$	$-1, 0, 1(\ l = 1; p)$	$4p$
	$2\ (n = 2, d)$	$-2, -1, 0, 1, 2\ (l = 2; d)$	$4d$
	$3\ (n = 3, f)$	$-3, -2, -1, 0, 1, 2, 3\ (l = 3; f)$	$4f$

Both Choices *A* ($l = 4$) and *D* ($l = 2$) can be eliminated because the value of the angular quantum number (l) is not equal to three ($l = 3$). The next difference between Choices *B* and *C* is the magnetic quantum number (m_l). Based on the table, the value of $m_l = -3$ is an allowable angular orientation, but not $m_l = +4$. The final value of the magnetic quantum number is determined by the following equation:

$$m_l: 2l + 1 = 2(3) + 1 = 7$$

For the f-shaped orbital, $l = 3$, there are 7 distinct orbital orientations designated by seven numbers:

$$-3, -2, -1, 0, +1, +2, +3$$

The spin quantum numbers $m_s = +\frac{1}{2}$ or $m_s = -\frac{1}{2}$ are allowable and will not impact Choice *B* as the correct answer.

6. A: Choice *A* is the correct answer. The number of moles must be determined from the average atomic mass. The periodic table can be used to find the atomic mass. After converting to moles, Avogadro's number can be used to determine the number of atoms for each substance.

The atomic mass for each substance is:

Carbon (C)	$12.01\frac{\text{g}}{\text{mol}} \times 1 = 12.01\frac{\text{g}}{\text{mol}}$
Nitrogen gas (N_2)	$14.01\frac{\text{g}}{\text{mol}} \times 2 = 28.02\frac{\text{g}}{\text{mol}}$
Chromium (Cr)	$52.00\frac{\text{g}}{\text{mol}} \times 1 = 52.00\frac{\text{g}}{\text{mol}}$
Sodium (Na)	$22.99\frac{\text{g}}{\text{mol}} \times 1 = 22.99\frac{\text{g}}{\text{mol}}$

Each substance can be converted as follows: grams → moles → number of atoms

Carbon:

$$(2.00\text{ g C})\left(\frac{1\text{ mol C}}{12.01\text{ g C}}\right)\left(\frac{6.022 \times 10^{23}\text{ C atoms}}{1\text{ mol C}}\right) = 1.00 \times 10^{23}\text{ C atoms}$$

Nitrogen gas: One last conversion ratio is used to convert molecules of nitrogen gas to nitrogen atoms.

$$(2.00\text{ g N}_2)\left(\frac{1\text{ mol N}_2}{28.02\text{ g N}_2}\right)\left(\frac{6.022 \times 10^{23}\text{ N}_2\text{ molecules}}{1\text{ mol N}_2}\right)\left(\frac{2\text{ N atoms}}{1\text{ molecule N}_2}\right) = 8.60 \times 10^{22}\text{ N atoms}$$

Chromium:

$$(2.00\text{ g Cr})\left(\frac{1\text{ mol Cr}}{52.00\text{ g Cr}}\right)\left(\frac{6.022 \times 10^{23}\text{ Cr atoms}}{1\text{ mol Cr}}\right) = 2.32 \times 10^{22}\text{ Cr atoms}$$

Sodium:

$$(2.00\text{ g Na})\left(\frac{1\text{ mol Na}}{22.99\text{ g Na}}\right)\left(\frac{6.022 \times 10^{23}\text{ Na atoms}}{1\text{ mol Na}}\right) = 5.24 \times 10^{22}\text{ C atoms}$$

The order of increasing atom numbers goes from chromium → sodium → nitrogen gas → carbon. Two grams of carbon contains the greatest number of atoms.

7. B: Choice *B* is the correct answer. The stoichiometric relationship between moles of iron to moles of iron (VI) oxide is 4:2. For every 4 moles of iron, two moles of iron (VI) oxide are produced.

$$4\text{ Fe(s)} + 3\text{ O}_2\text{(g)} \rightarrow 2\text{ FeO}_3\text{(s)}$$

Since oxygen gas is provided excess, iron is the limiting reactant, and only 5.50 moles of iron are present. First, set up the stoichiometric ratio to convert moles of iron to moles of iron (VI) oxide. Then convert to grams of iron (VI) oxide provided that the molar mass is:

$$\text{molar mass of Fe: } 55.85 \times 1\frac{\text{g}}{\text{mol}} = 55.85\frac{\text{g}}{\text{mol}}$$

$$\text{molar mass of O: } 16.00 \times 3\frac{\text{g}}{\text{mol}} = 48.00\frac{\text{g}}{\text{mol}}$$

$$\text{molar mass of FeO}_3 = 55.85\frac{\text{g}}{\text{mol}} + 48.00\frac{\text{g}}{\text{mol}} = 103.85\frac{\text{g}}{\text{mol}}$$

Convert moles of Fe → moles of iron (VI) oxide → grams of iron (VI) oxide

$$(5.50 \text{ mol Fe})\left(\frac{2 \text{ mol FeO}_3}{4 \text{ mol Fe}}\right)\left(\frac{103.85 \text{ g FeO}_3}{1 \text{ mol FeO}_3}\right) = 285.59 \text{ g FeO}_3$$

Choice *A* is incorrect since it uses an incorrect ratio of 4 moles FeO_3 to 4 moles Fe. Choice *C* is incorrect since it does not incorporate or multiply by the molar mass of FeO_3. Choice *D* is incorrect since it uses the ratio of 3 moles of O_2 to 2 moles of FeO_3.

8. D: Choice *D* is the correct answer. To determine the net ionic equation, determine the type of molecular equation. The reactants may participate in a precipitation (double-displacement) reaction. Use the solubility rules to determine the possible reaction products.

$$\overbrace{\text{K}_2\text{S(aq)}}^{\text{soluble}} + \overbrace{\text{Pb(C}_2\text{H}_3\text{O}_2)_2\text{(aq)}}^{\text{soluble}} \rightarrow \overbrace{2\ \text{KC}_2\text{H}_3\text{O}_2\text{(aq)}}^{\text{soluble}} + \overbrace{\text{PbS(s)}}^{\text{insoluble}}$$

To find the total ionic equation, separate the soluble compounds into dissociated ions. Insoluble compounds are kept together since they precipitate.

$$2\ \text{K}^+\text{(aq)} + \text{S}^{2-}\text{(aq)} + \text{Pb}^{2+}\text{(aq)} + 2\ \text{C}_2\text{H}_3\text{O}_2^-\text{(aq)} \rightarrow 2\text{K}^+\text{(aq)} + 2\ \text{C}_2\text{H}_3\text{O}_2^-\text{(aq)} + \text{PbS(s)}$$

Then cancel the spectator ions, potassium and acetate ion, which are found on the reactant and product side.

$$\cancel{2\ \text{K}^+\text{(aq)}} + \text{S}^{2-}\text{(aq)} + \text{Pb}^{2+}\text{(aq)} + \cancel{2\ \text{C}_2\text{H}_3\text{O}_2^-\text{(aq)}} \rightarrow \cancel{2\ \text{K}^+\text{(aq)}} + \cancel{2\ \text{C}_2\text{H}_3\text{O}_2^-\text{(aq)}} + \text{PbS(s)}$$

The final net ionic equation, Choice *D*, will show the formation of the precipitate.

$$\text{Pb}^{2+}\text{(aq)} + \text{S}^{2-}\text{(aq)} \rightarrow \text{PbS(s)}$$

Choice *A* is incorrect since it contains soluble ions. Choice *B* is incorrect since only one spectator ion, potassium, is removed. Choice *C* is incorrect since it represents the molecular equation.

9. D: Choice *D* is the correct answer. Determine the mass of carbon needed to release 25.5 kJ of heat for the reaction shown below.

$$C(s) + 2\,H_2(g) \rightarrow CH_4(g); \qquad \Delta H^{\circ}_{rxn} = -74.8\frac{kJ}{mol}$$

For every 1 mole of carbon that reacts with 2 moles of hydrogen gas, one mole of methane gas is produced. The production of one mole of methane releases –74.8 kilojoules (kJ) per mole (mol). A conversion factor between the amount of heat released and the moles of methane can be used to find the mass of carbon in grams. First, start with the desired amount of heat, which is 25.5 kilojoules (kJ).

$$(-25.5\text{ kJ})\left(\frac{1\text{ mol }CH_4(g)}{-74.8\text{ kJ}}\right)$$

Use another conversion factor to relate the moles of methane and carbon. The stoichiometric relationship between carbon and methane is 1:1 and is taken from the balanced equation.

$$(-25.5\text{ kJ})\left(\frac{1\text{ mol }CH_4(g)}{-74.8\text{ kJ}}\right)\left(\frac{1\text{ mole }C(s)}{1\text{ mol }CH_4(g)}\right)$$

Include the final relationship between moles of carbon and the mass of carbon using the molar mass taken from the periodic table.

$$(-25.5\text{ kJ})\left(\frac{1\text{ mol }CH_4(g)}{-74.8\text{ kJ}}\right)\overbrace{\left(\frac{1\text{ mole }C(s)}{1\text{ mol }CH_4(g)}\right)}^{\text{1:1 stoichiometric}}\left(\frac{12.01\text{ g C}}{1\text{ mol C}}\right) = 4.09\text{ g C}$$

Choice *A* is incorrect because it gives the mass of hydrogen instead. If the question asked for the mass of hydrogen, then:

$$(-25.5\text{ kJ})\left(\frac{1\text{ mol }CH_4(g)}{-74.8\text{ kJ}}\right)\overbrace{\left(\frac{2\text{ mole }H_2(g)}{1\text{ mol }CH_4(g)}\right)}^{\text{1:2 stoichiometric}}\left(\frac{2.016\text{ g }H_2(g)}{1\text{ mol }H_2(g)}\right) = 1.37\text{ g }H_2(g)$$

Choice *B* is incorrect since it gives the moles of carbon, and Choice *C* is incorrect since it gives the moles of hydrogen gas.

10. A: Choice *A* is the correct answer. One single chemical bond represents one sigma (σ) bond, which is represented by a single line in the structure shown below. A double bond represents a sigma bond (σ) and a pi (π) bond. A triple bond represents two sigma (σ) bonds and one pi (π) bond. The number of sigma (σ) and pi (π) bonds are shown below and are counted from left to right. There are a total of 16 sigma (σ) bonds and 4 pi (π) bonds. The number of lone pairs can be determined by looking at the group number of the specific element. Oxygen belongs to group VIA and will have six valence electrons. Each oxygen atom contains two bonds that share two valence electrons.

The remaining four valence electrons make up two lone pairs with two electrons per orbital or lone pair. Nitrogen belongs to group VA and will have five valence electrons. Each nitrogen atom has three sigma bonds that share three valence electrons. The remaining two valence electrons will make up the lone pair. There are two oxygen atoms, which means there are four lone pairs. There are four nitrogen atoms, so there are four lone pairs. Therefore, the total number of lone pairs is 8.

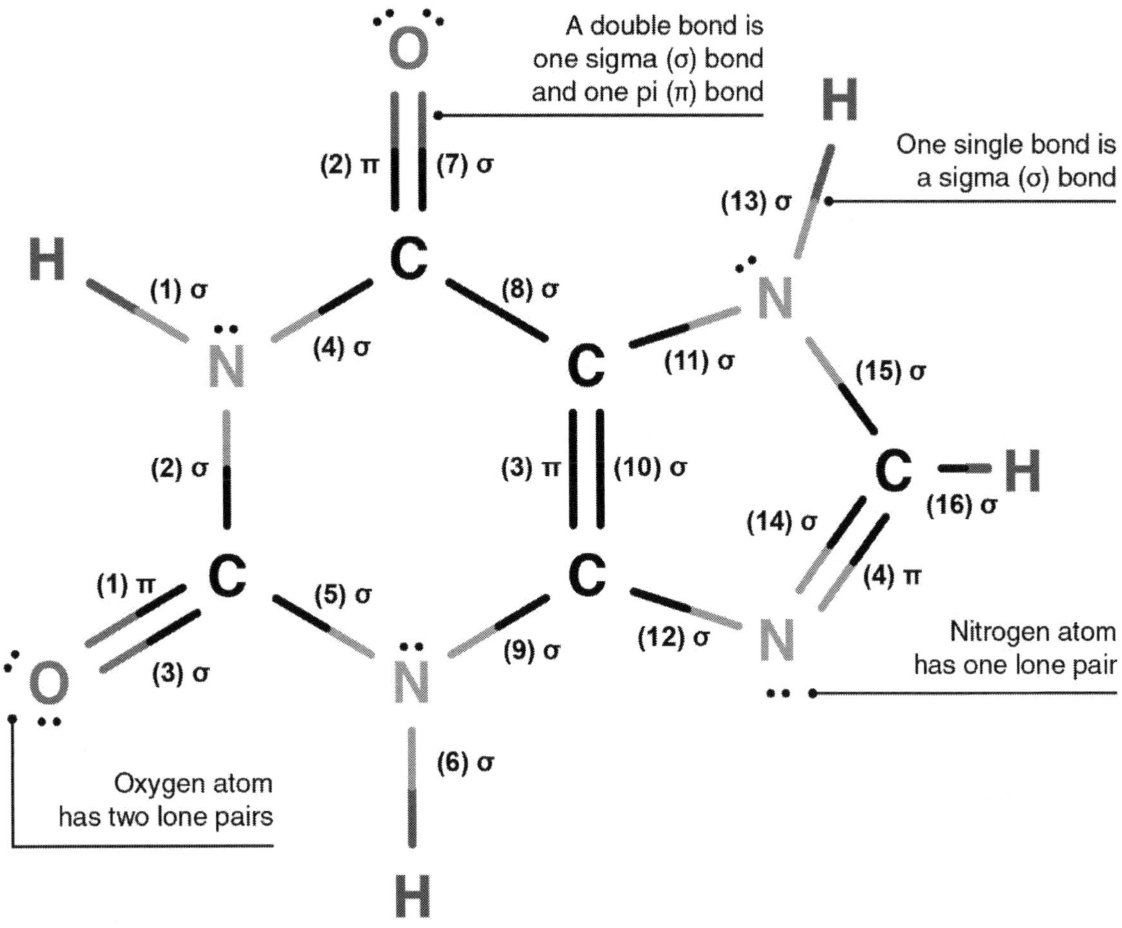

Choice *B* is incorrect since the sigma bonds are not included in the double bonds. Choice *C* is incorrect because the double bonds are counted as two pi bonds instead of counting as one sigma bond and one pi bond. The lone pair electrons are not included for nitrogen or oxygen. Choice *D* is incorrect since the lone pair electrons are not included for nitrogen or oxygen.

11. B: Choice *B* is the correct answer. 1-pentanol has stronger intermolecular forces compared to ethanol. There is a strong relationship between vapor pressure and intermolecular forces. The nature of the molecular forces can be determined by examining each structure. Both ethanol and 1-pentanol contain London dispersion forces (van Der Waals), dipole-dipole, and hydrogen bonding intermolecular forces. However, the molar mass between each substance is different. 1-pentanol has a greater molecular weight and, therefore, will have more electrons per molecule.

As the molar mass increases, so will the extent of the intermolecular forces. Specifically, there will be more dispersion forces in longer hydrocarbon chains ($-CH_2-$). As the number of intermolecular forces increases, there are fewer molecules or particles in the vapor phase above the liquid, since it requires more energy to break apart intermolecular forces; the vapor pressure will decrease. More energy (higher temperatures) is needed to transition to the vapor state for molecules with more intermolecular forces—the stronger or greater the intermolecular forces, the lower the number of particles in the vapor state. For 1-pentanol, at any temperature shown in the graph, it will have the lowest vapor pressure compared to ethanol. The weaker the intermolecular forces, the greater the number of particles in the vapor state. Since ethanol has fewer hydrocarbon chains, its intermolecular forces will be relatively weaker; it will have a higher vapor pressure compared to 1-pentanol.

Choice *A* is incorrect since the intermolecular forces of 1-pentanol are greater than ethanol. Choices *C* and *D* are incorrect because ethanol represents Curve A, the higher vapor pressure curve. Ethanol has weaker intermolecular forces, so at any temperature, its vapor pressure will be greater than 1-pentanol (Curve B).

12. D: Choices *A*, *B*, and *C* are incorrect because solids all increase solubility. Solids all increase solubility with Choices *A*, *B*, and *C*. Powdered hot chocolate is an example to consider. Heating, Choice *A*, and stirring, Choice *B*, make it dissolve faster. Regarding Choice *C*, powder is in chunks that collectively result in a very large surface area, as opposed to a chocolate bar that has a very small relative surface area. The powdered form dramatically increases solubility. Decreasing the solvent (usually water) will decrease solubility, therefore, Choice *D* is correct.

13. A: The quantity of a solute in a solution can be calculated by multiplying the molarity of the solution by the volume. The equivalence point is the point at which an unknown solute has completely reacted with a known solute concentration. The limiting reactant is the reactant completely consumed by a reaction. The theoretical yield is the maximum quantity of product produced by a reaction, according to stoichiometric ratios.

14. C: Choice *C* is the correct answer. Colligative properties will be dependent on the number of particles and not on the nature of the solute. The molality of a solution (solute and solvent) is given by the moles of solute per kilogram of solvent. The boiling point elevation can be given by the following formula:

$$\Delta T_b = m \times i \times k_b$$

In this equation, ΔT_b is the change in boiling point, m is the molality of the solution (moles of solute per kilogram of solvent), i is the Van't Hoff factor, and k_b is the molal boiling point constant.

The number of particles is reflected in the equation for boiling point elevation by the Van't Hoff factor. All concentrations are the same (0.5 m), and the solvent is the same (k_b =0.51°C /m). The main difference is the value of the Van't Hoff coefficient (i). Each substance or solute will have a different number of particles in the solution.

Given that $\Delta T_b \propto i$ (m and k_b are the same for all solutions), the largest change in the boiling point elevation will correspond to the solute with the greatest Van't Hoff factor. Choice *C*, aluminum (III) acetate, has a factor of 4 since the salt breaks up into one aluminum ion and three acetate ions; it is the correct answer. The remaining choices all have factors less than aluminum (III) acetate. Ethanol, potassium nitrate, and barium chloride have Van't Hoff factors of 1, 2, and 3, respectively.

15. D: Choice *D* is the correct answer. According to Le Chatelier's principle, the equilibrium of the chemical system will change when it's subjected to pressure and temperature changes. A change in pressure will shift the equilibrium and will be dependent on the gaseous moles of the reactant and products. There are two moles of gaseous reactant and three moles of gaseous products. When the pressure decreases, the equilibrium will shift in the direction that accommodates or maximizes the loss in pressure. The reaction shifts to the right, where there are more moles of the product.

$$2\ NO_2F(g) \rightarrow F_2(g) + 2\ NO_2(g)$$

When the gas pressure increases, the equilibrium will shift in a direction that minimizes the increase in pressure—the reaction shifts to the left towards the reactant where there are fewer moles of gas.

$$2\ NO_2F(g) \leftarrow F_2(g) + 2\ NO_2(g)$$

Therefore, if the pressure of the reaction is decreased, the equilibrium or reaction rate will shift to the right to produce a greater yield of F_2 and NO_2. Choice *D* is correct. Choice *A* is incorrect since the reaction rate would increase. Choices *B* and *C* are incorrect since the number of products will increase.

16. D: Choice *D* is the correct answer. The question requires finding the equilibrium concentration of the reaction product. The amount of initial reactants is provided but must be converted to a concentration unit. The concentration of a substance is expressed in mol/liter (molarity=mol/liter) and represented by brackets '[ ]'. Given 0.40 mol of N_2 and 0.40 mol of O_2 in a 2.0 L flask (assuming constant volume), the initial concentrations are:

$$[N_2] = \frac{0.40\ \text{mol}}{2.0\ \text{L}} = 0.20\ \text{M}$$

$$[O_2] = \frac{0.40\ \text{mol}}{2.0\ \text{L}} = 0.20\ \text{M}$$

A table of the initial, change, and equilibrium concentrations (ICE table) is shown below.

	$N_2(g)$ +	$O_2(g)$ ⇄	$2\ NO(g)$
Initial	0.20 M	0.20 M	0
Change	$-x$	$-x$	$+2x$
Equilibrium	$0.20\ \text{M} - x$	$0.20\ \text{M} - x$	$2x$

The equilibrium values are given by adding and subtracting the initial and change values. The equilibrium expression will incorporate the equilibrium values from the table. Note that $K_c = 0.10$

$$K_c = \frac{[NO]^2}{[N_2][O_2]} = 0.10$$

$$0.10 = \frac{[NO]^2}{[N_2][O_2]} = \frac{[2x]^2}{[0.20 - x][0.20 - x]} = \frac{[2x]^2}{[0.20 - x]^2} = \left(\frac{2x}{0.20 - x}\right)^2$$

The last term of the previous expression was further simplified by taking the perfect square.

$$0.10 = \left(\frac{2x}{0.20 - x}\right)^2$$

Take the square root of both sides:

$$\sqrt{0.10} = \frac{2x}{0.20 - x}$$

$$(0.20 - x)\sqrt{0.10} = 2x$$

$$0.20\sqrt{0.10} - x\sqrt{0.10} = 2x$$

$$0.20\sqrt{0.10} = x\sqrt{0.10} + 2x$$

$$0.20\sqrt{0.10} = x(\sqrt{0.10} + 2)$$

$$x = \frac{0.20\sqrt{0.10}}{\sqrt{0.10} + 2} = \frac{0.06324}{2.316} = 0.0273$$

Plugging this value into the equilibrium concentration of NO yields:

$$2x = [\text{NO}]$$

$$2(0.0273) = [\text{NO}] = 0.055\ \text{M}$$

The equilibrium concentration is 0.055 M, so Choice *D* is the best answer. Choice *A* is incorrect since it corresponds to an initial concentration of 0.40 M, which can occur if 0.40 mol is not divided by 2.0 L. Choice *B*, represents an answer choice where the change in NO in the ICE table is x instead of $2x$. Choice *C* is incorrect since it is half the equilibrium concentration of NO (0.0273), which must be multiplied by two.

17. A: Choice *A* is the correct answer. First, calculate the moles of the acid and base. The moles of NaOH and $\text{HC}_2\text{H}_3\text{O}_2$ is given by:

$$moles_{\text{NaOH}} = \text{Molarity} \times \text{Volume} = (0.500\ \text{M})(0.0250\ \text{L}) = 0.0125\ \text{moles of NaOH}$$

$$moles_{\text{HC}_2\text{H}_3\text{O}_2} = \text{Molarity} \times \text{Volume} = (0.250\ \text{M})(0.0500\ \text{L}) = 0.0125\ \text{moles of}\ \text{HC}_2\text{H}_3\text{O}_2$$

The reaction will result in the formation of 0.0125 moles of water and 0.0125 moles of the basic salt $\text{NaC}_2\text{H}_3\text{O}_2$. A basic salt is created from the reaction of a strong base and weak acid; it will produce a basic solution that has a pH greater than 7. The concentration of the salt must include the total volume, which is:

$$\text{Total volume} = 25.0\ \text{ml} + 50.0\ \text{ml} = 75.0\ \text{ml or}\ 0.0750\ \text{L}$$

Now find the molarity of the salt.

$$Molarity_{\text{NaC}_2\text{H}_3\text{O}_2} = \frac{0.0125\ \text{moles}}{0.0750\ \text{L}} = 0.167\ \text{M}$$

Set up an ICE table to write an equilibrium expression.

	$NaC_2H_3O_2$ +	$H_2O(l)$ ⇄	$HC_2H_3O_2$ +	OH^-
Initial	0.167 M		0	0
Change	$-x$		$+x$	$+x$
Equilibrium	$0.167\text{ M} - x$		x	x

Since the expression represents the formation of a hydroxide ion, find $K_b\ from\ K_a$

$$K_b = \frac{K_w}{K_a} = \frac{1 \times 10^{-14}}{1.8 \times 10^{-5}} = 5.55 \times 10^{-10}$$

Now set up the equilibrium expression:

$$K_b = \frac{[HC_2H_3O_2][OH^-]}{[NaC_2H_3O_2]} = \frac{[x][x]}{[0.167 - x]} \sim \frac{x^2}{0.167}$$

Since K_b is much less than 1, the last term assumes the value of x is relatively small compared to the concentration of the salt. Rearranging the expression:

$$x = \sqrt{K_b(0.167)} = \sqrt{5.55 \times 10^{-10} \times 0.167} = 9.63 \times 10^{-6}$$

Now find the pOH:

$$pOH = -\log([OH^-]) = -\log(9.62 \times 10^{-6}) = 5.016$$

The pH of the solution is basic due to neutralization with a strong base and weak acid, which forms a basic salt.

$$pH = 14 - pOH = 14 - 5.016 = 8.98$$

Choice *B* is incorrect and provides the pOH. Choice *C* is incorrect since it uses K_a and takes the pOH to give 2.76. Choice *D* is incorrect since it uses K_a and takes the pOH to give 2.76, followed by the calculation of the pH to give 11.23.

18. C: When dissolved into pure water, sodium hydroxide ($NaOH$) dissociates into Na^+ and OH^- ions. However, in a solution containing potassium hydroxide, there will be some hydroxide ions already present. Since there are already OH^- ions, the common ion effect takes place, reducing the effective solubility of $NaOH$, so Choice *B* is incorrect. Choice *A* is incorrect because if there's too much $NaOH$, it might not be able to completely dissociate. Choice *D* is incorrect because some amount of $NaOH$ will still dissolve, but potentially less than in pure water. Therefore, *C* is the correct choice.

19. C: These are the coefficients that follow the law of conservation of matter. The coefficient times the subscript of each element should be the same on both sides of the equation.

20. A: Choice *A* is the correct answer. First, determine the molarity of the solution.

$$\text{Molarity} = \frac{\text{moles of salt}}{\text{liters of solution}} = \frac{2.00\times10^{-3}\text{ mol}}{2.00\text{ L}} = 1.00 \times 10^{-3}\text{ M}$$

Set up an ICE table and the solubility product expression:

	MX_2 ⇄	M +	$2X^-$
Initial		0	0
Change		$+x$	$+2x$
Equilibrium		x	$2x$

$$K_{sp} = [M][X]^2$$

$$K_{sp} = [x][2x]^2$$

$$K_{sp} = (x)(4x^2)$$

$$K_{sp} = 4x^3$$

Substitute $x = 1.00 \times 10^{-3}$

$$K_{sp} = 4(1.00 \times 10^{-3})^3 = 4.00 \times 10^{-9}$$

Choice *B* is incorrect and corresponds to an expression given by $K_{sp} = [x][x]^2$. Choice C is incorrect and corresponds to the expression $K_{sp} = [x][x]^2/[x]$. Choice *D* is incorrect and corresponds to the expression $K_{sp} = [x][2x]^2/[x]$. Choices *C* and *D* should not include an expression for the salt since it does not change the solubility product expression.

21. A: Oxidation is when a substance loses electrons in a chemical reaction, and reduction is when a substance gains electrons. Any element by itself has a charge of 0, as iron and oxygen do on the reactant side. In the ionic compound formed, iron has a +3 charge, and oxygen has a −2 charge. Because iron had a zero charge that then changed to +3, it means that it lost three electrons and was oxidized. Oxygen gained two electrons and was reduced.

22. C: Fission occurs when heavy nuclei are split, and it is currently an energy source that fuels power plants. Fusion, on the other hand, is the combining of small nuclei and produces far more energy, and it is the primary nuclear reaction that powers stars like the sun. Harnessing the extreme energy released by fusion has proven difficult so far, which is unfortunate because its waste products are not radioactive, while waste produced by fission typically is.

23. B: Choice *B* is the correct answer. The relationship between the ΔG°_{rxn} and the equilibrium constant is given by the following equations:

$$K = e^{\left(\frac{-\Delta G^\circ_{rxn}}{RT}\right)} \text{ or } \Delta G^\circ_{rxn} = -RTln(K)$$

$$R = 8.314 \frac{\text{J}}{\text{mol} \times \text{K}} \text{ and } T \text{ (Kelvin)} = 273.15 + 25 = 298.15\text{K}$$

$$\Delta G^\circ_{rxn} = -\left(8.314 \frac{\text{J}}{\text{mol} \times \text{K}}\right)(298.15K) \times ln(4.50 \times 10^{-4}) = 19{,}102 \frac{\text{J}}{\text{mol}} \text{ or } 19.1 \frac{\text{kJ}}{\text{mol}}$$

Since the equilibrium constant is much less than zero, the forward reaction is not favorable; the reaction is not spontaneous since the standard Gibbs free energy is positive. Therefore, Choices *A* and *C* can be eliminated since these choices neglect one minus sign in the standard Gibbs free energy formula, making the value negative. Choices *C* and *D* are incorrect since the temperature used is given in Celsius.

24. D: Choice *D* is the correct answer. To predict if the reaction is spontaneous, the relationship between $\Delta G, \Delta H, \Delta S,$ and T must be understood. A reaction is spontaneous under standard conditions where ΔG° is negative. Recall that:

$$\Delta G^{\circ} = \Delta H^{\circ} - T\Delta S^{\circ}$$

The sign of ΔG° will be dependent on the magnitude and signs of ΔH° and S°, in addition to the temperature. The relationship between these values is shown below.

Outcome	ΔG°	ΔH°	$-T\Delta S^{\circ}$	ΔS°
Spontaneous at all temperatures	$-$(negative)	$-$(negative)	$-$(negative)	$+$(positive)
Nonspontaneous at all temperatures	$+$(positive)	$+$(positive)	$+$(positive)	$-$(negative)
Spontaneous at low temperatures but nonspontaneous at high temperatures	$-$(negative) or $+$(positive)	$-$(negative)	$+$(positive)	$-$(negative)
Spontaneous at high temperatures but nonspontaneous at low temperatures.	$-$(negative) or $+$(positive)	$+$(positive)	$-$(negative)	$+$(positive)

Given that the sign of ΔH° is negative, find the sign of $\Delta S^{\circ}$by looking at the molar entropy values. In the combustion of butane, there are 7.5 moles of reactant and 9 moles of product.

$$C_4H_{10}(g) + \frac{13}{2}O_2(g) \rightarrow 4\ CO_2(g) + 5\ H_2O(g)$$

The reaction will have a positive ΔS° since the entropy of gas increases. Therefore, in the first row of the table shown above, since enthalpy is negative and entropy is positive, the reaction will be spontaneous (negative Gibbs free energy) at increasing temperatures.

25. A: Choice *A* is the correct answer. The connection between the cell potential, E°, and the standard Gibbs free energy, ΔG°, is:

$$\Delta G^{\circ} = -RTln(K) \text{ where } -RTln(K) = -nFE^{\circ}$$

$$-nFE^{\circ} = \Delta G^{\circ} \rightarrow E^{\circ} = \frac{\Delta G^{\circ}}{-nF}$$

The value n is equal to the number of electrons transferred, and F is Faraday's constant.

$$E^{\circ} = \frac{\Delta G^{\circ}}{-nF} = \frac{(15.75 \text{ kJ})\left(\frac{1000\text{J}}{1 \text{ kJ}}\right)}{-(2 \text{ mol e}^-)\left(\frac{96485 \text{ C}}{1 \text{ mol e}^-}\right)} = -0.08162\frac{\text{J}}{\text{C}} \text{ or } -0.08162 \text{ V}$$

Choice *B* is incorrect since $n = 2$ is removed from the equation. Choice *C* is incorrect since the negative sign is dropped, and Choice *D* is wrong since the equivalency equation $1 \text{ kJ} = 1000 \text{ J}$ is not included.

26. C: The lower subscript to the left of the chemical symbol indicates the atomic number (Z), which is equal to the number of protons. There are 88 protons in radium and also 88 electrons because the number of electrons must equal to the number of protons in a neutral atom. The upper left superscript indicates the mass number (A), which is the sum of the protons and neutrons. To find the number of neutrons use the following equation:

$$\text{neutron number } (N) + \text{atomic number } (Z) = \text{mass number } (A)$$

$$N = A - Z$$

$$N = 226 - 88 = 138$$

27. D: The correct set of quantum numbers is determined according to the number of electrons for a given atom. The possible values of l and m_l are given by the formulas $l = n - 1$ and $m_l = 2l + 1$. For example, in Choice *A*, the possible quantum numbers are:

$$n = 2$$

$$l = n - 1 = 2 - 1 = 1$$

$$m_l = 2l + 1 = 2(1) + 1 = 3 \quad \{-1, 0, +1\}$$

Choices *A* and *B* contain an allowed set of quantum numbers. Choice *C* also shows a unique set of quantum number belonging to $n = 1$. However, for Choice *D*, $m_l = -2$ is not possible because $l = 1$.

28. C: The question is asking to find the number of oxygen atoms (not molecular oxygen, O_2). Use the following unit conversion roadmap to determine the number of oxygen atoms.

$$\text{liters of CO}_2 \rightarrow \text{moles of CO}_2 \rightarrow \text{moles of O} \rightarrow \#\text{ of O atoms}$$

$$0.500 \text{ L CO}_2 \times \frac{1 \text{ mol CO}_2}{22.4 \text{ L CO}_2} \times \frac{2 \text{ mol O atoms}}{1 \text{ mol CO}_2} \times \frac{6.022 \times 10^{23} \text{ O atoms}}{1 \text{ mol O atoms}} = 2.69 \times 10^{22} \text{ O atoms}$$

Note that the molar volume is used to convert liters of gas to moles. If the substance were a solid (e.g., dry ice or solid carbon dioxide), then one would use its molar mass to convert to moles. Then, using Avogadro's number, the moles of a substance can be converted to the number of gas molecules. However, there are two moles of O atoms per one mole of carbon dioxide, so this stoichiometric relationship must be accounted for in the equation above. Therefore, Choice *A* is incorrect. Choices *B* and *D* are not correct because those answers refer to molecular oxygen.

29. A: To find the mass of caffeine, use the following roadmap conversion:

$$\text{molecule of caffeine} \xrightarrow{\text{use } N_A} \text{moles of caffeine} \xrightarrow{\text{use molar mass}} \text{mass of caffeine}$$

The molar mass of caffeine is approximately 194.2 g/mol.

$$1 \text{ molecule caffeine} \times \frac{1 \text{ mol}}{6.022 \times 10^{23} \text{ molecules}} \times \frac{194.2 \text{ g caffeine}}{1 \text{ mol caffeine}} \times \frac{1 \text{ kg}}{1000 \text{ g}} = 3 \times 10^{-25} \text{ kg caffeine}$$

Choice *C* would have been a correct answer if the units were in grams. If the question asked for grams of one caffeine molecule, then formula above would have neglected the last conversion formula giving a value of 3×10^{-22} g.

30. A: The compound containing nitrogen and oxygen has an empirical formula of N_xO_y where x and y represent the whole number atom rations. If there are 1.51 g of oxygen, then the mass of nitrogen is:

$$\text{mass of nitrogen} = \text{mass of compound} - \text{mass of oxygen} = 2.04 \text{ g} - 1.51 \text{ g} = 0.53 \text{ g N}$$

The mass of each substance can now be converted to moles.

$$\text{Mass of nitrogen: } 0.53 \text{ g O} \times \frac{1 \text{ mol N}}{14.01 \text{ g N}} = 3.78 \times 10^{-2} \text{ mol N}$$

$$\text{Mass of oxygen: } 1.51 \text{ g O} \times \frac{1 \text{ mol O}}{16.00 \text{ g O}} = 9.44 \times 10^{-2} \text{ mol O}$$

To obtain x and y, divide by the smallest molar value between O and N, which is 3.78×10^{-2}.

$$x = \frac{3.78 \times 10^{-2} \text{ mol N}}{3.78 \times 10^{-2} \text{ mol}} = 1 \text{ for N}$$

$$y = \frac{9.44 \times 10^{-2} \text{ mol O}}{3.78 \times 10^{-2} \text{ mol}} = 2.5 \text{ for O}$$

The *y* term is not a whole number, so each term must be multiplied by two giving $x = 2$ and $y = 5$. Therefore, the empirical formula is N_2O_5.

31. C: The formula mass of the compound can be determined through the following computation:

$$7.61 \times 10^{20} \text{ molecules } (SO_2)_n \times \frac{1 \text{ mol}}{6.022 \times 10^{23} \text{ molecules}} = 1.26 \times 10^{-3} \text{ mol } (SO_2)_n$$

$$\text{molar mass} = \frac{0.162 \text{ g } (SO_2)_n}{1.26 \times 10^{-3} \text{ mol } (SO_2)_n} = 129 \text{ g/mol}$$

The value of n can then be calculated dividing the molar mass by the molar mass of the empirical formula.

$$n = \frac{\text{formula or molar mass (g mol}^{-1}\text{)}}{\text{empirical formula mass (g mol}^{-1}\text{)}}$$

$$n = \frac{129 \text{ g mol}^{-1}}{64.07 \text{ g mol}^{-1}} \approx 2$$

Therefore, using the value of n, the molecular formula can also be found:

$$(SO_2)_n = (SO_2)_2 = S_2O_4$$

32. D: To find the mass of oxygen, convert the molar amount of sucrose to the mass in grams, then multiply by the percentage of oxygen.

$$1.50 \text{ mol } C_{12}H_{22}O_{11} \times \frac{342.296 \text{ g } C_{12}H_{22}O_{11}}{1 \text{ mol } C_{12}H_{22}O_{11}} = 513 \text{ g } C_{12}H_{22}O_{11}$$

$$\text{mass \% O} = \frac{176.0 \text{ g O}}{342.296 \text{ g } C_{12}H_{22}O_{11}} \times 100\% = 51.42\%$$

Now multiply the mass of the sample and the fraction of oxygen in the sample.

$$\text{mass of oxygen in sample} = \frac{51.42\%}{100.0\%} \times \text{mass of sucrose} = 0.5142 \times 513 \text{ g} = 264 \text{ g O}$$

33. B: The maximum amount of carbon dioxide created from the reaction, according to its stoichiometry, is the theoretical yield. To find the theoretical yield, determine which reactant produces the least amount of carbon dioxide using the stoichiometry from the reaction.

$$3 \text{ mol CO} \times \frac{2 \text{ mol } CO_2}{2 \text{ mol CO}} = 3 \text{ mol } CO_2$$

$$1 \text{ mol } O_2 \times \frac{2 \text{ mol } CO_2}{1 \text{ mol } O_2} = 2 \text{ mol } CO_2$$

Oxygen is the limiting reactant because it produces fewer moles of carbon dioxide. The theoretical yield is only two moles of carbon dioxide. Carbon monoxide is the excess reactant because it is not entirely consumed and would produce one mole of carbon dioxide if the gas reacted to completion.

34. A: First determine the limiting reactant and theoretical yield of carbon monoxide.

$$2 \text{ mol } CO_2 \times \frac{2 \text{ mol CO}}{1 \text{ mol } CO_2} = 4 \text{ mol CO}$$

$$3 \text{ mol C} \times \frac{2 \text{ mol CO}}{1 \text{ mol C}} = 6 \text{ mol CO}$$

The limiting reactant is carbon dioxide, which means that the theoretical yield is four moles of carbon monoxide. Carbon (charcoal) is the excess reactant and produces two extra moles of carbon monoxide.

35. D: To find the correct theoretical yield of barium sulfate, determine the limiting reactant. The molar masses of aluminum sulfate and barium chloride are 342.14 g/mol and 208.23 g/mol.

$$3.52 \text{ g } Al_2(SO_4)_3 \times \frac{1 \text{ mol } Al_2(SO_4)_3}{342.17 \text{ g } Al_2(SO_4)_3} \times \frac{3 \text{ mol } BaSO_4}{1 \text{ mol } Al_2(SO_4)_3} = 3.09 \times 10^{-2} \text{ mol } BaSO_4$$

$$4.06 \text{ g } BaCl_2 \times \frac{1 \text{ mol } BaCl_2}{208.23 \text{ g } BaCl_2} \times \frac{3 \text{ mol } BaSO_4}{3 \text{ mol } BaCl_2} = 1.95 \times 10^{-2} \text{ mol } BaSO_4$$

It is not necessary to convert moles of barium sulfate to mass to find the limiting reactant. Barium chloride is the limiting reactant because it produces fewer moles of barium sulfate. To find the theoretical yield of barium sulfate in grams, convert the smaller molar amount of barium sulfate to grams.

$$1.95 \times 10^{-2} \text{ mol } BaSO_4 \times \frac{233.40 \text{ g } BaSO_4}{1 \text{ mol } BaSO_4} = 4.55 \text{ g } BaSO_4$$

On an important note, it's useful to perform the calculation in one operation to avoid any potential rounding error: For example, the previous calculations may be performed in one operation:

$$4.06 \text{ g } BaCl_2 \times \frac{1 \text{ mol } BaCl_2}{208.23 \text{ g } BaCl_2} \times \frac{3 \text{ mol } BaSO_4}{3 \text{ mol } BaCl_2} \times \frac{233.40 \text{ g } BaSO_4}{1 \text{ mol } BaSO_4} = 4.55 \text{ g } BaSO_4$$

In other words, if possible, rounding should be done at the end of a calculation. If the theoretical yield of barium sulfate in moles was asked for, then 1.95×10^{-2} mol $BaSO_4$ is acceptable.

36. C: The following equation gives the percent yield:

$$\text{percent yield} = \frac{\text{actual yield (experiment)}}{\text{theoretical yield}} \times 100\% = \frac{3.96 \text{ g}}{4.55 \text{ g}} \times 100\% = 87.0\%$$

Note that the percent yield is given as a percentage and that the theoretical yield, found by using stoichiometry, is always greater than the actual yield. Experimentally, it can be difficult to collect all the barium sulfate. Consider the scenario where you are baking a cake. Not all the batter (eggs, flour, etc.) goes into the cooking pan, as some of it gets left behind in the mixing bowl.

37. C: The balanced chemical equation is:

$$Al_2(SO_4)_3(aq) + 3 \text{ } BaCl_2(aq) \rightarrow 3 \text{ } BaSO_4(s) + 2 \text{ } AlCl_3(aq)$$

For simplification, rounding is shown in each step of the following calculation:

$$3.52 \text{ g } Al_2(SO_4)_3 \times \frac{1 \text{ mol } Al_2(SO_4)_3}{342.17 \text{ g } Al_2(SO_4)_3} \times \frac{3 \text{ mol } BaSO_4}{1 \text{ mol } Al_2(SO_4)_3} = 3.09 \times 10^{-2} \text{ mol } BaSO_4$$

$$4.06 \text{ g } BaCl_2 \times \frac{1 \text{ mol } BaCl_2}{208.23 \text{ g } BaCl_2} \times \frac{3 \text{ mol } BaSO_4}{3 \text{ mol } BaCl_2} = 1.95 \times 10^{-2} \text{ mol } BaSO_4$$

Aluminum sulfate is the excess reactant because it produces a greater molar amount of barium sulfate. One method to determine the excess amount is to perform the following calculations:

$$3.09 \times 10^{-2}\ \text{mol BaSO}_4 - 1.95 \times 10^{-2}\ \text{mol BaSO}_4 = 1.14\ \times 10^{-2}\ \text{excess moles of BaSO}_4$$

Now convert the excess moles of barium sulfate to grams of aluminum sulfate:

$$1.14\ \times 10^{-2}\ \text{excess moles of BaSO}_4 \times \frac{1\ \text{mol Al}_2(\text{SO}_4)_3}{3\ \text{mol of BaSO}_4} \times \frac{342.17\ \text{g Al}_2(\text{SO}_4)_3}{1\ \text{mol Al}_2(\text{SO}_4)_3} = 1.30\ \text{g Al}_2(\text{SO}_4)_3$$

Note that if rounding were done at the very last step, a value of 1.30 g of $Al_2(SO_4)_3$ would have also been obtained. Alternatively, the mass of barium chloride could have been used to calculate the limiting mass of aluminum sulfate. The difference between the two values would give the excess amount of aluminum sulfate.

$$4.06\ \text{g BaCl}_2 \times \frac{1\ \text{mol BaCl}_2}{208.23\ \text{g BaCl}_2} \times \frac{1\ \text{mol Al}_2(\text{SO}_4)_3}{3\ \text{mol BaCl}_2} \times \frac{342.17\ \text{g Al}_2(\text{SO}_4)_3}{1\ \text{mol Al}_2(\text{SO}_4)_3} = 2.22\ \text{g Al}_2(\text{SO}_4)_3$$

$$\text{excess mass of Al}_2(\text{SO}_4)_3 = \text{initial mass of Al}_2(\text{SO}_4)_3 - 2.22\ \text{g} = 3.52\ \text{g} - 2.22\ \text{g} = 1.30\ \text{g Al}_2(\text{SO}_4)_3$$

38. D: The reaction quotient will need to be determined and compared to the equilibrium constant to determine if a precipitate will form. First, write a balanced equation and calculate the amount of each reactant from their concentrations and initial volumes:

$$2\ \text{AgNO}_3(\text{aq}) + \text{Na}_2\text{SO}_4(\text{aq}) \rightarrow \text{Ag}_2\text{SO}_4(\text{s}) + 2\ \text{NaNO}_3(\text{aq})$$

$$\text{mol AgNO}_3 = 0.100\ \text{L} \times 0.05\ \frac{\text{mol AgNO}_3}{\text{L}} = 5.0 \times 10^{-3}\ \text{mol AgNO}_3 = 5.0 \times 10^{-3}\ \text{mol Ag}^+$$

$$\text{mol Na}_2\text{SO}_4 = 0.0500\ \text{L} \times 0.05\ \frac{\text{mol Na}_2\text{SO}_4}{\text{L}} = 2.5 \times 10^{-3}\ \text{mol Na}_2\text{SO}_4 = 2.5 \times 10^{-3}\ \text{mol SO}_4^{2-}$$

The total volume after adding sodium sulfate is 150 mL or 0.150 L. The molarity of each ion is:

$$[\text{Ag}^+] = \frac{5.0 \times 10^{-3}\ \text{mol AgNO}_3}{0.150\ \text{L}} = 0.0333\ \text{M}$$

$$[\text{SO}_4^{2-}] = \frac{2.5 \times 10^{-3}\ \text{mol Na}_2\text{SO}_4}{0.150\ \text{L}} = 0.0166\ \text{M}$$

Now write out the dissociation of silver sulfate and set up an ICE table:

$$Ag_2SO_4(s) \rightleftharpoons 2\,Ag^+(aq) + SO_4^{2-}(aq)$$

	$[Ag^+]$	$[SO_4^{2-}]$
Initial	0	0
Change	$+2S$	$+S$
Equilibrium	$2S$	S

Expressed in terms of molar solubility, the reaction quotient for the dissociation of silver sulfate is:

$$Q = [Ag^+]^2[SO_4^{2-}] = (2S)^2(S) = 4S^3$$

Now calculate Q:

$$Q = [Ag^+]^2[SO_4^{2-}] = (0.0333\,)^2(0.0166) = 1.85 \times 10^{-5}$$

Because $Q > K_{sp}$, this indicates that there will be a precipitate. The concentration of silver and the sulfate ion are both in excess. This can be proven by comparing the solution to the ion concentrations at equilibrium. Since $K_{sp} = 6.9 \times 10^{-15}$ for silver sulfate, solving for its molar solubility at equilibrium would give:

$$[SO_4^{2-}] = S = 1.2 \times 10^{-5}\text{M and } [Ag^+] = 2S = 2.4 \times 10^{-5}\text{ M}$$

For the molar solubility in the given solution, use the calculated reaction quotient $Q = 1.9 \times 10^{-5}$,

$$[SO_4^{2-}] = S = 1.7 \times 10^{-2}\text{ M and } [Ag^+] = 2S = 3.3 \times 10^{-2}\text{ M}$$

These concentrations are much greater, so the ions will be present in excess and form a precipitate of silver sulfate.

39. C: Choice *C* is the correct answer. First, assign oxidation states. Oxygen has a -2 oxidation state. There are three oxygen atoms, so $3x(-2) = -6$, which means nitrogen in nitrate ion has an oxidation of $+5$. For nitrogen monoxide, since oxygen has a -2 state, then nitrogen must have a $+2$ state since nitrogen monoxide is neutral.

$$\overbrace{NO_3^-}^{+5}(aq) \rightarrow \overbrace{NO}^{+2}(g)$$

Since the oxidation state for the reaction goes from +5 to +2, the reaction is reduced. Now balance the equation by adding electrons.

$$3\,e^- + \overbrace{NO_3^-}^{+5}(aq) \rightarrow \overbrace{NO}^{+2}(g)$$

Do not confuse the oxidation state of the nitrogen atoms with the overall charge. The reactant side has a charge of 1- from the nitrate ion and a charge of 3- from the three electrons. Because the reaction is in a basic solution, balance the charge of the reactant side with OH^-.

$$\overbrace{3\ \mathrm{e}^- + \overbrace{\mathrm{NO_3^-}}^{+5}\ \mathrm{(aq)}}^{4-\ \text{charge}} \rightarrow \overbrace{\overbrace{\mathrm{NO}}^{+2}\ \mathrm{(g)} + 4\mathrm{OH}^-}^{4-\text{charge}}$$

The reactant and product sides both have an overall charge of 4-. Now balance the half-reaction by adding water to the reactant side. A coefficient of two is placed in front of the water formula to balance the number of oxygen and hydrogen atoms.

$$2\ \mathrm{H_2O(l)} + 3\ \mathrm{e}^- + \mathrm{NO_3^-(aq)} \rightarrow \mathrm{NO(g)} + 4\ \mathrm{OH}^-$$

If the reaction was in an acidic solution, then a hydronium ion would be added to the reactant side (instead of a hydroxide ion to the product side, as shown above).

$$\overbrace{4\ \mathrm{H}^+ + 3\ \mathrm{e}^- + \overbrace{\mathrm{NO_3^-}}^{+5}\ \mathrm{(aq)}}^{0\ \text{charge}} \rightarrow \overbrace{\overbrace{\mathrm{NO}}^{+2}\ \mathrm{(g)}}^{0\ \text{charge}}$$

The reactant side has an overall net charge of zero like the product side. Now balance hydrogen by adding water to the product side. A coefficient of two is placed in front of the water formula to balance the number of oxygen and hydrogen atoms.

$$4\ \mathrm{H}^+ + 3\ \mathrm{e}^- + \mathrm{NO_3^-(aq)} \rightarrow \mathrm{NO\ (g)} + 2\ \mathrm{H_2O(l)}$$

Choice *B* is incorrect since that reaction is balanced in an acidic solution. Choice *A* is similar to Choice *B* and is incorrect since water is on the reactant side, while hydronium ion and electrons are on the product side. Choice *D* is incorrect since the hydroxide ion is placed in the reactant, while water and electrons are on the product side.

40. A: The mass of silver(I) chloride can be converted to a molar amount, which can then be equated to the known molality (m).

$$250.0\ \mathrm{g\ AgCl} \times \frac{\mathrm{mol\ AgCl}}{143.32\ \mathrm{g\ AgCl}} = 1.744\ \mathrm{moles\ AgCl}$$

The molality (m) is given by:

$$m = \frac{\text{moles of solute}}{\text{kilograms of solvent}}$$

The solvent in this case is water, and the solute is silver(I) chloride. The mass of the solvent can be found by rearrangement:

$$m = 0.35\ \mathrm{mol\ kg^{-1}} = \frac{1.744\ \text{moles AgCl}}{\text{kilograms of water}}$$

$$\text{kilograms of water} = \frac{1.744\ \mathrm{mol\ AgCl}}{0.35\ \mathrm{mol\ kg^{-1}}} = 5.0\ \mathrm{kg\ water}$$

Choices *A* and *D* represent answers with the correct units. Choice *D* is incorrect because it gives the incorrect mass of the solvent. Choices *C* and *B* are incorrect because the units of mass should be in kilograms.

41. B: We can use the following equation to determine the volume of concentrated acid that is needed:

$$M_{\text{initial}}V_{\text{initial}} = M_{\text{final}}V_{\text{final}}$$

The final volume and molarity are 350 mL and 2.00 M HNO_3, which represents the final diluted concentration. The initial molarity represents the more concentrated acid, 5.00 M HNO_3. Solving for the initial volume gives:

$$V_{\text{initial}} = \frac{M_{\text{final}}V_{\text{final}}}{M_{\text{initial}}} = \frac{2.00\text{ M } \times 350\text{ mL}}{5.00\text{ M}} = 140\text{ mL of } 5.00\text{ M HNO}_3$$

Note that units of mL can be used because the molarity units cancel. Choices *C* and *D* do not represent the correct volumes. To prepare 350 mL of a 2.00 M HNO_3 solution, add 140 mL of 5.00 M HNO_3 into a large graduated cylinder, and dilute with water up to the 350 mL marker or add 210 mL of water to make a 2.00 M solution of HNO_3.

42. C: The endpoint refers to a point where a titration is stopped due to a color change (from the addition of an acid-base indicator), indicating equivalence has been reached. Equivalence occurs when the concentrations of hydronium ions and hydroxide ions are equal, $[H^+] = [OH^-]$. Based on this, the molarity of the diprotic acid can be found as follows:

$$\text{mol KOH} = 1.500\text{ M KOH} \times 35.00\text{ mL KOH} \times \frac{1\text{ L}}{1000\text{ mL}} = 5.250 \times 10^{-2}\text{ mol KOH}$$

Then the moles of the base must be converted to moles of acid (equivalence). However, because the acid is diprotic, the stoichiometric relationship must be taken into account.

$$5.250 \times 10^{-2}\text{ mol KOH} \times \frac{1\text{ mol H}_2\text{SO}_4}{2\text{ mol KOH}} = 2.626 \times 10^{-2}\text{ mol H}_2\text{SO}_4$$

Finally, the concentration of the acid is given by the following equation:

$$\text{M H}_2\text{SO}_4 = \frac{2.626 \times 10^{-2}\text{ mol H}_2\text{SO}_4}{15.00\text{ mL } \times \frac{1\text{ L}}{1000\text{ mL}}} = 1.750\text{ M H}_2\text{SO}_4$$

Note that a volume of 15.00 mL is used because this is the initial volume of the acid corresponding to a concentration of 1.750 M. The volume is not the combined volume of the acid and base because that volume represents a neutral solution.

43. C: The physical process is exothermic because liquid water has a kinetic energy greater than solid ice. Because the average kinetic energy is proportional to the temperature, as water freezes heat will flow out of the system.

$$H_2O(l) \rightarrow H_2O(s) + \text{heat}$$

The reaction is exothermic because heat is released from the molecular system. Consequently, because heat is lost by the chemical system ($-q_{system}$), then heat must be released or gained by the surroundings ($+q_{surroundings}$). The surroundings include the plant and air around it. If a plastic bag is placed over the plant, it will be able to trap or absorb the heat, thereby keeping the plant from completely freezing.

44. B: The formation of each compound is exothermic, so Choices *C* and *D* could not be correct choices.

$$\mathrm{Li + Br \rightarrow LiBr + heat} \quad \Delta H_f^\circ = -351.2\ \mathrm{kJ/mol}$$

$$\mathrm{Li + Cl \rightarrow LiCl + heat} \quad \Delta H_f^\circ = -408.6\ \mathrm{kJ/mol}$$

Choice *B* is correct because the amount of heat produced by the formation of lithium chloride is greater in magnitude compared to lithium bromide.

45. D: Note that the enthalpy of reaction for the combustion of methane is –802.3 kJ/mol. The problem is asking how much heat (in kJ) is produced from 1.50 kg, so it is expected that the value will be relatively large. To determine how much heat is produced, use the following conversion roadmap:

$$\text{kilograms of } \mathrm{CH_4} \xrightarrow{\frac{1000\ \mathrm{g}}{1\ \mathrm{kg}}} \text{grams of } \mathrm{CH_4} \xrightarrow{\frac{1\ \mathrm{mole\ CH_4}}{16.042\ \mathrm{g\ CH_4}}} \text{moles of } \mathrm{CH_4} \xrightarrow{\frac{-802.3\ \mathrm{kJ}}{1\ \mathrm{mole\ CH_4}}} \text{kilojoules}$$

The last conversion factor is important because it relates the stoichiometric relationship for moles and energy.

$$1.50\ \mathrm{kg\ CH_4} \times \frac{1000\ \mathrm{g}}{1\ \mathrm{kg}} \times \frac{1\ \mathrm{mol\ CH_4}}{16.042\ \mathrm{g\ CH_4}} \times \frac{-802.3\ \mathrm{kJ}}{1\ \mathrm{mol\ CH_4}} = -7.50 \times 10^4\ \mathrm{kJ}$$

Choices *B* and *C* are not correct because these values indicate heat is absorbed. Choice *A* is not correct because $\Delta H_{rxn}^\circ = -802.3$ kJ per mole of methane. Choice *D* is correct because this value indicates that the combustion of 1.50 kg of methane produces -7.50×10^4 kJ.

46. A: Use the following equation to find ΔH_{rxn}°.

$$\Delta H_{rxn}^\circ = \sum n\Delta H_f^\circ(\text{products}) - \sum n\Delta H_f^\circ(\text{reactants})$$

$$\Delta H_{rxn}^\circ = \left[\overbrace{1 \times -1675.7\frac{\mathrm{kJ}}{\mathrm{mol}}}^{\mathrm{Al_2O_3}} + \overbrace{2 \times 0\frac{\mathrm{kJ}}{\mathrm{mol}}}^{\mathrm{Fe}}\right] - \left[\overbrace{2 \times 0\frac{\mathrm{kJ}}{\mathrm{mol}}}^{\mathrm{Al}} + \overbrace{1 \times -824.2\frac{\mathrm{kJ}}{\mathrm{mol}}}^{\mathrm{Fe_2O_3}}\right] = -851.5\ \mathrm{kJ/mol}$$

The reaction is known as a thermite reaction and is exothermic. The value of –851.5 kJ is also correct (energy released per mole unit) because the equation says that for every two moles of aluminum that reacts, –851.5 kJ is produced. Or, for every 1 mole of iron(III) oxide that reacts, –851.5 kJ is produced.

47. C: The heat of reaction equation to determine the amount of heat that is lost from the metal and transferred to the water bath.

$$q_{\text{water}} = m \times C_{\text{s, water}} \times \Delta T$$

$$q_{\text{water}} = 100.0\text{ g} \times 4.184\text{ J/(g °C)} \times T_f - T_i$$

$$q_{\text{water}} = 100.0\text{ g} \times 4.184\text{ J/(g °C)} \times (37.0\text{ °C} - 25.0\text{°C}) = +5.02 \times 10^3\text{ J}$$

Note that 100.0 g of water is equivalent to 100.0 mL of water because the density is 1 g/mL. The initial temperature used should be that of water. Because of the amount of heat that is absorbed, the heat of reaction should be positive for water but negative for the metal.

$$+q_{\text{water}} = -q_{\text{metal}}$$

The heat of reaction is used again, but this time to find the specific heat capacity of the metal. Note that metal loses -5.02×10^3 J.

$$q_{\text{metal}} = m \times C_{\text{s, metal}} \times \Delta T$$

$$C_{\text{s, metal}} = \frac{q_{\text{metal}}}{m\Delta T} = \frac{-5.02 \times 10^3\text{ J}}{43.0\text{ g} \times (37.0\text{ °C} - 100.0\text{ °C})} = 1.85\text{ J/(g °C)}$$

The final temperature will be that of the water bath; thermal equilibrium is reached at that temperature. Because the initial temperature is greater than the final one, the ΔT will be negative. However, the negative signs will cancel out and give a positive specific heat (it must be positive).

48. D: Entropy is a measure of disorder or randomness in a system. The contraction of a gas either due to cooling or compression is an example where the change in entropy is negative ($-\Delta S$). As the volume decreases, the gas molecules/particles will occupy fewer spaces. The randomness decreases. The freezing of water is an example of where water molecules that were free to occupy different positions within a liquid now become fixed and ordered in the form of a solid and fixed crystal lattice. There is more order (less disorder), meaning that the change in entropy is negative ($-\Delta S$).

The reaction of solid calcium oxide and carbon dioxide gas to form solid calcium carbonate is an example of a system that becomes more ordered. The products do not contain a gas which can occupy different points in space. The entropy change is negative ($-\Delta S$). Adding sugar to water is an example where the entropy change is positive ($+\Delta S$). The molecular structure of sugar does not break down, rather the crystal structure of table sugar breaks apart and dissolves in water. The sugar molecules are free to move around in solution and are not restrained to fixed positions. The disorder increases.

49. A: The table below indicates that when both the enthalpy and entropy change are positive, then the reaction will be spontaneous only when the temperature increases (Scenario 4, last row). Initially, at low temperatures, the positive ΔH term has a greater than the $-T\Delta S$ term, which makes the Gibbs free energy positive. However, as the temperature increases, the $-T\Delta S$ term becomes more negative and makes a more negative contribution than ΔH, which will make the Gibbs free energy more negative.

ΔG Sign conventions for different signs of ΔH and ΔS						
Scenario	**Spontaneity**	K	ΔG	ΔH	$-T\Delta S$	ΔS
1	Spontaneous	> 1	$-$	$-$	$-$	$+$
2	Nonspontaneous	< 1	$+$	$+$	$+$	$-$
3	Spontaneous (low T) Nonspontaneous (high T)	> 1 < 1	$-$ $+$	$-$	$+$	$-$
4	Nonspontaneous (low T) Spontaneous (high T)	< 1 > 1	$+$ $-$	$+$	$-$	$+$

50. C: Based on the table displaying free energy sign conventions, assuming that $\Delta G \approx \Delta G^{\circ}$, the reaction would correspond to Scenario 3. The entropy of reaction is negative because there is more order as two molecules of a gas form one molecule. The enthalpy of reaction is negative and exothermic. If the temperature is low enough, the magnitude of the $-\Delta H$ term will be greater than the positive $T\Delta S$ term, and the reaction will be spontaneous. However, as the temperature is increased, the magnitude of the $+T\Delta S$ term will outweigh the $-\Delta H$ term, which will make the Gibbs free energy positive and nonspontaneous.

51. B: The nitrogen atom has the orbital and electron configuration shown below.

N: $1s^2 2s^2 2p^3$

The atomic number of nitrogen is seven, which means there are seven electrons for a neutral nitrogen atom. Nitrogen is found in the p-block (group 3A to 8A elements with p orbitals) within Group 5A in the periodic table. There are five valence electrons (group 5A), and three of those electrons are found in the p subshell. Counting from left to right (3A to 5A) in the p block indicates there will be three electrons dispersed in the p subshell. Note that subshell and orbital don't necessarily have the same meaning for the p subshell. There are three p orbitals in one p subshell, which contains three electrons. This p subshell belongs to the L shell and is denoted 2p. There is another subshell in the L shell called the 2s subshell, which contains only one orbital and holds a maximum of two electrons. Therefore, there are five electrons in the L shell for the nitrogen atom, which is shown by the orbital diagrams. The sum of the superscripts given by the electron configuration also gives the total number of electrons in nitrogen.

52. D: The figure below shows several orbital diagrams and quantum numbers corresponding to different electrons.

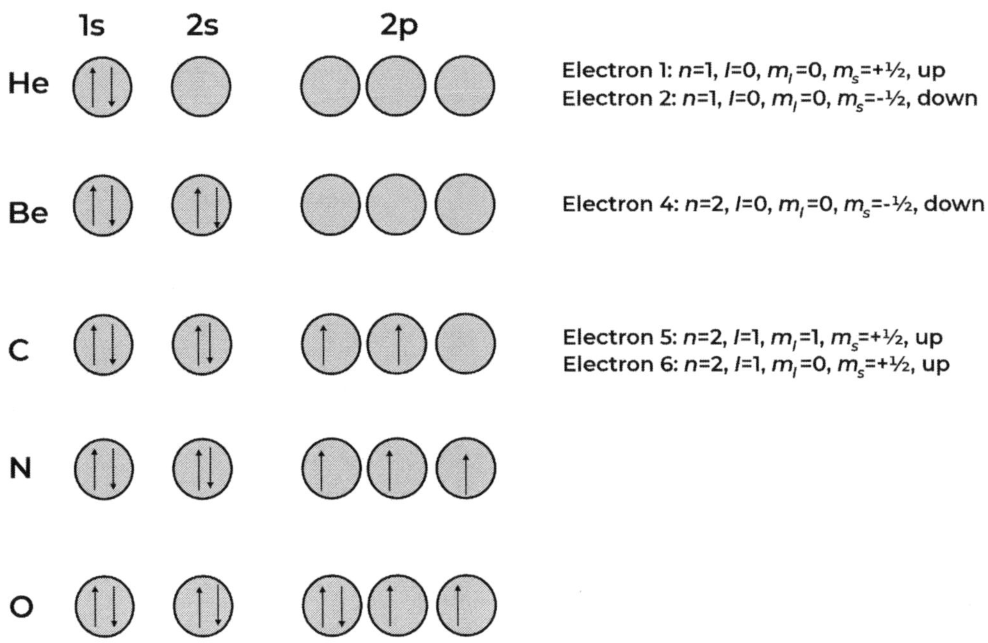

Recall that the Aufbau principle explains how electrons are added to orbitals, such that repulsion is minimized. Electrons are filled in the first three p orbitals with the same spin quantum number (i.e., $m_s = +\frac{1}{2}$). If a seventh electron were added to carbon, it would have the following set of quantum numbers:

$$n = 2, l = 1, m_l = +1, m_s = +\frac{1}{2}$$

Note that each answer choice has $n = 2$, meaning that only electrons are considered in the L shell or s and p subshells. The $l = 1$ quantum number is referring to the 2p subshell. Choices *A* and *C* could not be possible choices because each has $l = 0$, which corresponds to electrons in the 2s subshell. The eighth electron, based on the Aufbau principle, should be added to the p subshell. Choice *B* represents electron five (shown in the figure above) and has $m_s = +\frac{1}{2}$. Therefore, the answer choice must be *D*:

$$n = 2, l = 1, m_l = -1, m_s = -\frac{1}{2}$$

Note that, the magnetic quantum number ($m_l = -1$) will be the same as electron 5, but the spin quantum number must be $m_s = -\frac{1}{2}$ based on the Pauli exclusion principle.

53. A: Choices *B*, *C*, and *D* all represent possible electron configurations for nitrogen. However, Choice *A* does not represent a possible set of quantum number because the magnetic quantum number $m_l = -2$

is not an allowed value within the 2p subshell. The only permitted values when $l = 1$ are $m_l = -1, 0,$ and $+1$. Choices *B* and *C* correspond to electrons in the 1s and 2s subshells, while Choice *D* refers to an electron in the 2p subshell.

54. B: Nitrogen trifluoride is similar to ammonia (NH_3) and will have a molecular geometry that is trigonal pyramidal about the nitrogen atom. However, the electron-group geometry will be tetrahedral because there is a lone pair electron around the nitrogen atom, which will occupy space like a chemical bond. Three bonds and a lone pair will minimize repulsion by pointing or aligning to the corners of a tetrahedron.

55. B: The formal charges for each structure are shown below, according to the following formula:

$$\text{formal charge (FC)} = \text{\# of valence e}^- - \left(\frac{1}{2}\text{\# of bonding e}^- + \text{\# of nonbonding e}^-\right)$$

I II III

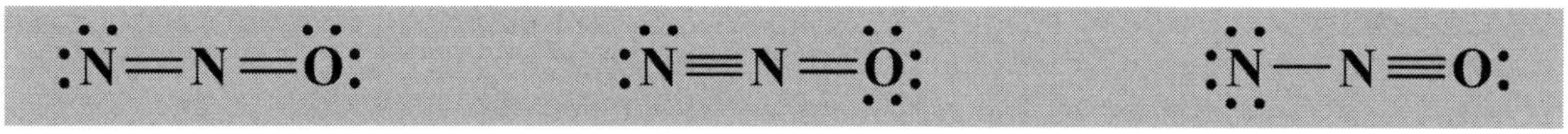

Structure I:

$$\text{formal charge for outer nitrogen atom} = 5 - \left(\frac{1}{2}(4) + 4\right) = -1$$

$$\text{formal charge for cental nitrogen atom} = 5 - \left(\frac{1}{2}(8) + 0\right) = +1$$

$$\text{formal charge for oxygen atom} = 6 - \left(\frac{1}{2}(4) + 4\right) = 0$$

Structure II:

$$\text{formal charge for outer nitrogen atom} = 5 - \left(\frac{1}{2}(6) + 2\right) = 0$$

$$\text{formal charge for central nitrogen atom} = 5 - \left(\frac{1}{2}(8) + 0\right) = +1$$

$$\text{formal charge for oxygen atom} = 6 - \left(\frac{1}{2}(2) + 6\right) = -1$$

Structure III:

$$\text{formal charge for outer nitrogen atom} = 5 - \left(\frac{1}{2}(2) + 6\right) = -2$$

$$\text{formal charge for central nitrogen atom} = 5 - \left(\frac{1}{2}(8) + 0\right) = +1$$

$$\text{formal charge for oxygen atom} = 6 - \left(\frac{1}{2}(6) + 2\right) = +1$$

All structures are neutrally charged. Structure II or Choice *B* is the most likely structure because the oxygen atom, the most electronegative, bears the negative charge, while the central nitrogen contains a positive charge. Choice *C* includes a positive charge on the oxygen atom, which makes the structure more unstable. Choice *A* has a structure with a negative charge on the outer nitrogen atom, the least electronegative atom. Choice *D* is also incorrect because it lists the formal charges incorrectly.

56. C: Choices *A*, *B*, and *D* are all true. In Choice *A*, the A to B phase transition corresponds to sublimation, a solid to gas transition. In Choice *B*, the change from C to B represents a liquid to gas transition called evaporation. In Choice *D*, the A to C transition is a solid to liquid transition called melting. Choice *C* is incorrect because although the slope of the provided phase diagram is positive, the slope of the solid-liquid equilibrium of water is negative. If the slope were positive for the phase diagram of water, then ice skating would be difficult or impossible. Because the solid-liquid equilibrium line has a negative slope, the pressure of the skates over the ice causes a solid to liquid phase transition, melting a small portion of ice under the skates, and thus reducing friction with the solid ice. However, if the slope was positive, at 0 °C, increasing the pressure would not result in a phase transition.

57. A: To determine the freezing point depression, first calculate the molality of the solution.

$$m = \frac{\text{moles of solute}}{\text{kilograms of solvent}} = \frac{1.00 \times 10^3 \text{ g } C_2H_6O_2 \times \frac{1 \text{ mol } C_2H_6O_2}{62.07 \text{ g } C_2H_6O_2}}{5.00 \times 10^3 \text{ g } H_2O \times \frac{1 \text{ kg}}{1000 \text{ g}}} = 3.22 \ \frac{\text{mol}}{\text{kg}}$$

Solving for the freezing point depression gives:

$$\Delta T_f = m \times K_f = 3.22 \text{ mol kg}^{-1} \times 1.86 \ \frac{°\text{C}}{\text{mol kg}^{-1}} = 5.99 \ °\text{C}$$

The actual freezing point can be found by expanding the left-hand side of the previous equation, and accounting for the negative sign.

$$\Delta T_f = T_{\text{solvent}} - T_{\text{solution}} = 0.00 \ °\text{C} - 5.99 \ °\text{C} = -5.99 \ °\text{C}$$

Note that 0.00 °C corresponds to the freezing point of pure water or the solvent.

58. C: The following form of the Arrhenius equation can be used to find the factor or ratio at which the rate constant increases.

$$\ln \frac{k_2}{k_1} = \frac{E_a}{R}\left(\frac{1}{T_1} - \frac{1}{T_2}\right)$$

The ratio or factor is given by the following rearrangement of the previous equation:

$$\frac{k_2}{k_1} = e^{\frac{E_a}{R}\left(\frac{1}{T_1}-\frac{1}{T_2}\right)}$$

Note that $E_a = 125\ \text{kJ/mol}$, $R = 8.314\ \text{J/(mol K)}$, $T_1 = 25.0 + 273.15\ \text{K}$, and $T_2 = 50.0 + 273.15\ \text{K}$.

First, evaluate the term within the exponent:

$$\frac{E_a}{R}\left(\frac{1}{T_1}-\frac{1}{T_2}\right) = \frac{125\ \text{kJ mol}^{-1}}{8.314\ \text{J mol}^{-1}\ \text{K}^{-1}} \times \frac{1000\ \text{J}}{1\ \text{kJ}} \times \left(\frac{1}{298.15\ \text{K}} - \frac{1}{323.15\ \text{K}}\right) = 3.901$$

Now evaluate the following expression:

$$\frac{k_2}{k_1} = e^{3.901} = 49.5$$

Increasing the temperature to 50.0 °C increases the rate by nearly 50 times the original rate.

59. B: Use the following equations to determine the time it takes for the element X to decay to 35.0 percent of its original amount:

$$\ln[\text{B}]_t = -kt + \ln[\text{B}]_0 \text{ and } t_{1/2} = \frac{0.693}{k}$$

First, find the rate constant:

$$k = \frac{0.693}{t_{1/2}} = \frac{0.693}{7.95\ \text{days}} = 0.087170\ \text{days}^{-1}$$

Now solve for t using the rearranged equation above.

$$\ln[\text{B}]_t = -kt + \ln[\text{B}]_0$$

$$\ln[\text{B}]_t - \ln[\text{B}]_0 = -kt$$

$$t = -\ln\left(\frac{[\text{B}]_t}{[\text{B}]_0}\right)\frac{1}{k}$$

The terms $[\text{B}]_t$ and $[\text{B}]_0$ represent the amount at time t (35%) and the initial amount at time zero. For simplification, suppose that $[\text{B}]_0 = 1$, then $[\text{B}]_t = 0.350([\text{B}]_0) = 0.350$. Regardless of the amount, the term within the natural logarithm will be 0.350.

$$t = -\ln\left(\frac{0.350(\cancel{[\text{B}]_0})}{\cancel{[\text{B}]_0}}\right)\frac{1}{0.087170\ \text{days}^{-1}} = 12.0\ \text{days}$$

60. D: The overall equilibrium expression will be the product of each constant or expression. First, determine the equilibrium constant expression for the first reaction, followed by the second one.

$$2\ \mathrm{CO}(g) + \mathrm{O}_2(g) \rightleftharpoons 2\ \mathrm{CO}_2$$

$$K_1 = \frac{[\mathrm{CO}_2]^2}{[\mathrm{CO}]^2[\mathrm{O}_2]}$$

$$\mathrm{CO}_2(g) + \mathrm{C}(s) \rightleftharpoons 2\ \mathrm{CO}(g)$$

$$K_1 = \frac{[\mathrm{CO}]^2}{[\mathrm{CO}_2]}$$

Now multiply each equilibrium constant to obtain the overall K value.

$$K_1 \times K_2 = K_{\text{overall}} = \frac{[\mathrm{CO}_2]^2}{[\mathrm{CO}]^2[\mathrm{O}_2]} \times \frac{[\mathrm{CO}]^2}{[\mathrm{CO}_2]} = \frac{[\mathrm{CO}_2]}{[\mathrm{O}_2]}$$

This expression could have also been obtained if both equations from above were combined.

$$2\ \mathrm{CO}(g) + \mathrm{O}_2(g) \rightleftharpoons 2\ \mathrm{CO}_2$$

$$\mathrm{CO}_2(g) + \mathrm{C}(s) \rightleftharpoons 2\ \mathrm{CO}(g)$$

$$\mathrm{O}_2(g) + \mathrm{C}(s) \rightleftharpoons \mathrm{CO}_2(g) \quad K_{\text{overall}} = \frac{[\mathrm{CO}_2]}{[\mathrm{O}_2]}$$

61. D: The equilibrium expression of the reaction is:

$$K = \frac{1}{[\mathrm{SO}_2]}$$

The solid reactant and products are not included in the expression and will not impact the equilibrium constant or direction of equilibrium. Therefore, Choices *A* and *B* are not correct. A decrease in SO_2 pressure at equilibrium means that the reaction must shift to the right because fewer gas particles exert fewer forces over an area and lead to lower pressure. If the volume of the reaction vessel, containing the chemical system, was decreased, then the equilibrium will shift to the right where there are no gaseous products. In contrast, in Choice *C*, increasing the volume of the reaction vessel will initially decrease the pressure, but when equilibrium is reestablished, the reaction will shift to the left to produce more SO_2. Heat can be considered a product of the reaction. If heat is removed from the system, such as chilling the reaction vessel, then the reaction will shift to the right, reducing the overall pressure. If the temperature is reduced, then heat is removed, and the reaction will proceed to the right. At equilibrium, the pressure of SO_2 will be lower.

62. C: First set up the equilibrium constant expression for the reaction of ammonia in water.

$$\underbrace{NH_3(aq)}_{\text{Brønsted–Lowry base}} + \underbrace{H_2O(l)}_{\text{Brønsted–Lowry acid}} \rightleftharpoons \underbrace{OH^-(aq)}_{\text{conjugate base}} + \underbrace{NH_4^+(aq)}_{\text{conjugate acid}}$$

$$K_b = \frac{[OH^-][NH_4^+]}{[NH_3]} = 1.8 \times 10^{-5}$$

Set up an ICE table to formulate an expression in terms of x or the hydroxide concentration.

	$[NH_3]$	$[OH^-]$	$[NH_4^+]$
Initial	0.35	0	0
Change	$-x$	$+x$	$+x$
Equilibrium	$0.35 - x$	x	x

$$K_b = \frac{(x)(x)}{(0.35 - x)} = \frac{x^2}{0.35 - x} = 1.8 \times 10^{-5}$$

Assuming x is much smaller than 0.35, then:

$$1.8 \times 10^{-5} = \frac{x^2}{0.35}$$

$$x = \sqrt{1.8 \times 10^{-5} \times 0.35} = 0.0025$$

Applying the 5 percent rule or substituting into the original equation gives:

$$\frac{0.0025}{0.35} \times 100\% = 0.71\% \qquad \frac{(0.0025)^2}{0.35 - (0.0025)} = 1.8 \times 10^{-5}$$

The value of x is reasonable because its less than 5 percent with respect to the initial concentration. The pOH can be found from the hydroxide concentration:

$$0.0025 = [OH^-]$$

$$pOH = -\log(0.0025) = 2.6$$

The pH of ammonia can then be found using the pOH:

$$pOH + pH = 14.00$$

$$pH = 14.00 - pOH = 14.00 - 2.6 = 11.4$$

63. A: First set up the equilibrium constant expression.

$$K_c = \frac{[HI]^2}{[H_2][I_2]}$$

Note that the concentration of each reactant is $1.00 \text{ mol}/1.0 \text{ L} = 1.0 \text{ M}$. Next, set up an ICE table.

	$[H_2]$	$[I_2]$	$[HI]$
Initial	1.0	1.0	0
Change	$-x$	$-x$	$+2x$
Equilibrium	$1.0 - x$	$1.0 - x$	$2x$

Then, substitute into the equilibrium expression:

$$49.7 = \frac{(2x)^2}{(1.0 - x)(1.0 - x)} = \frac{(2x)^2}{(1.0 - x)^2}$$

The right-hand side of the equation is a perfect square. Taking the square root of both sides gives:

$$\sqrt{49.7} = \sqrt{\frac{(2x)^2}{(1.0 - x)^2}}$$

$$\pm 7.0498 = \frac{2x}{1.0 - x}$$

Both positive and negative values must be considered. Rearranging the equation gives:

Case 1 $(+7.0498)$

$$x_1 = 0.78$$

Case 2 (-7.0498)

$$x_2 = 1.4$$

The second value (1.4) is not a possible choice because it's greater than the initial concentration, so the first value (0.78) is the correct answer. The equilibrium concentrations are:

$$[H_2] = [I_2] = 1.0 - 0.78 = 0.22 \text{ M}$$

$$[HI] = 2(0.78) = 1.6 \text{ M}$$

64. C: The radioactive decay process describes electron capture, because it's the only type of decay that involves electron absorption.

$$^{92}_{44}\text{Ru} + {}^{0}_{-1}\text{e} \rightarrow {}^{92}_{43}\text{Tc}$$

Ruthenium-92 will accept an electron from its inner orbitals, transforming one of its protons to a neutron. Consequently, the atomic mass will decrease from 44 to 43, while the mass number remains the same. Choices *A* and *B* are not correct because the mass number changes, and because ruthenium does not decompose to rhodium. Instead, the atom that has an atomic number of 43 is technetium. Choice *D* is incorrect because electron capture does not produce an alpha particle.

65. B: First find the N/Z ratio of Pb-212, which has $Z = 82$ (see exact values in the periodic table). The number of neutrons is $A - Z = 212 - 82 = 130$. The N/Z ratio is $130/82 = 1.59$. Based on the valley of stability, it lies slightly outside the shaded region. Because the N/Z ratio is too high, beta decay will occur, and a neutron will be converted to a proton.

$$^{212}_{82}\text{Pb} \rightarrow {}^{212}_{83}\text{Bi} + {}^{0}_{-1}\text{e}$$

The number of neutrons in bismuth-212 is $A - Z = 212 - 83 = 129$, which is one less than the parent nuclide. The N/Z ratio is $129/83 = 1.55$.

66. B: Choice *A* is incorrect because MnO_4^- is reduced in the reaction:

$$\overbrace{\text{MnO}_4^-}^{\substack{x+4(-2)=-1 \\ x=+7}} \rightarrow \overbrace{\text{MnO}_2}^{\substack{x+2(-2)=0 \\ x=+4}}$$

The oxidation state of manganese changes from Mn^{+7} to Mn^{+4}, which indicates a reduction took place. Because manganese is reduced, it acts as an oxidizing agent, making Choice *B* the correct choice. Iodide changes from I^- to I_2, meaning that its oxidation state changes from −1 to 0, indicating oxidation took place. The iodide ion, therefore, acts as the reducing agent.

67. B: The aluminum half-reaction has a relatively more negative potential compared to nickel. Therefore, aluminum will act as the anode and proceed in the reverse direction, thereby repelling electrons and becoming oxidized in the process. In contrast, nickel will act as the cathode and accept electrons because it has a more positive potential.

$$\text{Cathode (reduction): Ni}^{2+}(\text{aq}) + 2\text{e}^- \rightarrow \text{Ni(s)} \quad E^\circ = -0.23\text{ V}$$

$$\text{Anode (oxidation): Al(s)} \rightarrow \text{Al}^{3+}(\text{aq}) + 3\text{e}^- \quad E^\circ = +1.66\text{ V}$$

Because aluminum is oxidized, the sign of E° changes from negative to positive. Each equation must be multiplied by a factor such that the net equation will have an equal number of electrons on each side.

$$3 \times \left(\text{Ni}^{2+}(\text{aq}) + 2\text{e}^- \rightarrow \text{Ni(s)}\right) \quad E^\circ = -0.23\text{ V}$$

$$2 \times (\text{Al(s)} \rightarrow \text{Al}^{3+}(\text{aq}) + 3\text{e}^-) \quad E^\circ = +1.66\text{ V}$$

The spontaneous net equation is:

$$3\text{Ni}^{2+}(\text{aq}) + 6\text{e}^- \rightarrow 3\text{Ni(s)} \quad E^\circ = -0.23\text{ V}$$

$$2\text{Al(s)} \rightarrow 2\text{Al}^{3+}(\text{aq}) + 6\text{e}^- \quad E^\circ = +1.66\text{ V}$$

$$3\text{Ni}^{2+}(\text{aq}) + 2\text{Al(s)} \rightarrow 3\text{Ni(s)} + 2\text{Al}^{3+}(\text{aq}) \quad E^\circ_{\text{cell}} = -0.23\text{ V} + 1.66\text{ V} = +1.43\text{ V}$$

Note that the electrode cell potentials, E°, for each half-cell reaction were not multiplied by a factor. The reason is that E° is an intensive property and does not depend on the molar amount. E° remains the same regardless of the factor that is used to multiply the equation.

68. B: First calculate the molar concentration (units of mol/L) of silver chloride from its solubility. The molar mass of silver chloride is 143.32 g/mol.

$$1.9 \times 10^{-3} \frac{\text{g}}{\text{L}} = \frac{1 \text{ mol AgCl}}{143.32 \text{ g AgCl}} = 1.326 \times 10^{-5} \text{ mol/L}$$

First, write out the dissociation of silver chloride in water:

$$\text{AgCl(s)} \rightleftharpoons \text{Ag}^{+}\text{(aq)} + \text{Cl}^{-}\text{(aq)}$$

Now set up an ICE table and solve for K_{sp}:

	$[\text{Ag}^+]$	$[\text{Cl}^-]$
Initial	0	0
Change	$+S$	$+S$
Equilibrium	S	S

The K_{sp} of silver chloride can be then found from the concentration of dissolved silver chloride:

$$K_{\text{sp}} = [\text{Ag}^+][\text{Cl}^-]$$

$$K_{\text{sp}} = (S)(S) = (S)^2 = (1.326 \times 10^{-5})^2 = 1.758 \times 10^{-10} \approx 1.8 \times 10^{-10}$$

69. C. The equilibrium constant can be used to predict the extent and direction of the reaction. For example, a large K value ($> 10^3$) would indicate that the reaction proceeds strongly to the right, toward the products. By knowing the initial concentrations and equilibrium constant, an ICE table can be used to help set up a mathematical expression of the equilibrium expression in terms of the equilibrium concentrations. There is no information on the kinetics or how long it will take a reaction to proceed within the equilibrium constant

70. B: Choice *B* is the correct answer. To determine the missing particle for the nuclear fission reaction, express the reaction as a nuclear reaction equation.

$$^{235}_{92}\text{U} + ^{1}_{0}\text{n} \rightarrow ^{95}_{36}\text{Kr} + 2\ ^{1}_{0}\text{n} + \_\_\_\_\_$$

There are a total of 92 protons on the reactant side (92 from uranium and 0 from a neutron). There are 36 protons on the product side (36 from krypton and 0 from the two neutrons). Based on the conservation of mass, the missing particle must have $92 - 36$ protons, which equals 56 protons. Now balance the mass number (found on the superscript) in the equation. The mass number is $235 + 1 = 236$ (^{235}U and ^{1}n) on the reactant side and $95 + 2 = 97$ from the product side (^{95}Kr and two ^{1}n). The mass number of the missing particle is $236 - 97 = 139$. The unknown atom $^{139}_{56}\text{X}$ is Choice *B*, $^{139}_{56}\text{Ba}$. All other answer choices can be eliminated since the mass number and proton numbers will not balance the nuclear equation.

$$^{235}_{92}\text{U} + ^{1}_{0}\text{n} \rightarrow ^{95}_{36}\text{Kr} + 2\ ^{1}_{0}\text{n} + ^{139}_{56}\text{Ba}$$

Practice Test #2

1. What happens to the rate constant of a reaction if the activation energy is decreased by half?
    a. It increases.
    b. It remains the same.
    c. It goes to zero.
    d. It decreases slightly.

2. Four different gases of the same concentration are filled into sealed plastic bags. If the bags are all punctured to create a small hole of the same size in each, which gas will escape its bag at the highest rate?
    a. CO_2
    b. Xe
    c. Cl_2
    d. NO_2

3. 50 g of 150 K water is added to 60 g of 200 K water. What will be the equilibrium temperature of the mixed water system? (Note that $c_{water} = 1$).
    a. 145.2 K
    b. 177.3 K
    c. 198.5 K
    d. 210.0 K

4. According to the Brønstad-Lowry theory, an acid is described as what?
    a. A species that is capable of accepting a lone pair
    b. A species that increases the concentration of OH^- ions in a solution
    c. A species that increases the concentration of H^+ ions in a solution
    d. A species that is able to donate a proton to another molecule

5. During a reaction, two electrons are transferred and the $E°_{cell} = -1.5$ V. What is the $\Delta G°$ for this reaction?
    a. 290 kJ
    b. 450 kJ
    c. –320 kJ
    d. 580 kJ

6. If CuS has a K_{sp} of 8×10^{-37}, what is the approximate concentration of Cu^{2+}?
    a. 9.8×10^{-8}
    b. 4.2×10^{-37}
    c. 5.7×10^{-2}
    d. 8.9×10^{-19}

7. A chemical reaction yields 5 moles of potassium chloride. How many grams of potassium chloride is this?
   a. 372.8 g
   b. 10 g
   c. 27.3 g
   d. 745.5 g

8. Which compound is most likely to be useful in a salt bridge?
   a. CH_3OOH
   b. NH_3
   c. C_7H_8
   d. $MgSO_3$

9. What bond angles can be observed in a sulfur trioxide molecule (SO_3)?
   a. 90°, 120°, and 180°
   b. 180°
   c. 90° and 180°
   d. 120°

10. An atom has six protons and an atomic mass of 14 amu. Which element is this?
   a. Nitrogen
   b. Oxygen
   c. Boron
   d. Carbon

11. A reaction occurs at 650 K and has an equilibrium constant of 5.21. What is the $\Delta G°$ for the reaction?
   a. 8.31 kJ
   b. 5.21 kJ
   c. –4.42 kJ
   d. –8.92 kJ

12. Which of the following would increase the chance of a liquid vaporizing?
   a. Lower atmospheric pressure
   b. Stronger intermolecular forces
   c. Lower atmospheric temperature
   d. Increased humidity

13. For the following reaction, what is the $\Delta H°$?

$$PCl_5 \rightarrow PCl_3 + Cl_2 \quad \Delta H = ?$$

$$P_4 + 6\ Cl_2 \rightarrow 4\ PCl_3 \quad \Delta H = -2500\ kJ$$

$$4\ PCl_5 \rightarrow P_4 + 10\ Cl_2 \quad \Delta H = 3500\ kJ$$

   a. 250 kJ
   b. 1000 kJ
   c. 500kJ
   d. –350 kJ

14. For a reaction there is a 0.05 M concentration of the product and a 1.2 M concentration of the reactant. The K_{eq} is 5×10^{-3}. Which of the following statements is true?
   a. The reaction is at equilibrium.
   b. The reaction proceeds toward the products.
   c. The ΔG is positive.
   d. It is a combustion reaction.

15. A scientist manipulates temperature and pressure on a substance to make it change phases. They note that the calculated entropy decreased drastically. Which process most likely occurred?
   a. Evaporation
   b. Sublimation
   c. Freezing
   d. Deposition

16. Which of the following determines the order that electrons fill orbitals of an atom in its ground state?
   a. Pauli exclusion principle
   b. Aufbau principle
   c. Rutherford-Bohr model
   d. Hund's rule

17. What is the electronic geometry of ammonia (NH_3)?
   a. Tetrahedral
   b. Trigonal pyramidal
   c. Trigonal planar
   d. Trigonal bipyramidal

18. For the following reaction, the $\Delta S°$ is –200 $\frac{J}{K}$. The entropy $(S°)$ for A_2 is 190 $\frac{J}{mol \cdot K}$, B_2 is 128 $\frac{J}{mol \cdot K}$, and AB_3 is 191 $\frac{J}{mol \cdot K}$. What is the $\Delta S°$ for this reaction?

$$A_2 + 3\ B_2 \leftrightarrow 2\ AB_3$$

   a. 192 $\frac{J}{K}$
   b. –192 $\frac{J}{K}$
   c. 574 $\frac{J}{K}$
   d. –574 $\frac{J}{K}$

19. How many moles are there in 10 g of sodium chloride?
   a. 0.17 mol
   b. 0.43 mol
   c. 5.84 mol
   d. 0.11 mol

20. For the following Daniell cell diagram, which of the following is the cathode?

$$Zn\ (s)\ |\ Zn^{2+}\ (2\ M)||\ Cu^{2+}\ (2\ M)|\ Cu\ (s)$$

a. Zn
b. Zn^{2+}
c. Cu^{2+}
d. Cu

21. An unknown material is deemed radioactive by researchers. They observe that it ejects electrons from its nucleus. Which conclusion is consistent with the observation?

a. The emission is a beta particle.
b. Nuclear fission is occurring.
c. It has a half-life of over three centuries.
d. It is emitting alpha particles.

22. A scientist detects a very high energy electromagnetic wave of radiation. What should the scientist identify it as?

a. Alpha particle
b. Beta decay
c. Gamma ray
d. Ultraviolet ray

23. Which term describes the phenomena in which there is an electrostatic interaction between the molecules of a solvent and those of a solute?

a. Saturation
b. Precipitation
c. Le Châtelier's principle
d. Solvation

24. A reaction at 25° C has a $\Delta H°$ of –43.1 kJ and a $\Delta S°$ of $-129\,\frac{J}{K}$. What is the $\Delta G°$ for the reaction?

a. –4.66 kJ
b. 3.21 kJ
c. –2.11 kJ
d. 0.03 kJ

25. For the following redox reaction, which component is the oxidizing agent?

$$Zn + Cu^{2+} \rightarrow Zn^{2+} + Cu$$

a. Zn
b. Cu
c. Zn^{2+}
d. Cu^{2+}

26. In an experiment, 5.0 g of sodium reacts with atmospheric oxygen to yield 6.6 g of Na_2O. Use the following balanced chemical formula to find the percent yield of this experiment:

$$4\,Na(s) + O_2(g) \rightarrow 2\,Na_2O(s)$$

a. 98.5 %
b. 90.0 %
c. 95.2 %
d. 96.8 %

27. Two hydrogen atoms form a bond with an oxygen atom by sharing electrons. What type of bond is this between the hydrogen and oxygen atoms?

a. Covalent bond
b. Ionic bond
c. Metallic bond
d. Hydrogen bond

28. Which of the following elements is an s-block element?

a. Silver
b. Carbon
c. Lithium
d. Uranium

29. Given the following hypothetical reactions, determine the enthalpy of: $A + \frac{1}{2}B_2 \rightarrow AB$.

$$A + B_2 \rightarrow AB_2 \qquad \Delta H = -325\frac{kJ}{mol}$$

$$AB + \frac{1}{2}B_2 \rightarrow AB_2 \qquad \Delta H = -250\frac{kJ}{mol}$$

a. $-575\ kJ/mol$
b. $175\ kJ/mol$
c. $75\ kJ/mol$
d. $-75\ kJ/mol$

30. 20 grams of octane is burned in a bomb calorimeter that contains 500 g of water. The heat absorbed by the water was 35.23 kJ. If 15,430 J were absorbed by the calorimeter, what is the amount of heat released by the reaction ($q_{reaction}$)?

a. 19.8 kJ
b. −50.66 kJ
c. 35.23 kJ
d. −25.33 kJ

31. A scientist sets up an exothermic reaction. They decrease the temperature in the room drastically. Which of the following will be observed?

a. The reverse reaction rate increases.
b. The reaction stops because it is at equilibrium.
c. The reaction proceeds forward, but becomes endothermic.
d. The product formation is favored.

32. For the reaction:

$$CaCl_2 + 2\ AgNO_3 \rightarrow Ca(NO_3)_2 + 2\ AgCl$$

If 6.5 g of $CaCl_2$ is reacted with 7.1 g of $AgNO_3$ to make 6.9 g of $Ca(NO_3)_2$ and 11.9 g of $AgCl$, which compound is the limiting reactant?

a. $CaCl_2$
b. $AgNO_3$
c. $Ca(NO_3)_2$
d. $AgCl$

33. For the following reaction and corresponding graph that shows the kinetic curves for the components of the reaction, which curve corresponds to the reactant B_2?

$$A_2 + 2\ B_2 \rightarrow 2\ B_2A$$

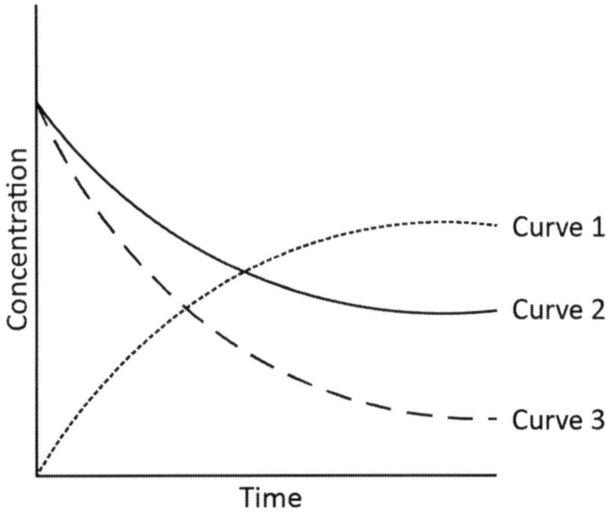

a. Curve 1
b. Curve 2
c. Curve 3
d. Cannot be determined

34. Which of the following is a weak base?

a. $NaOH$
b. NH_3
c. H_2SO_4
d. $HCOOH$

35. Which of the following is the correct expression for the equilibrium constant for this reaction?

$$N_2 + 3\,H_2 \leftrightarrow 2\,NH_3$$

a. $K_{eq} = [N_2][H_2]^3$
b. $K_{eq} = \frac{[N_2][H_2]^3}{[NH_3]^2}$
c. $K_{eq} = [NH_3]^2$
d. $K_{eq} = \frac{[NH_3]^2}{[N_2][H_2]^3}$

36. Glucose has a molecular formula of $C_6H_{12}O_6$. What is the empirical formula of glucose?
a. CH_2O
b. $C_6H_{12}O_6$
c. $C_3H_6O_3$
d. $C_2H_4O_2$

37. Which of the following illustrates the correct electronic configuration of lithium using spdf notation?
a. $1s^22s^1$
b. $1s^21p^1$
c. $1s^12p^13d^1$
d. $[He]\ 2s^2$

38. Which of the following is a true statement?
a. The purity of a solid substance cannot be determined by its melting point.
b. Impure and pure samples of the same substance have the same melting point.
c. Each pure substance has a unique melting point.
d. Two different pure metals may have the same melting point.

39. Which of the following is not an example of a substance that acts as a Lewis acid?
a. $BaCl_2$
b. Cu_2
c. H^+
d. BF_3

40. Six half-lives decay an atom into what percentage of the original?
a. 0.25%
b. 1.56%
c. 2.31%
d. 3.01%

41. Relating to the rules of solubility, which of the following statements is INCORRECT?
a. All salts containing ammonium are water-soluble.
b. Most halides are water-soluble.
c. Most hydroxides are water-soluble.
d. Most metal oxides are insoluble.

42. A compound containing nitrogen and hydrogen is found to contain 82.2% nitrogen and 17.8% hydrogen. What is the empirical formula of the compound?
   a. NH_4
   b. N_2H_3
   c. NH_3
   d. N_3H

43. A lab tech is told to prepare 500 mL of 1.5 *M* NaOH from a 6 *M* stock solution. What volume of the stock solution should the lab tech dilute with DI water?
   a. 50 mL
   b. 100 mL
   c. 115 mL
   d. 125 mL

44. A molecule has no net charge. Which term best describes the molecule?
   a. Nonbonding
   b. Isoelectric
   c. Basic
   d. Nonpolar

45. 15 g of NaCl is dissolved in to 200 mL of water. What is the molality of the resultant solution?
   a. 0.2 m
   b. 0.5 m
   c. 1.0 m
   d. 1.3 m

46. A student determines that the ion product of a salt is less than the salt's K_{sp}. What can be concluded from this information?
   a. The salt is acidic.
   b. The solution is unsaturated.
   c. The salt precipitates in the solution.
   d. The solution is at equilibrium.

47. Which of the following processes has the least exothermic standard heat of combustion?
   a. Combustion of propane
   b. Combustion of hexane
   c. Combustion of ethane
   d. Combustion of pentane

48. 25 g of table salt is added to 100 g of water. What is the mole fraction of the water?
   a. 0.08
   b. 0.93
   c. 0.72
   d. 0.10

49. How many hydrogen atoms are in 2 moles of H_2O?
   a. 1.204×10^{24} atoms
   b. 2.408×10^{24} atoms
   c. 3.322×10^{24} atoms
   d. 6.645×10^{24} atoms

50. 10 g of methane reacts with atmospheric oxygen to create 27.4 g of carbon dioxide and 22.5 g of water. Which compound is the limiting reagent of this reaction?
   a. CH_4
   b. O_2
   c. CO_2
   d. H_2O

51. A student in a laboratory class is instructed to attempt to increase the rate of a reaction. Which of the following should the student do?
   a. Decrease concentration of reactants.
   b. Add a heterogenous catalyst to the reaction.
   c. Decrease the temperature.
   d. Increasing the energy barrier of the reaction.

52. How many grams of H_2O can be made from the complete combustion of 10.0 g of methane?
   a. 16.9 g
   b. 33.7 g
   c. 11.2 g
   d. 22.5 g

53. For the following equation, calculate the K_{sp} of $A(BC)_2$, given that its molar solubility is 3.6×10^{-5} M.

$$A(BC)_2 \rightarrow A^{2+} + 2\ AB^-$$

   a. 4.0×10^{-12}
   b. 3.2×10^{12}
   c. 2.1×10^{-14}
   d. 1.9×10^{-13}

54. Which of the following would indicate a strong acid?
   a. A K_a of 5.9×10^{-2}
   b. A pH of 14
   c. A pK_a of –5.9
   d. A pH of 3

55. What volume would 50 g of neon gas occupy at 300 K and 1.5 atm? $\left(R = 0.0821 \frac{L \times atm}{mol \times K}\right)$
   a. 37 L
   b. 41 L
   c. 45 L
   d. 52 L

56. Some chemists want to react two molecules together to create $FeCl_3$. They calculate that the theoretical yield of their reaction should be 25 g of $FeCl_3$. To consider the experiment a success, they want a percent yield equal to or greater than 92%. What is the minimum actual yield they can obtain to consider the experiment a success?

a. 23.8 g
b. 23.0 g
c. 22.5 g
d. 24.8 g

57. For the following reactions, If K_{eq} for Reaction 1 is 0.5, what is the K_{eq} of Reaction 2?

$$\text{Reaction 1:} \quad 2\text{ A} + 1\text{ B} \leftrightarrow 2\text{ C} + 2\text{ D}$$

$$\text{Reaction 2:} \quad 2\text{ C} + 2\text{ D} \leftrightarrow 2\text{ A} + 1\text{ B}$$

a. 0.5
b. 2
c. 5
d. 50

58. A reaction has the following rate law. What is the order of the entire reaction?

$$\text{rate} = \text{k}[\text{x}]^0[\text{y}]^1[\text{z}]^2$$

a. 0
b. 1.5
c. 2
d. 3

59. What is the correct molecular geometry of the compound methane?

a. Trigonal planar
b. Linear
c. Tetrahedral
d. Trigonal bipyramidal

60. Which term describes an electron that is emitted from a nucleus during radioactive decay?

a. Beta particle
b. Gamma ray
c. Isotope
d. Alpha particle

61. Which of the following statements about covalent bonds is correct?

a. As bond order decreases, bond strength increases.
b. As bond order increases, bond length decreases.
c. As bond energy increases, bond length increases.
d. As bond energy decreases, bond order increases.

62. A 15 g gas occupies 18.9 L at STP. Which of the following is the molecular weight of the gas?
  a. $6.6\ \frac{\text{g}}{\text{mol}}$
  b. $10.1\ \frac{\text{g}}{\text{mol}}$
  c. $12.6\ \frac{\text{g}}{\text{mol}}$
  d. $14.3\ \frac{\text{g}}{\text{mol}}$

63. Which of the following refers to a conversion of one element into a different element from the emission of radiation from an unstable nucleus?
  a. Nuclear reaction
  b. Transmutation
  c. Nuclear fusion
  d. Alpha decay

64. The $\Delta G°$ of a reaction was determined to be 52.4 kJ. Given this information, which of the following statements is true?
  a. The reaction is at equilibrium.
  b. The forward reaction is spontaneous at high temperatures.
  c. The reverse reaction is spontaneous.
  d. The reaction cannot reach its activation energy.

65. A newly discovered isotope of an element has 135 protons and an atomic mass of 269 amu. How many neutrons does this isotope have?
  a. 135
  b. 134
  c. 270
  d. 269

66. 1.0 g of hexane (C_6H_{14}) is burned within a bomb calorimeter containing 800 g of water. The initial temperature of the water is 25.0° C and the specific heat of water is $4.186\ \frac{\text{J}}{\text{g}\cdot°\text{C}}$. If the heat absorbed by water is 16.74 kJ, what is the temperature of the water after the reaction?
  a. 25.5 °C
  b. 28.1 °C
  c. 30.0 °C
  d. 33.2 °C

67. Which term describes moles of solute per kilograms of solvent?
  a. Mole fraction
  b. Molarity
  c. Molality
  d. Normality

68. Which of the following is always the same between two structural isomers of a molecule?
  a. Arrangement of the atoms
  b. Bond angles
  c. Molecular formulas
  d. Bonding arrangements

69. The p orbitals of two different atoms combine to form a certain type of bond. Which type of bond do they form?
   a. Sigma
   b. Hydrogen
   c. Pi
   d. Ionic

70. For an electron to move from an energy state to another, an atom must do what with energy?
   a. Absorb energy
   b. Create energy
   c. Destroy energy
   d. Release energy

Answer Explanations

1. A: The activation energy would increase. When activation energy decreases, the rate constant of a reaction will increase. When activation energy decreases, the barrier blocking a reaction from occurring is reduced, making the rate constant increase. This can also be confirmed mathematically using the Arrhenius equation to compare what the rate would be at any activation energy and what it would be at half of that activation energy.

2. A: CO_2 is the correct answer. Carbon dioxide has the smallest molar mass at 44.01 g/mol. Since it is the smallest gas molecule, more of it can escape at a time compared to the larger molecules. Choice *B*, Xe, is incorrect because it has a molar mass of 131.29 g/mol. Choice *C*, Cl_2, is incorrect because it has a molar mass of 70.91 g/mol. Choice *D*, NO_2, is incorrect because it has a molar mass of 46.01 g/mol.

3. B: 177.3 K is the correct answer. The two portions of water undergo thermal exchange in this example, meaning that the heat given off of one liquid will be absorbed by the other liquid. The first step is to note that:

$$q_{\text{cold}} = -q_{\text{hot}}$$

Referring to the lower temperature water as cold and the higher temperature water as hot, expand this further and solve for final equilibrium temperature:

$$(m_{\text{cold}})(c_{\text{H}_2\text{O}})(T_{\text{final}} - T_{\text{cold}}) = (m_{\text{hot}})(c_{\text{H}_2\text{O}})(T_{\text{hot}} - T_{\text{final}})$$

$$(50\text{ g})\left(1\frac{\text{cal}}{\text{g} \times \text{K}}\right)(T_{\text{f}} - 150\text{ K}) = (60\text{ g})\left(1\frac{\text{cal}}{\text{g} \times \text{K}}\right)(200\text{ K} - T_{\text{f}})$$

$$50T_{\text{f}} - 7{,}500 = 12{,}000 - 60T_{\text{f}}$$

$$T_{\text{f}} = 177.3\text{ K}$$

4. D: "A species that is able to donate a proton to another molecule" is the correct answer because the Brønstad-Lowry theory of acids and bases describes an acid as a species that can donate a proton, while a base is a proton acceptor molecule. Choice *A*, a species that is capable of accepting a lone pair, is incorrect because that is how the Lewis theory of acids and bases describes an acid. Choice *B*, a species that increases the concentration of OH^- ions in a solution, is incorrect because that is how the Arrhenius theory of acids and bases describes an acid. Choice *C*, a species that increases the concentration of H^+ ions in a solution, is incorrect because that is how the Arrhenius theory of acids and bases describes a base.

5. A: 290 kJ is the correct answer. Set up and solve the problem using the following steps:

$$\Delta G° = -nFE°_{\text{cell}} = -(2\text{ mol e}^-)(96{,}485\frac{\text{C}}{\text{mol} \times \text{e}^-})(-1.5\text{ V})$$

$$\Delta G° = 289{,}455\text{ J} = 290\text{ kJ}$$

6. D: 6.0×10^{-9} is the correct answer. The first step is to write the balanced chemical equation, then use the K_{sp} to solve for the concentrations:

$$\mathrm{Cu\ (s)} \leftrightarrow \mathrm{Cu^{2+}(aq)} + \mathrm{S^{2-}\ (aq)}$$

$$\mathrm{K_{sp}} = 8.0 \times 10^{-37} = [\mathrm{Cu^{2+}}][\mathrm{S^{2-}}] = (\mathrm{x})(\mathrm{x}) = \mathrm{x}^2$$

$$\mathrm{x} = \sqrt{8 \times 10^{-37}} = 8.9 \times 10^{-19}\ \mathrm{M}$$

$$\text{Since } (\mathrm{x})(\mathrm{x}) = [\mathrm{Cu^{2+}}][\mathrm{S^{2-}}], \mathrm{x} = [\mathrm{Cu^{2+}}]$$

$$[\mathrm{Cu^{2+}}] = 8.9 \times 10^{-19}\ \mathrm{M}$$

7. A: 372.8 g is the correct answer. To determine the mass of something in grams when given moles produced, the amount of moles must be multiplied by the molar mass of the molecule. The molar mass of potassium is 39.1 $\mathrm{g/mol}$, and the molar mass of chlorine is 34.45 $\mathrm{g/mol}$. Therefore, the molar mass of potassium chloride (KCl) is:

$$39.1\frac{\mathrm{g}}{\mathrm{mol}} + 34.45\frac{\mathrm{g}}{\mathrm{mol}} = 74.55\frac{\mathrm{g}}{\mathrm{mol}}$$

Thus, the number of grams of KCl is:

$$5\ \mathrm{mol} \times 74.55\frac{\mathrm{g}}{\mathrm{mol}} = 372.8\ \mathrm{g}$$

8. D: $MgSO_3$ is the correct answer because it is a strong electrolyte and an ionic compound that dissociates completely in solution. Salt bridges contain electrolytes to function properly. Choice *A*, CH_3OOH, is incorrect because it is acetic acid, a weak electrolyte. Choice *B*, NH_3, is incorrect because it is ammonia, another weak electrolyte. Choice *C*, C_7H_8, is incorrect because it is the cyclic hydrocarbon toluene. Toluene does not dissolve or ionize in aqueous solutions.

9. D: 120° is the correct answer because sulfur trioxide has a trigonal planar shape, and trigonal planar molecules only have 120° bond angles. Choice *A* is incorrect because 90°, 120°, and 180° are the bond angles present in trigonal bipyramidal molecules. Choice *B*, 180°, is incorrect because it is the only bond angle that is seen in linear molecules. Choice *C*, 90° and 180°, is incorrect because they are bond angles present in octahedral structures.

10. D: Carbon is the correct answer because carbon is defined by having 6 protons. Although the most common form of carbon is carbon-12, which has an approximate atomic mass of 12 amu, isotopes of carbon with 13 amu and 14 amu do exist in exceptionally small amounts. Choice *A*, nitrogen, is incorrect because nitrogen has 7 protons, even though its most common form has an atomic mass of 14 amu. Choice *B*, oxygen, is incorrect because oxygen has 8 protons. Choice *C*, boron, is incorrect because it has 5 protons.

11. D: –8.92 kJ is the correct answer. It can be determined using the equation following equation:

$$\Delta G° = -\mathrm{R}T\ln(K_{\mathrm{eq}})$$

$$\Delta G° = -(8.314 \times 10^{-3})(650)\ln(5.21)$$

$$\Delta G° = -8.92 \text{ kJ}$$

12. A: Lower atmospheric pressure is the correct answer because when less air pressure is on the surface of a liquid, it is more easily able to vaporize. Choice *B*, stronger intermolecular forces, is incorrect because stronger intermolecular forces means stronger attraction between molecules in a liquid. More attraction means the molecules are less able to leave the others as a gas. Choice *C*, lower atmospheric temperature, is incorrect because liquids are less likely to vaporize at lower temperatures. Choice *D*, increased humidity, is incorrect because liquids are more likely to vaporize into drier air than humid air.

13. A: 250 kJ is the correct answer. It can be solved by using Hess's law to rewrite and combine the given reactions to match the unknown reaction. The two reactions simplify and combine to give:

$$4\ \mathrm{PCl_5} \rightarrow 4\ \mathrm{PCl_3} + 4\ \mathrm{Cl_2} \quad \Delta\mathrm{H} = 1000 \text{ kJ}$$

It can be further simplified to match the unknown equation by dividing by 4, giving the correct answer:

$$\mathrm{PCl_5} \rightarrow \mathrm{PCl_3} + \mathrm{Cl_2} \qquad \Delta\mathrm{H} = 250 \text{ kJ}$$

14. C: "The ΔG is positive" is correct. ΔG is positive and the reaction proceeds toward the reactants when the value of the reaction quotient, Q, is greater than the equilibrium constant, K_{eq}. Therefore, to solve this problem, Q must be found and compared to the given value for K_{eq}.

$$\mathrm{Q} = \frac{[\text{Products}]}{[\text{Reactants}]} = \frac{0.05 \text{ M}}{1.2 \text{ M}} = 4.2 \times 10^{-2}$$

$$4.2 \times 10^{-2} > 5.0 \times 10^{-3}$$

Given this information it can be determined that for this reaction, it is not at equilibrium, it proceeds towards the reactants, and the ΔG is positive. This makes answer choices *A* and *B* incorrect, while answer choice *C* is left as the correct answer. Choice *D*, it is a combustion reaction, is incorrect because that cannot be determined from the information given.

15. D: Deposition is the correct answer because it is the largest decrease in disorder, or entropy. Deposition is the phase change of a gas to a solid. Choice *A*, evaporation, is incorrect because that is an increase in entropy. Evaporation is a liquid changing to gas phase, so it is an increase in entropy. Choice *B*, sublimation, is incorrect because it is a massive increase in entropy. Sublimation is a change from the solid to the gas phase. Choice *C*, freezing, is incorrect because, although it is a decrease in entropy, it is not the most correct answer choice. Freezing is the change of a substance from a liquid to a solid, which is less of a decrease in entropy than deposition is.

16. B: The Aufbau principle is the correct answer because it states the order in which electrons fill subshells: they fill the lowest energy subshells before the higher energy subshells. Choice *A*, the Pauli exclusion principle, is incorrect because it states that two or more identical particles cannot occupy the same quantum state simultaneously. Choice *C*, the Rutherford-Bohr model, is incorrect because it is a proposed description of the structure of atoms. Choice *D*, Hund's rule, is incorrect because it states that each orbital is occupied before any other orbital is doubly occupied by electrons.

17. A: Tetrahedral is the correct answer because ammonia (NH_3) has a lone pair of electrons, which is included as a region of electron density when determining the electronic geometry. Choice *B*, trigonal pyramidal, is incorrect because although it is the molecular geometry of ammonia, it is not its electronic geometry. Choice *C*, trigonal planar, is incorrect because ammonia has four regions of electron density when including the lone pair while trigonal planar molecules have three regions of electron density. Choice *D*, trigonal bipyramidal, is incorrect because it has five regions of electron density.

18. B: $-192\ \text{J/K}$ is the correct answer. Solve for this answer using the following equation:

$$\Delta S^\circ = \sum S^\circ{}_{\text{products}} - \sum S^\circ{}_{\text{reactants}}$$

$$\Delta S^\circ = \left[2\ \text{mol AB}_3 \times 191\frac{\text{J}}{\text{mol} \times \text{K}}\right] - \left[1\ \text{mol A}_2 \times 190\frac{\text{J}}{\text{mol} \times \text{K}} + 3\ \text{mol B}_2 \times 128\frac{\text{J}}{\text{mol} \times \text{K}}\right]$$

$$\Delta S^\circ = -192\frac{\text{J}}{\text{K}}$$

19. A: 0.17 mol is the correct answer. To find the moles in 10 g of sodium chloride, determine the chemical formula for sodium chloride and find its molar mass. The chemical formula for sodium chloride is NaCl. To find its molar mass, add the molar masses of sodium ($22.99\ \text{g/mol}$) and chlorine ($35.45\ \text{g/mol}$) together: $22.99\ \text{g/mol} + 34.45\ \text{g/mol} = 58.44\ \text{g/mol NaCl}$. To find the correct number of moles in 10 grams of NaCl, divide the molar mass of NaCl from the 10 grams:

$$10\ \text{g NaCl} \times \frac{1\ \text{mol NaCl}}{58.44\ \text{g NaCl}} = 0.17\ \text{mol NaCl}$$

20. D: Cu is the correct answer because it is in the far right of the cell diagram, meaning that it is the cathode. Choice *A*, Zn, is incorrect because it is the anode. Choice *B*, Zn^{2+}, is incorrect because it is the anode solution. Choice *C*, Cu^{2+}, is incorrect because it is the cathode solution.

21. A: "The emission is a beta particle" is the correct answer because beta particles are single electrons ejected from a nucleus. Choice *B*, nuclear fission is occurring, is incorrect because fission occurs when an atom's nucleus completely breaks apart and releases a massive amount of energy. Choice *C*, it has a half-life of over three centuries, is incorrect because not enough information is provided to determine the half-life. Choice *D*, it is emitting alpha particles, is incorrect because alpha particles are composed of two protons and two neutrons.

22. C: Gamma ray is the correct answer because a gamma ray is a high-energy electromagnetic wave of radiation. Gamma radiation is similar to the lower energy radiation of X-rays. Choice *A*, alpha particle, is incorrect because that is an emitted particle consisting of two protons and two neutrons. Choice *B*, beta decay, is incorrect because that is a form of radioactive disintegration. Choice *D*, ultraviolet ray, is incorrect because that is a form of electromagnetic radiation that is much lower energy.

23. D: Solvation is the correct answer because it describes the interaction between a dissolved solute and the solution it is dissolved in. Choice *A*, saturation, is incorrect because, in the context of solutions, it is the point in a solution when no more solute can dissolve into the solvent. Choice *B*, precipitation, is incorrect because it is the process of an aqueous changing into a solid within a solution. Choice *C*, Le Châtelier's principle, is incorrect because it states that if dynamic equilibrium alters from a change in a variable of a system, the position of equilibrium changes to counteract the variation.

24. A: –4.66 kJ is the correct answer. Use the following equation for Gibbs free energy to reach this answer:

$$\Delta G = \Delta H - T\Delta S$$

$$\Delta G = (-43.1\text{ kJ}) - \left(298\text{ K} \times \left(-129 \times 10^{-3}\frac{\text{kJ}}{\text{mol}}\right)\right)$$

$$\Delta G = -4.66\text{ kJ}$$

25. D: Cu^{2+} is the correct answer because it gains two electrons and becomes a reduced product, thus making it the oxidizing agent. Choice *A*, Zn, is incorrect because that is the reducing agent. Choice *B*, Cu, is incorrect because that is the reduced product. Choice *C*, Zn^{2+}, is incorrect because that is the reducing agent.

26. A: 98.5 % is the correct answer. The first step to solving this problem is to find the theoretical yield:

$$5\text{ g Na} \times \frac{1\text{ mol Na}}{22.99\text{ g Na}} \times \frac{2\text{ mol Na}_2\text{O}}{4\text{ mol Na}} \times \frac{61.98\text{ g Na}_2\text{O}}{1\text{ mol Na}_2\text{O}} = 6.7\text{ g Na}_2\text{O}$$

The final step is to use the given actual yield and the calculated theoretical yield to find the percent yield:

$$\%\text{ yield} = \frac{\text{Actual yield}}{\text{Theoretical yield}} \times 100 = \frac{6.6\text{ g Na}_2\text{O}}{6.7\text{ g Na}_2\text{O}} \times 100 = 98.5\ \%$$

27. A: Covalent bond is the correct answer because covalent bonds form when two atoms with incomplete valence shells complete them by sharing electrons to pair together. Choice *B*, ionic bond, is incorrect because an ionic bond is formed by an electrostatic attraction between oppositely charged ions. Choice *C*, metallic bond, is incorrect because it forms from electrostatic attraction between a positively charged metal ion and conduction electrons. Choice *D*, hydrogen bond, is incorrect because it is an electrostatic attraction between a hydrogen atom that is bound to an electronegative atom and another electronegative atom that has a lone pair of electrons.

28. C: Lithium is the correct answer because its last valence electrons reside within an s subshell. S-block elements are those with their last valence electrons in the s subshell. The s-block elements are those from periodic groups 1 and 2. Choice *A*, silver, is incorrect because it is in group 11 and period 5, making it a d-block element, as its valence electrons are present in a d subshell. Choice *B*, carbon, is incorrect because its last valence electron is within a p subshell, making it a p-block element. Choice *D*, uranium, is incorrect because its last valence electrons are within an f subshell, making it an f-block element.

29. D: –75 kJ/mol is the correct answer. To achieve the net equation of $\text{A} + \frac{1}{2}\text{B}_2 \rightarrow \text{AB}$, the second provided reaction must be reversed, which will result in the reaction enthalpy's sign becoming positive.

$$A + B_2 \rightarrow AB_2 \qquad \Delta H = -325\frac{\text{kJ}}{\text{mol}}$$

$$AB_2 \rightarrow AB + \frac{1}{2}B_2 \qquad \Delta H = +250\frac{\text{kJ}}{\text{mol}}$$

Adding the enthalpies together provides the answer:

$$-325\frac{\text{kJ}}{\text{mol}} + 250\frac{\text{kJ}}{\text{mol}} = -75\frac{\text{kJ}}{\text{mol}}$$

30. B: –50.66 kJ is the correct answer. The total heat released by the reaction can be calculated from the heat absorbed by the water and the calorimeter. It is important to note that the amount of heat released by the reaction will be a negative number.

$$q_{\text{reaction}} = -(\text{heat absorbed by water and calorimeter}) = -(35.23\text{ kJ} + 15.43\text{ kJ})$$

$$q_{\text{rxn}} = -50.66\text{ kJ}$$

31. D: "The product formation is favored" is the correct answer because decreased temperature around exothermic reactions increase the forward rate of the reaction, favoring product formation. Choice *A*, the reverse reaction rate increases, is incorrect because when the forward reaction increases, the reverse reaction rate decreases. Choice *B*, the reaction stops because it is at equilibrium, is incorrect because with the temperature drop, product formation increases, which pushes this reaction further away from equilibrium. Choice *C*, the reaction proceeds forward, but becomes endothermic, is incorrect because it is impossible for an exothermic reaction to simply become endothermic.

32. B: $AgNO_3$ is the correct answer because it is the limiting reactant. It can be found by determining how much $CaCl_2$ is needed to react with the 7.1 g of $AgNO_3$. If the amount of $CaCl_2$ needed is less than the 6.5 g of $CaCl_2$ available, $AgNO_3$ is the limiting reactant and $CaCl_2$ is in excess. The following calculation can find the answer:

$$7.1\text{ g }AgNO_3 \times \frac{1\text{ mol }AgNO_3}{169.87\text{ g }AgNO_3} \times \frac{1\text{ mol }CaCl_2}{2\text{ mol }AgNO_3} \times \frac{110.98\text{ g }CaCl_2}{1\text{ mol }CaCl_2} = 2.32\text{ g }CaCl_2$$

Because 2.32 g $CaCl_2$ is less than the 6.5 g $CaCl_2$ available, $CaCl_2$ is in excess and $AgNO_3$ is the limiting reactant.

33. C: Curve 3 is the correct answer. The third curve is correct because it has the steepest downhill slope, and therefore has the highest disappearance rate. B_2 has the highest disappearance rate due to the "2" coefficient, meaning that two molecules combine with one molecule of A_2 to form the product. Thus, it disappears at twice the rate of A_2. Choice *A*, Curve 1, is incorrect because it corresponds to B_2A. Curve 1 shows the concentration growing over time, meaning that it is the product. Choice *B*, Curve 2, is incorrect because it corresponds to the reactant A_2. Choice *D* is incorrect because B_2 is shown by curve 3.

34. B: NH_3, ammonia, is the correct answer because it is a weak base that does not fully dissociate in water. Choice *A*, NaOH, is incorrect because it is sodium hydroxide, a very common strong base. Choice *C*, H_2SO_4, is incorrect because it is sulfuric acid, a very strong acid. Choice *D*, HCOOH, is incorrect because it is formic acid, a common weak acid.

35. D: $K_{eq} = \frac{[NH_3]^2}{[N_2][H_2]^3}$ is the correct answer. The law of mass action states that for a reversible reaction, such as: $aA + bB \leftrightarrow cC + bB$, if a system has a constant temperature and is at equilibrium, then the equilibrium constant is found with this equation:

$$K_{eq} = \frac{[C]^c[D]^d}{[A]^a[B]^b}$$

36. A: CH_2O is the correct answer because it is the simplest whole-number ratio of the atoms in glucose. An empirical formula has the same proportions of elements as the molecular formula, but in the smallest possible whole number amounts.

37. A: $1s^22s^1$ is the correct answer because lithium has one complete s orbital and one partially full s orbital. Electrons fill into orbitals in the order of 1s, 2s, 2p, 3s, 3p, 4s, 3d, 4p, 5s, 4d, etc. Choice *B*, $1s^21p^1$, is incorrect because there is no 1p orbital. Choice *C*, $1s^12p^13d^1$, is incorrect because the 1s orbital will fill completely before electrons are added to any other orbital. Choice *D*, $[He]\ 2s^2$, is incorrect because it represents the electron configuration of beryllium.

38. C: "Each pure substance has a unique melting point" is the correct answer. Choice *A*, purity of a solid substance cannot be determined by its melting point, is incorrect because finding the melting point is the primary method for determining a substances purity. Choice *B*, impure and pure samples of the same substance have the same melting point, is incorrect because impurities within a substance change the melting point, typically increasing the melting point from that of a pure substance. Choice *D*, two different pure metals may have the same melting point, is incorrect because different substances all have their own unique melting points.

39. A: $BaCl_2$ is the correct answer because it has no empty orbitals, which means it is unable to accept electrons. A Lewis acid is a compound with the ability of accepting an electron pair from a different compound. Choice *B*, Cu_2, is incorrect because it is a Lewis acid due to it being an electrophile. Cu_2 can accept lone pairs of electrons from Lewis base compounds such as ammonia. Choice *C*, H^+, is incorrect because it has no valence electrons and can readily accept a lone pair from a base to form a bond. Choice *D*, BF_3, is incorrect because it is electron deficient. BF_3 has an incomplete p-orbital, so it is able to accept a lone pair.

40. B: 1.56% is the correct answer. A half-life is the time it takes for an atom to decay by half its original form. Therefore, if six half-lives occurred, the percentage can be found by multiplying 0.5 by itself 5 times:

$$\%\text{ after 6 half} - \text{lives: } (0.5 \times 0.5 \times 0.5 \times 0.5 \times 0.5 \times 0.5) \times 100 = 1.56\%$$

41. C: "Most hydroxides are soluble" is the correct answer because all hydroxides are insoluble, except for those that are formed with Ca^{2+}, Sr^{2+}, Ba^{2+}, alkali metals, and ammonium. Choice *A*, all salts containing ammonium are water-soluble, is incorrect because all salts that contain ammonium and alkali metal cations are water-soluble. Choice *B*, most halides are water-soluble, is incorrect because halides, excluding fluorides, are always water-soluble unless they are formed with Ag^+, $Pb_2{}^+$, or $Hg_2{}^{2+}$. Choice *D*, most metal oxides are insoluble, is incorrect because all metal oxides are insoluble, with the exception of when they are formed with alkali metals, ammonium, CaO, SrO, or BaO.

42. C: NH_3 is the correct answer. The best way to approach a problem like this is to assume it is a 100 g sample and convert each percentage into grams. That would be 82.2 g of nitrogen and 17.8 g of hydrogen. The next step is to convert those figures into moles:

$$82.2 \text{ g N} \times \frac{1 \text{ mol N}}{14 \text{ g N}} = 5.87 \text{ mol N}$$

$$17.8 \text{ g H} \times \frac{1 \text{ mol H}}{1.01 \text{ g H}} = 17.62 \text{ mol H}$$

To find the empirical formula, both moles must be divided by the smaller of the two:

$$\text{N: } \frac{5.87 \text{ mol}}{5.87} = 1$$

$$\text{H: } \frac{17.62 \text{ mol}}{5.87} \approx 3$$

Therefore, the correct empirical formula is NH_3.

43. D: 125 mL is the correct answer. This can be found using the equation:

$$M_i V_i = M_f V_f$$

$$V_i \times 6\ M = 500\ mL \times 1.5\ M$$

$$V_i = \frac{500\ mL \times 1.5\ M}{6\ M} = 125\ mL$$

44. B: Isoelectric is the correct answer because it refers to having no net electrical charge. When a molecule is at its isoelectric point, it has no net charge. Choice *A*, nonbonding, refers to something incapable of forming a bond with another atom or molecule. Molecules with no net charge can bind to others through several different process, such as hydrogen bonding. Choice *C*, basic, is incorrect because a basic molecule is one that is capable of accepting an electron pair from another molecule. Choice *D*, nonpolar, is incorrect because it refers to a chemical that has no separation of charge.

45. D: 1.3 m is the correct answer. It can be found by taking the following steps:

$$\text{Molality} = m = \frac{\text{moles of solute}}{\text{kilograms of solvent}}$$

$$\text{kg of solvent: } 200 \text{ mL } H_2O = 200 \text{ g } H_2O = 0.2 \text{ kg } H_2O$$

$$\text{Moles NaCl: } 15 \text{ g NaCl} \times \frac{1 \text{ mol NaCl}}{58.44 \text{ g NaCl}} = 0.26 \text{ mol NaCl}$$

$$\text{Molality of solution} = m = \frac{0.26 \text{ mol NaCl}}{0.2 \text{ kg } H_2O} = 1.3 \text{ m}$$

46. B: "The solution is unsaturated" is the correct answer because when the ion product (IP) is less than the K_{sp}, the solution is not at equilibrium and can further dissolve the salt, making it unsaturated.

Choice *A*, the salt is acidic, is incorrect because acidity cannot be determined from IP and K_{sp}. Choice *C*, the salt precipitates in the solution, is incorrect because a solute typically will not precipitate out of a solution when the solution is not saturated, and no additional compound has been added. Choice *D*, the solution is at equilibrium, is incorrect because it would be at equilibrium if the IP was equal to the K_{sp}.

47. C: Combustion of ethane is the correct answer. Combustion reactions of hydrocarbons with oxygen yield water and carbon dioxide, while producing heat. Longer-chain hydrocarbons produce larger amounts of heat, as more bonds are broken. Therefore, combustion of ethane produces the least exothermic standard heat of combustion, since it is the shortest-chain hydrocarbon out of the available choices. All other answer choices are incorrect since they are larger-chain hydrocarbons than ethane.

48. B: 0.93 is the correct answer. The mole fraction (X) of a compound is found with the following equation:

$$X_{\mathrm{A}} = \frac{\text{moles of A}}{\text{total moles of all species}}$$

First, find the moles for both water and table salt. Then, use them in the following equation:

$$25\mathrm{g\ NaCl} \times \frac{1\ \mathrm{mol\ NaCl}}{58.44\ \mathrm{g\ NaCl}} = 0.43\ \mathrm{mol\ NaCl}$$

$$100\ \mathrm{g\ H_2O} \times \frac{1\ \mathrm{mol\ H_2O}}{18.015\ \mathrm{g\ H_2O}} = 5.55\ \mathrm{mol\ H_2O}$$

$$X_{\mathrm{water}} = \frac{5.55\ \mathrm{mol\ water}}{(5.55 + 0.43)\ \mathrm{mol\ total}} = 0.93$$

49. B: 2.408×10^{24} atoms of hydrogen is the correct answer. The first step is to use Avogadro's number to find the number of molecules in 2 moles of H_2O:

$$2\ \mathrm{mol}\ \times \frac{6.022 \times 10^{23}\mathrm{molecules}}{1\ \mathrm{mol}} = 1.204 \times 10^{24}\ \mathrm{molecules\ H_2O}$$

To find the number of hydrogen atoms present, the number of H_2O molecules must be multiplied by 2, since there are 2 hydrogen atoms in every H_2O molecule:

$$1.204 \times 10^{24}\ \mathrm{molecules\ H_2O}\ \times \frac{2\ \mathrm{atoms\ H}}{1\ \mathrm{molecule\ H_2O}} = 2.408\ \mathrm{atoms\ H}$$

50. A: CH_4 is the correct answer because there are only 10 g of methane available and unlimited O_2. No calculations are necessary in this problem, since it mentions atmospheric oxygen. Choice *B*, O_2, is incorrect because there is no limit to the atmospheric oxygen. Choices *C* and *D*, CO_2 and H_2O, are incorrect because they are products of the reaction.

51. B: "Add a heterogenous catalyst to the reaction" is the correct answer because adding any catalyst, heterogenous or homogenous, will decrease the activation energy, which will in turn increase the reaction rate. Choice *A*, decrease concentration of reactants, is incorrect because decreased concentrations result in fewer collisions between reactant molecules. Choice *C*, decrease the temperature, is incorrect because decreased temperatures decrease the kinetic energy of the molecules, which in turn decreases the number of collisions and the reaction rate. Choice *D*, increase the energy barrier, is incorrect because the energy barrier, also known as the activation energy, decreases the reaction rate as it increases.

52. D: 22.5 g is the correct answer. The first step is to write the balanced chemical equation for the combustion of methane:

$$\mathrm{CH_4\ (g) + 2\ O_2\ (g) \rightarrow CO_2(g) + 2\ H_2O\ (l)}$$

Next, to calculate the resultant mass of water, the grams of methane must be converted into moles of methane, moles of water, then grams of water, using the chemical equation and molar masses:

$$\mathrm{Mass\ H_2O = 10\ g\ CH_4 \times \frac{1\ mol\ CH_4}{16.04\ g\ CH_4} \times \frac{2\ mol\ H_2O}{1\ mol\ CH_4} \times \frac{18.02\ g\ H_2O}{1\ mol\ H_2O} = 22.5\ g\ H_2O}$$

53. D: 1.9×10^{-13} is the correct answer. The first step is to determine that the molar solubility (S) represents $\mathrm{A(BC)_2}$ dissociating into $\mathrm{A^{2+}}$ (S) and $\mathrm{BC^-}$ ($2S$). Next, the equation for K_{sp} can be made, plugging in the values for S to solve:

$$K_{\mathrm{sp}} = [\mathrm{A^{2+}}][\mathrm{BC^-}]^2 = \mathrm{x(2x)^2}$$

$$K_{\mathrm{sp}} = (3.6 \times 10^{-5})\left((2)(3.6 \times 10^{-5})\right)^2$$

$$K_{\mathrm{sp}} = 1.87 \times 10^{-13} = 1.9 \times 10^{-13}$$

54. C: "A $\mathrm{p}K_\mathrm{a}$ of –5.9" is the correct answer because strong acids will always have a $\mathrm{p}K_\mathrm{a}$ that is less than 0. Choice *A*, a K_a of 5.9×10^{-2}, is incorrect because a strong acid always will have a K_a that is greater than 1. Choice *B*, a pH of 14, is incorrect because a high pH (greater than 7) is indicative of something basic. Choice *D*, a pH of 3, is incorrect because pH alone cannot be used to determine the strength of an acid. pH only indicates the concentration of hydrogen ions within a solution. To determine the strength of an acid, one must know the concentration of the initial chemical, the concentration of dissociated hydrogen ions, and the concentration of conjugate base for the acid to determine if the hydrogen ions are fully dissociating in a solution. Strong acids completely dissociate within water.

55. B: 41 L is the correct answer. Use the ideal gas law to solve this. Since all given units in the problem match those in the given expression of the gas constant, no unit conversions are necessary. The first step is to find the number of moles of neon, then solve for volume using the ideal gas law:

$$\mathrm{Moles\ of\ neon} = n = \mathrm{50\ g \times \frac{1\ mol}{20\ g} = 2.5\ mol\ Ne}$$

$$PV = n\mathrm{R}T$$

$$\mathrm{(1.5\ atm)V = (2.5\ mol)\left(0.082\frac{L \cdot atm}{mol \cdot K}\right)(300\ K)}$$

$$\mathrm{V = 41.05\ L}$$

56. B: 23.0 g is the correct answer. The percent yield is found by dividing the actual yield from the theoretical yield and multiplying by 100. When given the theoretical yield and the desired minimum percent yield, the formula can be rearranged to solve for actual yield:

$$\frac{\text{Actual yield}}{25\text{ g}} \times 100 = 92\%$$

$$\text{Actual yield} = 0.92 \ \times 25\text{ g} = 23.0\text{ g}$$

57. B: 2 is the correct answer. Reaction 2 is the exact reverse of Reaction 1. Therefore, the expression for the Reaction 2 K_{eq} is the inverse of Reaction 1 K_{eq}. Furthermore, this means that the Reaction 2 K_{eq} is simply the inverse of the Reaction 1 K_{eq}:

$$\text{Reaction 2 } K_{\text{eq}} = \frac{1}{0.5} = 2$$

58. D: 3 is the correct answer. The overall order of a reaction is found by adding each individual order within the reaction:

$$\text{rate} = 0 + 1 + 2 = 3$$

59. C: Tetrahedral is the correct answer because molecules that are tetrahedral in shape have four regions of electron density from the four hydrogens bonded to the carbon. Choice *A*, trigonal planar, is incorrect because it has three regions of electron density. Choice *B*, linear, is incorrect because it has two regions of electron density. Choice *D*, trigonal bipyramidal, is incorrect because it has five regions of electron density.

60. A: Beta particle is the correct answer because during radioactive decay, electrons emitted from a nucleus are known as beta particles. Beta-radiation from beta particles are capable of penetrating skin to cause damage such as burns. Choice *B*, gamma ray, is incorrect because gamma particles in gamma rays are emitted photons that arise from radioactive decay. Choice *C*, isotope, is incorrect because an isotope is an atom which has a different number of protons and neutrons. Choice *D*, alpha particle, is incorrect because an alpha particle is a positively charged bundle of two protons and two neutrons that is emitted from a nucleus in radioactive decay.

61. B: "As bond order increases, bond length decreases" is the correct answer because when bond order increases (e.g., a single bond increases to a double or triple bond), each bond's length is shorter than if it were a lower bond order. Choice *A*, "as bond order decreases, bond strength increases," is incorrect because as bond order decreases, bond strength will decrease due to being lower energy, longer, and fewer in number. Choice *C*, "As bond energy increases, bond length increases," is incorrect because shorter bonds are higher-energy bonds. Choice *D*, "As bond energy decreases, bond order increases," is incorrect because when bond order increases, bond energy increases.

62. C: 12.6 g/mol is the correct answer. The ideal gas law can find the solution. Standard pressure and volume is used here, so the temperature is 273 K and the pressure is 1 atm.

$$PV = nRT$$

$$(1\text{ atm})(18.9\text{ L}) = \text{n}\left(0.082\frac{\text{L} \cdot \text{atm}}{\text{mol} \cdot \text{K}}\right)(273\text{ K})$$

$$n = 1.185 \text{ mol}$$

Lastly, find the molecular weight:

$$\text{Molecular weight} = \frac{15 \text{ g}}{1.185 \text{ mol}} = 12.65 \frac{\text{g}}{\text{mol}}$$

63. B: Transmutation is the correct answer because it refers to the way elements change into others from the emission of radiation from unstable nuclei. Choice *A*, nuclear reaction, is incorrect because that is an interaction between atomic nuclei and/or subatomic particles that results in a change in the properties of particles. Choice *C*, nuclear fusion, is incorrect because that occurs when two small nuclei combine to make a heavier nucleus. This process releases a large amount of energy. Choice *D*, alpha decay, is incorrect because that refers to radioactive decay where alpha particles are emitted.

64. C: "The reverse reaction is spontaneous" is the correct answer. When the ΔG is positive, the forward reaction is nonspontaneous, and the reverse reaction is spontaneous. Choice *A*, the reaction is at equilibrium, is incorrect because for a system to be at equilibrium, the ΔG must be zero. Choice *B*, the forward reaction is spontaneous at high temperatures, is incorrect because there is not enough information to determine that. Reactions are spontaneous at high temperatures when the ΔH and ΔS are both positive. Choice *D*, the reaction cannot reach its activation energy, is incorrect because there is not enough information to determine that.

65. B: 134 is the correct answer because the number of protons added to the number of neutrons in an atom is equivalent to its atomic mass. Choice *A*, 135, is incorrect because if this element had 135 neutrons, its atomic mass would be 270 amu $(135 \text{ protons} + 135 \text{ neutrons} = 270 \text{ amu})$. When an atom is in its most common form, it has equal protons and neutrons and it is not an isotope. Choice *C*, 270, is incorrect because a hypothetical atom with 270 neutrons and 135 protons would have an atomic mass of 405 amu. Choice *D*, 269, is incorrect because it is the atomic mass of the isotope.

66. C: 30° C is the correct answer. To solve this problem, use the following equation for heat transfer:

$$q = mc\Delta T$$

The first step is to take inventory of what is given and relevant within the problem, and make sure the units match in their prefixes and cancel out to give the desired answer:

$$m = 800 \text{ g}$$

$$T_{\text{i}} = 25.0 \text{ °C}$$

$$c_{\text{water}} = 4.186 \frac{\text{J}}{\text{g} \times \text{°C}}$$

$$q_{\text{water}} = 16.74 \text{ kJ} = 16{,}740 \text{ J}$$

Lastly, solve for final temperature:

$$16{,}740\text{ J} = (800\text{ g})\left(4.186\frac{\text{J}}{\text{g}\times{}^{\circ}\text{C}}\right)(T_{\text{f}} - 25.0\ {}^{\circ}\text{C})$$

$$T_f - 25.0\ {}^{\circ}\text{C} = 5.0$$

$$T_f = 30.0\ {}^{\circ}\text{C}$$

67. C: Molality is the correct answer because molality is found by dividing the moles of a solute by the kilograms of a solvent. Choice *A*, mole fraction, is incorrect because it is a term that describes the ratio of the moles of one component in a solution to the total moles of all components in the solution. Choice *B*, molarity, is incorrect because it is moles of solute per liters of solution. Choice *D*, normality, is incorrect because it is the number of gram equivalents of solute per liters of solvent.

68. C: Molecular formulas is the correct answer because the only constant similarity between different structural isomers is the number of atoms of each element within the molecules. Choice *A*, arrangement of the atoms, is incorrect because structural isomers differ in their shape. An example of this would be 1-propanol and 2-propanol. The alcohol group is attached to different carbons on the alkane structure, but they both have the same chemical formula (C_3H_8O). Choice *B*, bond angles, is incorrect because when atoms bind to different locations on a molecule, the electronegativity of newly positioned atoms can change the bond angle through interactions with adjacent atoms. Choice *D*, bonding arrangements, is incorrect because structural isomers are the same atoms with different bonding arrangements. Structural isomers can often contain different functional groups as well, due to bonds being rearranged.

69. C: Pi is the correct answer because a pi bond is formed from the combination of two p orbitals from different atoms. Choice *A*, sigma, is incorrect because a sigma bond forms when the s orbitals of two different atoms combine. Choice *B*, hydrogen, is incorrect because hydrogen bonding is a dipole-dipole attraction that occurs between a hydrogen atom that is bound to an electronegative atom, and another highly electronegative atom. Choice *D*, ionic, is incorrect because an ionic bond is an electrostatic attraction between two oppositely charged ions.

70. A: Absorb energy is the correct answer; an atom must absorb energy to get from its ground state to an excited state. An atom is in its excited state when an electron moves from one energy state to a higher energy level. Choices *B* and *C*, creates energy and destroys energy, are both incorrect because by the first law of thermodynamics, energy can neither be created nor destroyed. Choice *D*, release energy, is incorrect because when an excited atom releases energy, electrons return to the ground state. This process is known as emission.

Index

Dear ACS General Chemistry Test Taker,

We would like to start by thanking you for purchasing this study guide for your ACS General Chemistry exam. We hope that we exceeded your expectations.

Our goal in creating this study guide was to cover all of the topics that you will see on the test. We also strove to make our practice questions as similar as possible to what you will encounter on test day. With that being said, if you found something that you feel was not up to your standards, please send us an email and let us know.

We would also like to let you know about this other book in our catalog that may interest you.

GRE

This can be found on Amazon: amazon.com/dp/1637759622

MCAT

This can be found on Amazon: amazon.com/dp/1637752091

We have study guides in a wide variety of fields. If the one you are looking for isn't listed above, then try searching for it on Amazon or send us an email.

Thanks Again and Happy Testing!
Product Development Team
info@studyguideteam.com

FREE Test Taking Tips Video/DVD Offer

To better serve you, we created videos covering test taking tips that we want to give you for FREE. **These videos cover world-class tips that will help you succeed on your test.**

We just ask that you send us feedback about this product. Please let us know what you thought about it—whether good, bad, or indifferent.

To get your **FREE videos**, you can use the QR code below or email freevideos@studyguideteam.com with “Free Videos” in the subject line and the following information in the body of the email:

a. The title of your product

b. Your product rating on a scale of 1-5, with 5 being the highest

c. Your feedback about the product

If you have any questions or concerns, please don’t hesitate to contact us at info@studyguideteam.com.

Thank you!

Test Prep Books

SCAN HERE

Made in the USA
Columbia, SC
16 March 2023

13846312R00107